Christianity
without
Fetishes

Christianity
without
Fetishes

*An African Critique and Recapture
of Christianity*

F. EBOUSSI BOULAGA

Translated from the French by Robert R. Barr

ORBIS BOOKS
Maryknoll, New York 10545

The Catholic Foreign Mission Society of America (Maryknoll) recruits and trains people for overseas missionary service. Through Orbis Books Maryknoll aims to foster the international dialogue that is essential to mission. The books published, however, reflect the opinions of their authors and are not meant to represent the official position of the society.

Originally published as *Christianisme sans fétiche*, copyright © 1981 by Editions Présence Africaine, 25 bis, rue des Ecoles, 75005 Paris

English translation copyright © 1984 by Orbis Books, Maryknoll, NY 10545
Manufactured in the United States of America

Manuscript Editor: Lisa McGaw

Library of Congress Cataloging in Publication Data
Eboussi Boulaga, F. (Fabien)
  Christianity without fetishes.

  Translation of: Christianisme sans fétiche.
  Includes index.
  1. Christianity—Africa. 2. Christianity and other religions. 3. Christianity—Essence, genius, nature.
I. Title
BR1360.E3613   1984   209′.6   84-5807
ISBN 0-88344-432-1

Contents

Foreword

"Inculturation" is becoming a fad. In the jargon of contemporary religious or theological discourse the word keeps popping up—but without ever a clear definition. Lexicographers will have a field day with it. It is fast becoming a catchall for any number of sundry agendas. And it takes on different hues depending on the cultural or ideological matrix in which it is used. But to dismiss it as therefore transitory or inconsequential would be disastrous, as this book by Eboussi perhaps unwittingly demonstrates.

The terminology does not interest the author; the substance surely does. Though Eboussi is perhaps the leading theologian of francophone west Africa, he has not published much and this is his first book to be translated into English. We of the English-speaking world are the poorer for that, since Eboussi, as this book demonstrates, is a brilliant thinker, one who is quite comfortable in discourse which ranges from the simplest of concrete experiences to the headiest of subtle abstractions.

And from start to finish he is addressing, in a serious and radical way, the fundamental underpinnings of the inculturation debate. And "debate" it truly is as churchpersons in Third World regions start vigorously to take issue with Rome and the European-American theological axis that still dominates theological discourse.

Perhaps nowhere is this debate more lively and demanding than in Africa, particularly among French-speaking scholars of whom Eboussi is a leader. Already long familiar with the cry for authenticity and *négritude* issuing from west and central African sources, theologians there have gone beyond the superficial critiques of colonialism and cultural imperialism to plumb the deeper dimensions of their African-ness in ways both creative and challenging. One need only instance the publications of the Ecumenical Association of African Theologians within the last five years.

And Eboussi, perhaps more than any other, given both his superb competence as a savant and philosopher and his own personal hegira, is able effectively to question the very nature of Christianity as we of the West have come to know it and impose it on Africa.

Not really content with the way the whole debate was being carried on, yet anxious to be both thoroughly honest and unrelentingly authentic in his contributions, Eboussi left the academic and bourgeois circles of his normal ambience as a Jesuit professor of theology several years ago to return to his native village to re-think the whole Christian project as it encounters a new Africa. He then departed both the Society of Jesus and the priesthood.

This book is partly the result of that personal journey. It is not easy reading. Indeed, the reader is forewarned to be patient, to exert every effort to listen to what Eboussi is saying. Some of his remarks in the opening chapters are so lapidary and negative as to be shocking to ears unfamiliar with the sharp language of rejection common among some Africans. But to stay with him and *listen* attentively, with more than just one's intellect, is a truly rewarding experience, one that can help English-speaking readers realize both how serious African intellectual leaders are in their challenge to the West *and* how desperately we need to relativize our own thinking about what Christianity is.

Once the depth of Eboussi's critique begins to sink in, once one realizes that inculturation has precious little to do with liturgical vestments and musical instruments but rather with very basic worldviews, with basic human values, and indeed with the sharing of power, then the significance of this book begins to dawn. This is a threatening book. It cuts to the quick.

But radical surgery is what is needed right now if the inculturation debate is to bear any fruit. What is at stake is not the "winning" or "losing" of African peoples for Christianity, nor similar questions of "church growth," nor even getting down to defining some supposed "essence of Christianity" (Eboussi demonstrates once again that that task is otiose). Rather the whole question of inculturation has to do with identities, that of Jesus Christ and those of you and me and every person and people. It has to do with the whole human project itself.

And it is the genius of Eboussi that he advances the debate by getting underneath the usual superficialities and "turf" where it has hitherto been discussed.

In so doing, he also offers elements of reconstruction. Not content with critique and negation, he prefers finally to build. His tools are not ones we are used to. His language is often hard to follow. But the game is worth the candle.

What comes through more than anything else in this uniquely different approach to inculturation and to Christianity itself is the very authenticity of the project. Change is painful. The pain experienced by Eboussi and the anger it provoked signal us of the West that we, too, have yet much pain to endure if we are to transcend the sometimes petty dimensions of the inculturation debate.

SIMON E. SMITH, S.J.
Jesuit Refugee Service,
Nairobi, Kenya

Introduction

Revelation and Absolute Knowledge-and-Power

The purpose of the present work is to explicate and base an African critique and recapture of Christianity. Both the critique and the "reprise" are intended as nondoctrinal. In order to understand "the words of faith" and bestow a meaning on them, both moments will be limited to the circumstances and context of their use—the attitudes and manners of living that they imply or that sustain them.

A description of what *actually occurs* in these concrete circumstances, in this particular conjuncture, will make it plain that the claims residing in a self-definition of Christianity are expressions devoid of content. They give themselves the lie, they "turn around and go the other way" as soon as they are reduced to their effects. Conversely, such a description will demonstrate how human beings believe *otherwise*—not just believe that which is opposed to the dogmas. That is, it will demonstrate the use they make of what they believe when they pose and resolve the problems of existence without recourse to the binary logic of yes-or-no, true-or-false, proper to "truths" that determine definitive significations of the ultimate destination of individuals and humanity.

This observation will make it evident that the approach will not be merely pragmatic. Nor will it be a cynical one, in the sense in which one is sometimes satisfied with observing the habitual and inevitable distance between the ideal and the reality. The very questions we are about to pose will confirm this, as will their discussion and then the answers we shall propose.

1

Here, then, are the questions:

1. Can the status and functioning of dogmas acculturated in Western Christianity and civilization still be the same when Christianity is transplanted elsewhere, to another universe? Have the "truths to be believed" the same unambiguous weight of credibility everywhere?

2. Can what Christianity *should be,* the identity of Christianity, be conceived and thought, necessarily and sufficiently, from within the same Credo, the same rites, and with reference to one Scripture and one sole Lord?

3. Can tribal human beings, who have known the critique of their certitudes, have lived the death of both their myths and the irrefutable universe of those myths, seriously accept Christianity's pretension to be the foreordained truth and norm of all authentic existence and the solitary matrix of genuine human beings? Further: How is one to think and to live the necessity, supremacy, and universality of Christianity when the latter is imposed as the dominant religion, or the religion of the dominant? How are the truths, commandments, and rites to be inscribed in one's flesh, when they are received from below, in a state of social, political, economic, and cultural subordination and minority of age?

4. Finally, does not the God proposed by Christianity in the exercise of its symbolic domination, as its foundation, suffer in his representation from the taint of a partisanship that makes him necessarily an "other people's god"—the god of the privileged, with which he has struck an alliance, the law of one group, the principle of membership in, and therefore of exclusion from, this group? How is it possible to take the metaphors of "Revelation" and "Word of God" literally when they authorize a like human conception, too human a conception, and make of monotheism a political problem?

This entire book will be an uninterrupted sojourn in these problems. The answers we shall give, over and over again and in various forms, are topical and need to be reinserted into the developments in which they have first appeared. In taking the risk of abstracting from these developments in order to compose a global presentation of the answers in each of the discussion themes listed above, I should like first to indicate what is at stake in each, along with what cannot be done—the roadblocks in my undertaking that its set of problems imposes—in the hope of sparing the reader of good will the greatest risk of all: a misunderstanding of the overall conception.

1. Christianity enjoys a massive evidence bestowed upon it by longevity, numbers, and "success." It is the phenomenon of twice a thousand years. Multitudes of all nations, races, and conditions give it their allegiance. Finally, it is forever the customary religion of that civilization which has been the agent of the scientific and technological revolution, and which has thereby dominated the rest of humanity for three centuries. One does not demand vouchers of what exists with such constancy, such expansive force, and such brilliance!

This is the contingent, but apodictical, situation in the life and status of Western Christianity. Christianity is milieu, it is historical environment, it is almost atmospheric. It is of a system with other constitutive elements of civilization, and adjusts to their positions and shifts. Just as no one decides to be born of such-and-such parents, or in such-and-such a country, all *are* of this culture, of which Christianity is an integral part. Each one appropriates, in one way or another, the legacy of Christian garb. Side by side with those who endeavor to don it whole are those who are content with bolts, which they think of as without seams and needlework. There are the nonpracticing "believers," and then there are the non-believing "practicers," regular and occasional, especially occasional. And of course there is an infinity of little sects and odd cults.

The most remarkable situation is that of atheists who define themselves as "post-Christian." For the "post-Christian," Christianity is the last, the ultimate religion. After it, no other is possible, because it possesses to perfection whatever the others have, or ever could have. The only step from Christianity that would not be a regression is atheism. Atheism is Christianity's true realization and accomplishment. It suppresses it and preserves it all at the same time. It does not refute it—the ripe fruit does not refute the flower. Thus theism and atheism are but opposite species within the same "genus," sharing the same presuppositions. In each, Christianity legitimates the inherited identities of a common tradition. In this perspective, paradoxically, theism and atheism are each the key to

the other, hand in hand at the heart of Western Christian civilization.

Clearly, in a Christianity forming part of the same system as
atheism, deep within the same world, teachings and rites will find
their necessity and signification in the immanence of this common
identity. They will be the functions and efficacious symbols of its
continuity. Dogmas and sacraments, in this context, operate as
ritualizing agents of the inscription of individuals into the substance of a tradition. In the constitution of a family and cultural
genealogy, they are, for the person, foundational myths, at once
transcended and true, commemorated in their incredible distance,
but constantly brought back and actualized as the expression of
that person's being in the world, in his or her historical difference,
and as the bond among relationships antecedent to moral and
economic transactions and social roles.

The logic of membership, confronted with the problem of temporal continuity and discontinuity, does not proceed according to
the binary logic of true or false. A living community's past cannot
be contradistinguished from its present as "true" or "false." What
has given one's ancestors reasons for living and dying cannot simply be reputed as absurd and senseless by one who finds oneself in
human continuity with them. The living person will bring into play
all the resources of hermeneutics, that art of demonstrating one's
participation in the same moral, intellectual, and esthetic community with those of the past in spite of distance and differences. The
interpretation will have the ethical value of care and concern bestowed upon one's dead—the value of the acknowledgment of the
historicity of one's own particularity.

What occurs when this Christianity, acculturated in Western
civilization, is exported? We might put it this way: It is incapable of
surviving elsewhere unless it is transported whole, transported "as
is," bearing with it its lifestyle, and implicating the whole universe
that permits it to reproduce the material and symbolic conditions in
which it is accustomed to grow. It will thrive where there prevail the
financial, economic, and political lifestyle and power of the West,
whose way it has prepared or followed.

It also transports with it all its variations. Because these latter are
defined and asserted in terms of a mutual relationship within a
single historical world, they call for one another in virtue of a struc-

tural necessity. Missionary zeal is the external projection of an internal differentiation, with all its debates and rivalries, and without any adaptation whatever. None of the forms of Christianity is capable of envisaging its non-necessity, its contingency. It presents itself as the only authentic form, or the most authentic. Actually this certitude is not measured against its reference to the gospel, but polemically, by comparison with the other confessions. Since one is Christian by custom, what is directly targeted is the denomination; the faith is aimed for only indirectly. It even happens that faith is absent, and that no scruple is felt in propagating a manner of living that is still esteemed as the highest, as it forms a single system with the dominant civilization.

The pity is the misunderstanding consecrated by a like "package," a like displacement of religion. A teaching and practice torn from their global moorings, which are not only ecclesial and religious but also literary, artistic, familial, and biological, evaporate in abstractions, in a subtle spiritual essence incapable of being grasped. Deprived of their sociocultural infrastructure and their immunological milieu, dogmas are proposed for pure credence. Their content, imposed in their compact literalness or watered down by reappropriating exegeses, issues in the fantastic, the legendary, the magical, or the allegorical. It calls either for the sacrifice of the intelligence or for duplicity. Only a genealogical Christianity can avoid both the one and the other, or join them together without contradiction. Apart from such a Christianity, integralism is impossible. It will take the form of the irrefutable universes that we have all seen die. Progressivism, for its part, is insupportable and offhand. It thinks it comes off by reducing the number of beliefs or by proposing the *contrary* of what has lately been held, pronouncing the latter passé, transcended, and demonstrating that the opposite of the prevailing obvious sense is the only true one, the one based on Scripture, the Fathers, and the Reformers. One is forced to conclude that the status of beliefs and rites is not the same for us as for those for whom Christianity is the genealogical, cultural religion.

2. But, we shall be told, what Christianity *should be* remains untouchable. Despite the weaknesses and inconsistencies of Christians, their churches have indefectibly handed on the *essentials* of the revealed message, self-identical, necessary for salvation, uni-

versal, and in no way tied to any civilization whatever.

Can one define the essence of Christianity apart from its historical realizations, so diverse that they are mutually irreducible, and sometimes indifferent, incomprehensible, or hostile toward one another? Can the message be presented cut off from the effect it produces? Is it not recognizable as the tree only by its fruits? Paradoxically, the answer is contained in the question. It is precisely what these Christianities have in common that divides them—and this is the message.

All the Christianities have the *form of certitude.* Each is sure of its facts and cannot admit that it may have been wrong. For each, the multiplicity of content, or of Christianities, is nonsense, because only one is true and the others are false. Each is absolute, convinced that its categories are true and its ways of acting best suited to all humanity—although of course it is clear that the inequality of abilities and aptitudes and the difference in ethnic and climatic conditions indicate their administration in small doses, and counsel adaptation. But the divisions among Christians show that certitude survives as an abstract ideal, precisely in taking on different concrete content. What abides as common to all its forms, then, is the pure form of a given Christianity.

All the Christianities repeat the same thing. The meaning of things and beings has been unveiled once and for all. Their essence is that dependence on the Creator. The human being has fallen by having sought to be emancipated from this dependence, but has been graciously saved from this ruin by Jesus Christ, the incarnate Son of God. Henceforth this salvation is realized for each person by and in the obedience of the faith, a life according to the Spirit of the gospel at work in the preaching and sacraments of the church founded by Jesus. Thus all that is just, good, and true, today as yesterday and tomorrow, attaches to this church, and thus belongs to Christianity; it emanates from its saving superabundance, or else is its prefiguration. Outside the visible or invisible pale of the Christian religion, which includes virtual, implicit membership, there is but error, ignorance, and evil. It is the duty of Christianity to propose this message to all—to spread it everywhere, without alteration, and to make of all men and women its faithful. Its privilege, for its part, is thus to be the only Christianity to be the vessel of the truth of everything and everyone, the only vehicle to be able to posit acts coextensive with all humanity and to speak in its name.

Precisely in what respect does the consciousness of being the sole beneficiaries of the mystery of the world, the human being, and God, now at last revealed, constitute the element that sets these Christianities in opposition to one another? The answer is the affirmation by each of them, via these common formulas, that it is what it is, absolutely. Thus Christianity's self-definition is a tautological affirmation of its identity, in the form of a certitude.

Tautology, it has been said, is that which is common to all classes of propositions having nothing in common. Let us make free application of this notion as follows: the meaning and import of a reference to one and the same Creed, one and the same Scriptures, one sole Lord, and a single faith remain indeterminate and leave room for divergent interpretations. What is professed in these confessions of faith or common acts is withdrawn from any possible comparison with other realities as incommensurable with them. Thus it can only be referred to itself, measured by itself, and self-designated, tautologically. Dogmas and rites have no other content or functions than this formal definition of Christianity as itself.

What is proper in the Christian divisions is that each church, each sect takes the formal definition of Christianity as the description of what it itself is, *in itself*—the shape in which it *appears* or *ought to appear* to itself and to others. Thus each substitutes for what it really is or does, what it holds to be its essence, its raison d'être—that is, the self-definition of Christianity as tautological identity and pure, empty form of certitude. But this identity and this form are capable of receiving any content whatever. And they are the common possession of Western civilization, which is thus able to maintain them through laicization and atheism. Its own ways of thinking and living, this civilization believes, are true and suit all humanity, which has need of them in order to come to the light, to be delivered from ignorance, misery, and oppression. Thus humanity attains to the dignity and bliss of true human beings. After the propagation of the true faith comes that of the true civilization, and then that of revolutionary truth: verbal or military intervention by the whites always takes on, in the eyes of the whites, the sense of a "mission"—the necessary, obligatory propagation of the meaning of existence, revealed to them and entrusted to them as a monopoly to be wielded by them alone.

Nothing else flows from dogmatico-ritual tautology but this pretension, which is reputed as the essence, the *ratio essendi,* of Christianity. "Dogma" and "rite" are inalterable not only because they
reduplicatively express the Christian identity, but because they express the divine authority and the definitively manifested essence of
existence as owing to that authority. Church and believer are subject to the Word, or revelation, and this means concretely that they
are not free with respect to vocabulary, images, accounts, mythical
structures, formulas, or the schemata of Scripture and tradition,
which today actualize and comment upon this Word and revelation
by symbol—by dogma and ritual. Immutability is the index, the
icon, of the transcendence of God and the essence of the real as
these now present themselves to the intuition. The dogmatico-ritual
configuration is the two-layer univocal reflection of the structure
of the spiritual realities, independently and in themselves, that are
the foundation, sense, and truth of what is sensible and temporal.

Thus the believer and the church are shut within the boundaries
of this "discourse" to which they adhere, and by which they are as
it were possessed. To be sure, they receive a ready-made language,
capable of expressing and effectuating the meaning of everything
that happens, capable of judging it globally and peremptorily. But
in the face of brand-new, complex situations and strange new mental universes, the unvarying repetition of formulas, references, and
a consecrated vocabulary speedily reveal their limits. It becomes
either impossible or an exercise in bad faith to try to make the
multiple experiences of individuals and economic, religious, and
cultural collectivities correspond with a predetermined structure of
sense and meaning, and with a Christianity considered a priori to be
the agent of all salvific transformations and the inventive principle
of all creative decisions and solutions. The course of the world and
the Christian claim to be everything get progressively out of phase.
Owing to this verbal and conceptual screen, dogmatic Christianity
ends by detaching from the real and manifesting a genuine inability
to understand. What is simply incredible, in the proper sense of the
word, is the kind of truth it wields—a truth given in advance once
and for all, deprived of any heuristic dimension, expressing no
meaning in a nascent state, in the course of being effectuated; expressing no interaction and exchange between the mind and its objects. Thus the enterprise of being true, of building truth, lacks

credibility as it constructs itself from without, from a preexistent, intangible corpus of words, concepts, images, legends, and transhistorical existential scenarios serving to capture the real, interpret it, and transform it.

3. The result is that a truth or belief is defined in such a way as to confront only itself, and so becomes "irrefutable." It can maintain itself indefinitely, as it has foreseen even the reasons and the meaning of any failure it might encounter; and any rejections that might lie across its path, when these occur, only serve to reinforce its certitude. Besides, dogmatic enunciations are not simply "declarative." They are not content merely to observe or inform. They are imperatives, performatives. True knowledge is obedience to the sovereignty of God. One recognizes it only in submitting and worshiping it. Not to understand is to disobey, to rebel, by preferring the human to the divine and ultimately preferring oneself to one's Creator and Savior. Thus the proof from Scripture comes down to the argument from authority. The correct interpretation is the one that finds the dogmas in the texts, and more generally the self-definition of Christianity, the church, and their certainty in those texts. A hermeneutical tradition that has used always and everywhere the same catenae of citations, the same loci, to prove the same assertions, or as solutions to the same problems and in the same intentionality, creates a prescription of meaning, however it may be that we can only understand the texts so adduced in a different sense today. Their probative force resides not in themselves, but in the fact-of-the-church, in the globalism of what it is, and in the understanding it has of itself as a divine institution of meaning. The intrinsic authority of the church gives validity to interpretations and lines of reasoning that of themselves are neither evident nor constraining. They enlighten and convince because the church brings them forward and teaches them.

We fall into the paradoxes and the perils of dictated understanding, of evidence acquired by proxy or substitute, of authority devouring the content of knowledge and the thing-in-itself as well as it rejects all criteria of truth except obedience, institutional self-reproduction, ecclesial utility, and conformity to the system of unconditional acceptance. Bible and church are substituted for intelligence and conscience. The monopoly of the absolutely true and divine language gives to those who enjoy it an infinite and unlimited power over the world, history, and conscience.

The symbolic domination that results is such as to provoke the paralysis of the soul and the most total alienation of the spirit. Every success will be justification and confirmation of the revealed truths, while all lack of success, all misfortune, and all danger will be laid to the account of enemies from without, possessed by demons—and, still more, will call for self-accusation and a sense of guilt from those within: the lukewarmness of their faith and the laxity of their morals are the cause of Christianity's lack of success and the world's unhappiness. These constitute a proof *e contrario* of the urgent need for the restoration of ascetic rigor and doctrinal intransigence. Those who accept such teachings and such "megalomaniac" guilt, and are in a condition of a social minority and economic, cultural, and political subordination, cannot help but seize upon a sense of their helplessness before an essential violence situated in an inaccessible origin within the inmost recesses of the soul—a violence of which actual, daily violence is but the sequel, the consequence, and the exterior, superficial manifestation. These people, then, are driven to work violence upon themselves, voluntarily, self-destructively, a violence of flesh on flesh. Thus they are at the mercy of those who bear the visible marks of salvation and who have the mission to announce the Good News thereof.

Was there ever any doubt? From the moment of God's "intervention" in the world, the institution claiming to be his lieutenant, literally—the institution in his place and stead, his vicarious presence—will naturally appropriate divine rights. When God becomes incarnate he takes on the history and culture into which he enters and confers upon them, by reason of his person and in his person, a divine nature and foundation. The collectivity with which he thus enters into alliance and strikes a pact of blood will be found to be exempt from the common norms of legality, morality, criticism, and interpretation. It will be "holy," beyond good and evil, and produce a type of human being of unforfeitable innocence, and of good conscience and self-assurance that cannot be confounded—and a collectivity particularly dangerous for the others. The imperialistic, totalitarian, and sectarian potentialities of the doctrine of the incarnation receive their full development in situations of dependency and religious exploitation of human misery.

Is this doctrine still to be believed? The culprit here is the foundational and authorizing principle of such a dangerously anthropomorphic conception. What is this principle?

4. The notion of "revelation" rests on the premise that there are empirically observable realities that are substantially sacred and afford direct access to God—that symbols exist expressing God's nature, symbols *of* God. From these one can ascend toward him, know what he is, know what he wills and what he does. They can occur in the form of persons, words, formulas, books, defined behavior, or inward sentiments or certitudes.

This writer fails to see in what respect a like premise differs from that of fetishism, which localizes the sacred or the divine, and endows persons, affects, or things with supernatural characteristics and powers. In the case before us, what God alone is, what he cannot communicate in any fashion—that is, his ipseity, his holiness, his difference—is actually attributed to these symbols. An immediate relation to God is precisely idolatry. Strictly speaking, one must say that nothing, and no one, is *of himself, herself, or itself* a mediation for arriving at God—not Scripture, not sacraments, not prayer, not suffering, and not the "certitude of faith." Human beings themselves are said to be in the image and likeness of God only insofar as they are in the form of word and in process of love: *in quantum invenitur in eis verbum conceptum et amor procedens,*[1] that is, inasmuch as they are concrete liberties in the process of becoming, discursively, by the mediation of the world and their own acknowledgment of one another, and not in any immediacy of their empirical naturalness.

We shall escape the fetishism of revelation only if we *admit*, with all its theoretical and practical consequences, the metaphorical character of the notion or expression of "revelation" or "Word *of* God." What do we mean by this?

When we assert that God calls, chooses, hears, speaks, is appeased or converted, we have to admit that we are using metaphors—that is, we are *transferring* to God what transpires within human beings, who, granted, "depend" on God for their own being. But from what we adduce by way of oracle, from "visions" or "revelations" to the effect that our prayer is heard, it does not follow that God inspires us, reveals himself, and hears us in the sense that he now accomplishes for our benefit what he has not already done. God does not manifest himself in the sense that he ceases to be hidden *after* having been so for thousands of years, now divulging secrets he has kept locked in his bosom from the foundation of the world. This would be to posit a change in God correlative to the one taking place in the "creature." This would be to measure his action *secundum prius et posterius*, that is, according to the duration proper to the created universe, proper to human beings, who are not only situated in time, but who are themselves temporal and historical. As conceivable by us, the action of God is absolute (and that is a tautology): it is situated in a duration proper to him alone, that of his difference, which we call "eternity." Accordingly, if we have revelations, they can never be in transitive cause-and-effect relation with his revelation. We predicate this latter of him only by reason of and in the form of our ascending relations of creature to Creator. We cannot place ourselves at God's standpoint and perspective, and see how things, and ourselves, issue from him, and then express this in a language of *descending relations*, except fictively or metaphorically.

Why does this classic doctrine of the transcendence of God, and the nature and language of creaturely relations to him, seem never to have been applied to "sacred history"? Why, indeed, has it been thought that a positivism, or fetishism, of revelation can be avoided in fixing God's manifestation not in a piece of wood but in a slice of time—two thousand years, or thirty years? Why do those who willingly admit that "we know *that* God is, but not *what* he is" pretend to know something about his intentions, acts, and deeds, on the grounds that *agere sequitur esse*—activity betrays the nature of its supposite? They will tell us with all assurance that God has acted with such-and-such an intention, or at such-and-such a moment of history, even in their own lives. What persuades them that they have abandoned metaphorical language when they pretend to be privy to the express will, the "customary ways," of God? Do they mean they might possess the knowledge he has of himself, the world, and the human being?

The illusion is a natural one: to make creation an event of the past, something that happened in the "beginning," and to consider "continuing creation" as the conservation of substances, essences completed and constituted in their first origin. Since then, nothing occurs but accidents, accidentals—of which grace is one. Anything coming upon the scene as a result of action, passion, the choices of freedom and human interaction apparently escapes the order of substances and essences, hence of creation, but not of the divine omnipotence. That omnipotence intervenes in this domain of novelty, of the unforseeable. In order to mark the transcendence of these interventions as the foundation of what is occurring, they will have another history created for them, as it were—an atemporal substrate for the history that impinges on the senses. The latter, then, will fall in the category of appearances, nature, or prehistory.

All that remains is to base this duality in the very being of God. In nature, God "hides" in his transcendence. But from what vantage can the human being plumb the depths of the divine immanence and transcendence, and so distinguish them and understand them? Is it true that history "declares the glory of God" (Ps. 19:2) more than do the heavens? Even in the life of Jesus, and after Jesus, we still have to repeat that "we do not know what God is, but what he is not, and what relationship is maintained with him by all things besides"—that we have not attained to the knowledge he has of himself, the human being, and the world.

The African religious experience is long since in possession of the datum that there are no symbols to express the nature of God. That language about God is, and can only be, anthropomorphic and metaphorical is itself an ancient legacy of reflective thought. The need to make these an active dimension of the common consciousness and of emancipating practice is incumbent as a historical task, merely from the fact that the missionary religions have hidden these by their "success," making the positivism of revelation the foundation of their claim to a hegemony and monopoly of the meaning of existence. To be sure, they have tolerated negative theologies as a privilege reserved to those rare virtuosos of speculation and mysticism on the margins of the institution, while the institution itself has been organized and functions according to the principle of authoritarian and substantive mediation. Here we have as it were a double-truth theory, in the service of the power of those who know over those who neither can nor ought to, and an institutionalization of duplicity—both of which seem to us who pay the bill for such an order of things to be difficult to defend.

What use ought we to attempt to make of Christianity in this situation of unequal encounter, in the transverse dimension of a radical historicity, without parallel worlds, without the possibility of gathering up a "revealed datum," intact, behind the backs of the historical, temporal human beings who are its vehicles and who speak of it and transform it ceaselessly? For the relationship passes through them as they are, and not as they say they are, and it passes through them by the exchange, conflict, and communication that we establish with them. But it also passes by way of those to whom we are attached by a pact of history and blood. One must take account of the human costs, psychological, intellectual, and material, to these latter from the use made of the beliefs to which we give our assent. These beliefs would have no truth value if we were to appropriate them all by ourselves, "even breaking human relationships, and the ties of life and history."

An ethics of historical responsibility for thought, truth, and belief commands us to subject to discussion, and to the judgment of our experience, what the dominators' *activism of the offerer*, of importunity, does not cease imperiously to propose to us. Thus, in this book, we have had to demand of the Christianity soliciting us that it enter into the framework of our movement for liberty in its most concrete expressions, and that it take the form of "African power," of self-determination rediscovered and rectified. We have not been able to exempt from examination either the gospel or the conception of God, under pain of uprooting, but then at once ourselves restoring the certitude and pretension to the universal that belong to the corpus of discourses and practices, institutions and lifestyles of an imperialistic civilization.

This is the approach we feel to have been counseled by what is at stake in the debates conducted throughout the chapters of this book. In Part One we shall expound the logic of the discourse and practice of Christianity as a dominant religion, with the effects these produce. We shall also describe the resistance of the "African reaction" in opposing them, and isolate the lines of force according to which this reaction is organized and expresses its historical and cultural difference.

In Part Two we shall seek to identify a reading of the gospel that will be possible for us without being the vain attempt of a "return to the founts," or of a "personal contact" that leaps across time and the abysses of history and culture. We shall deliberately take our point of departure in the present and its interests, without seeking to arrive at a motionless "datum" or "kernel" lying hidden in the recesses of the origin. Instead, we shall ask ourselves only what effect in terms of meaning these accounts still produce when they are heard today from within our historical reality.

Part Three will be the attempt to situate this effect with reference to the order of discourse and practices. It will neither propose programs nor prophesy. It will describe what actually occurs when one undertakes to ask oneself the following question: What is to be made of Christianity in the framework of an ethics of historical responsibilty, and in view of the experience of language limitations that forbid us to speak from "God's viewpoint"?

If we have in revelation the paradigm, or prime analogate, and progenitor of all subsequent ideologies *of last appeal*, then this work of critical review, still too much like that of the theologian for our liking, will have further implications, and reach into other spheres.

Part One

DOMINATION AND THE
ESTRANGEMENT OF BELIEF

The following backward glance is that cast by Africans on finding themselves essentially "locked out," lost, strangers to themselves. Our African's focus on the past here is not intended as an indictment for indictment's sake. The concern is for the present, in which one must live and act. The old forms of alienation are cited in order to promote a new departure, in order to denounce the persistence and latent presence of these forms today and to close off the avenues of their resurgence in other shapes. Further, what we here seek to express in the form of their negations are but the same positive, constructive approaches that will claim our attention throughout the remainder of this book.

In Part One we shall show how a Christianity of empire imposes itself only by tearing up its converts by the roots, out of where-they-live, out of their being-in-the-world, presenting them with the Faith only at the price of depriving them of their capacity to generate the material and spiritual conditions of their existence. Henceforward these dominated persons will be able to find their truth only outside themselves, as the utterly-other-from-themselves-and-their-universe. The missionary discourse has a habit of propounding God, or the content of the faith, as the irruption into one's world of the purest Strangeness, and conversion as the snatching of the candidate for Christianity from the jaws of perdition, which is confused with one's traditional mode of living and being human.

17

However, the methods and argumentation employed to discredit the beliefs, rites, and institutions of the "pagans" run the risk of backfiring and wrecking Christianity's credibility. The dominator-dominated relationship that operates in evangelization renders societies present—and hence generates manners, modes, and mores —that are *heterogeneous*, "foreign in their kind." The Christianity mounting the African shore is that of "bourgeois society." It will crash against the religiousness of societies altogether removed from its own. These societies will resist and set up a counterideal to such traits and tendencies, which for them are unbinding, individualistic, and monetaristic and invoke "in the name of the Scriptures" other values and another expressiveness. The latter will now play the role of unmasker of the partialities and particularities of a religion that pretends to universality.

Let us be wary, however, of overestimating the value of the manner of religion that spontaneously takes shape behind the popular practices of African resistance. Assuredly it is full of things for us to learn. But rarely does it mount to the level of the situation marked or determined by the arrival of Africans, and their disquieting newness. It is irrelevant, by its anachronism, precisely where its "imaginary praxis" and the immediacy of its recourse to the Powers are in default. The hour of the Son of man has struck.

Chapter 1

Uprooting, Alienating Praxis

Whence comes the right and the duty to extirpate the customs and usages of peoples to be converted?[1] What is the end result of such an operation? These are the questions to be examined in this chapter.

FOUNDATIONS OF THE POWER OF ERADICATION

The traditional African manner of living is interpreted as "paganism." The latter, in its turn, is characterized as "unfaith," faithlessness, the condition of the *infidelis*. Finally, the latter is ignorance and misconception of the true God, the One who has personally revealed himself. Consequently the traditional African manner of living is an evil life, and disinheritance.

The logic is ineluctable. The obliteration or absence of the correct understanding of God as he is either entails the degradation of the human being or is its nefarious consequence. Human beings who suffer the loss of their perception of "values" lose as well a perception of the God who constitutes the basis of these values, or rather, who prescribes them. The converse is equally true: the one who, explicitly or implicitly, denies the true nature of God falls prey to passions and vices.

It follows that paganism is not a neutral state, a lack to be made up. It is a state of guilt, of rebellion against God, and of fall beneath the threshold of humanity. Incorrectly to worship God is necessarily to have recourse to substitutes and simulacra. Idolatry, fetishism, and animism are the necessary forms and concrete shapes of error. We are not dealing here with intellectual error merely; this is error lived, existential error, which causes the human being to fall beneath the level of human "nature." Because it is against nature, paganism is inhuman. Inevitably it is accompanied by slavery, infanticide, cannibalism, polygamy, and all manner of other aberration and imperfection. This being the case, to Christianize will mean to humanize, to civilize the degraded human being. It will mean the taming of human beings, and their progressive rearing to a normal state by education, by tutelage as if of minors, until such time as they may attain to their majority and win emancipation.

This is a point to be insisted upon. What arouses missionary enthusiasm, the exhilarating thrust of being sent, is not simply the command to go preach the gospel to all nations. It is also the distress of the retarded pagan peoples. The most striking thing about Africa is its misery, moral as well as physical. Slavery, ignorance, superstition, immorality rage about in the most unbridled fashion. Corporeal afflictions fairly swarm. The appalling force of this degradation is a demonstration *e contrario* of the humanizing power of Christianity. Where the latter is lacking, stagnation reigns and regression is just in the offing.

This regression is, in the first instance, of an intellectual order. Human beings will become, or continue to be, "big babies" in their concepts, in their modes of reasoning (or rather, of not reasoning), in their beliefs. Second, this regression will be moral. A human being becomes a package of instincts—and what is worse of depraved, unnatural instincts. Now, as animality has got the upper hand, as human beings have turned into dangerous beasts in certain respects, it is evident that the only language they will understand in the beginning will be that of constraint and discipline, the language of immediate sanction by chastisement or reward. This constraint is imposed upon them as it is imposed upon children or the infirm: for their own good. Indeed it is themselves they must be shielded from, for they have in effect forfeited their rights and become incapable of their responsibilities. They are morally incompetent.

Hence the authority exercised over them is twofold: natural and religious, in indissolubility. It is the authority at once of reason and of revelation, of civilization and of faith, the former being both condition and product of the latter in each pair. For what is original and unique with Christianity is that these tandems are unified and circular. Here we have the reason why evangelization and colonialism are inseparable. In themselves they are very different but they are not opposed. Indeed they coincide with respect to the task of the rehabilitation of the retarded, fallen human being. Moreover, the West, despite appearances, is Christian. Its ethics, its sensitivity, the very fibers of its being are steeped in Christianity. Atheists in the West practice more true religion in their daily round, professional ethics, family life, and elevated concept of God than do baptized Africans. Whence emerge a number of attitudes or norms of conduct, as logical as they are arresting.

First, the constant collaboration, since the sixteenth century, between mission and colonial power, and the dependency of the former on the secular arm of empire, wherever it may stand in need of its protection, material means, or safe conduct in order to carry on a successful work of rehabilitation, has not, to be sure, been without a certain violence, in some of its modalities, upon its beneficiaries.

Second, whatever their merits, the new Christians cannot be placed on equal footing with the Western colonials; and those colonials, be they the most vicious of miscreants, will be more deserving of respect and consideration than their protégés. Why? Because in either, there is an inalienable substratum that changes the meaning of visible, surface manifestations. The black is still a pagan, and rather a child, despite baptism; and the white Occidental is still a Christian, a rational, reasonable being, despite transgressions and straying. The Christianity of the former is a veneer, something adventitious, an accident. The Christianity of the latter is substrate and substance.

The proper pedagogy for the African, then, will be one of "firmness." It will inculcate obedience and gratitude. Firmness is necessary for the taming of the animal in the African. The Africans' obedience cannot be one that issues from the human "rational will." These creatures are sensitive only to the subjugating values of prestige or to fear—for them, literally the beginning of wisdom.

The African virtue par excellence, then, will be the one that flows from fear: docility. After all, has the African nothing to learn? One will avoid, then, prematurely awakening in this person a sense of autonomy. Pride will be crushed. Without diffidence, in other words without self-contempt, Africans will sin by temerity and presumption. Haste makes waste. This slow caution is for their own good.

Another virtue is necessary here as well. It is called gratitude. Africans must recognize what is being done for them, what it means to leave one's homeland and to place oneself at their service under such hard conditions. This gratitude should extend even to the missionaries' parents, who have so generously consented to their children's exile. It should extend to the mother country, which has dispatched them hither—the nation-mediatrix of civilization and the faith. No chauvinism this, no natural, inordinate project. Surely not. The nations of Europe are lovable, and are loved, because they have been sanctified by the faith and watered by the blood of martyrs, and thus have been incorporated into the framework and substance of salvation history. It may seem paradoxical, but it is for this very reason—because attachment to their own countries will be tantamount to attachment to a pagan land and a pagan past—that these new Christians must be deterred from any nationalism of their own.

Finally, it is also out of profound considerations of religion that the missionary is a person of such stern rigor—a real crusader. After all, the missionary's struggle is not merely with these sullied human persons, but with the evil spirits themselves, everywhere abroad, penetrating all things and dominating everyone. In Christendom demons wear masks. Here in heathendom, their last bastion, they show their face. They work in the open, they maintain their tyranny without the trammels imposed upon them by the omnipresence, in civilized climes, of the church and its efficacious spiritual instruments. Here the devil is despot, and his crown of empire is studded with his obsessed, his possessed, his devotees, and his oracles. Against him and his minions, the missioner is engaged in total, inexorable war, and naked violence is not merely a matter of principle but of practice.

The conclusions are inescapable. The faith, in this context, calls for neither freedom nor comprehension. We are dealing with minors—degraded beings, instruments of the forces of evil. Constraint is not only licit, it is obligatory. Or to put it another way, the faith of the colonial protégé is an effect of domination. It is a faith under tutelage, a faith by proxy. Faith becomes the credit accorded the missioner and the colonial by the native on grounds of their prestige and superiority. It is the native's state of subjugation, dramatized as if for the theater.

TORN UP BY THE ROOTS: NO MORE OF THIS WORLD

> For the worship of infamous idols
> is the reason and source and extremity of all evil
> [Wisd. 14:27].

Behold the maxim of the missionary enterprise.

The existence of a pagan world is *ultimately* to be explained in the cult of idols. All the faces of paganism are ultimately reducible to idolatry. One single intentionality informs and pervades its life in all its aspects. Hence the Christian is on the horns of a dilemma: either yield or resign from social life.

Actually, of course, *datur tertium*: Destroy the pagan institutions and substitute Christian ones. When Christianity was a minority and powerless, it could only shrink into an exile within itself and send its adepts physically into the desert, to solitude. But then Christendom was born from the ashes of the Roman empire. By the time it reached Africa it was in a position of strength and power. Now it could afford to implement its second strategy: the eradication of paganism by violence. Converts must abandon their world and live in villages built expressly for them—"reductions." Or they must form a ghetto community within their old villages. In fact, their world must be destroyed in all its family, political, and economic institutions. The Good News of Christianity is not the proclamation of a pink cloud. It is not a message of beatific peace. It is a piercing sword and a devouring fire. It is the judgment of an angry God bursting upon history. Before he justifies and sanctifies, God condemns. Before he builds or sows, he levels and uproots.

Ancient institutions and ancient society, we shall be told, were transformed from within by the slow, patient toil of the Spirit. To be sure. But that was then. Providence knows divers ways. The power of the Spirit is institutionalized now. It operates within the organizations and mores of a civilization. The Roman Empire, for all its brutality, had been an objective and providential preparation for the propagation of Christianity. Today the Pax Moderna, the spread of the moral notions of the West, respect for the human person, rational monotheism, the separation of sacred and profane, the monogamous family, the asceticism of productive labor—all are better than preparation: they *are* Christianity, anonymous but ready to drop the disguise on first interrogation.

The historian can easily add to this list. Justification of this sacred enterprise of eradication is easy. What is reaching out to the South from Old Europe and the New World is but the extension of the North's own continuous, glorious, inquisitorial struggle against witches, heretics, and the possessed. Extirpation, conscious and explicit in days gone by, today is couched in euphemisms and metaphors.

There is only one flaw in the enterprise: its whole existential operation. Let us examine how it tears up, how it shatters.

Space

Extirpation is the negation of the pagan's living space and the substitution of another, more abstract or even totally chimerical living space. There are familiar vectors in life—directions one is wont to go, calculated to provide one with a locus of presence to oneself as a corporeal being. Extirpation is a mode of disorientation via the suppression of one's points of reference. It is disorientation by disjunction. A whole group, as we well know, will convert to Christianity, as to Islam, only upon transplantation to new villages. Here in the "reductions" everything is within the Christian's easy reach. But everything is *for* the new converts—never *by*. They are strangers to themselves—rejected in what constitutes them as selves. Henceforward the converts are to live in borrowed space— and this borrowed space imposes a strange and unfamiliar personhood, to which they must conform. And what is this borrowed space? The institutionalized judgment and ceaseless condemnation of all that the persons have been of and for themselves, the imposition of an extraterritorial administration.

In this universe of silent reproach, the new Christians perceive themselves suddenly stripped naked and despoiled. The result is a geography of fantasy and theological dichotomy. There are holy lands, and there are other, not holy lands. The latter have their truth and genuineness only in their effort to copy the former—the lands where the holiness of God hath dwelt. The new Christian is condemned to strive for an absent goal. The unreal is not that which does not exist; the unreal is that which *ought* not exist, that whose being is only apparent or borrowed. Pagan space is unreal. Thus the pious thing to do is to snatch oneself forth from it, at least in spirit. The heavenly Jerusalem on high has its projections here on earth, but they are very far from home.

Time

The pagan has no past, unless it be a past of wandering, a desperate search for deliverance. If, after conversion, one preserves any memory of it, let it be to one's shame. Let it be an occasion of gratitude to God for having at last inserted one into sacred history. To present the pagan past in any other light is to idealize it and consciously or unconsciously to yield all the more to anti-Christian sentiments—to a satanic hatred of the light. Any ethnology that fails in the unmasking of what it means to be native falls prey to this idealist illusion, this anti-Christian conspiracy. The Christian notion of history is altogether clear and simple: a pagan past is wholly and entirely disinheritance, deprivation, and distress. The degradation of paganism goes without saying, just as does the superiority of Christianity.

And yet, awash in the aberrations and distortions, what do we see? Traces, vestiges of the state of innocence, of a "primitive revelation"! Yes, there are providential seeds, stones half-upright in the rubble, where one can sit and wait. All this will come to light when the great Christian tree appears, once the church rises from darkness into its destined dawn. Then shall day banish the shadow of night, and the burgeoning tree absorb all the tentative seedlings unto itself. The pagan past has no value in itself. The fullness of Christianity acknowledges its value by suppressing it. The continuation of a promise after the promise has been fulfilled is a contradiction. Leave a like scandal to Jews. Let proclamation and prophecy now fade and die: breach with one's past is an absolute imperative of conversion to Christianity. Christian time admits of no interruptions. Its advance is rectilinear: its strides from the age of Judaism to our own, passing by way of the primitive church, the

Middle Ages, the Renaissance, and modernity. Conversion means integration into this current. The only history Christianity has consists in a radial diffusion, outward from a primitive focal point, being solely and exclusively the dissemination of completed forms and fully constituted truths whose identity admits of variation only in their degree of repetition and expression. The converts are half-breeds, adopted ones. Their temporal continuity and unity are shattered. They becomes a mass of confusion, unable to differentiate between the time of mystery—the life of Jesus as commemorated in today's sacred festivals—and the history of the West, which they now will wish to sacralize and "repeat" for their salvation's sake.

Since it cannot present itself to other ways of being human except from without, Christianity becomes an exoticism, a time-before-time, where one enters oblivion and expatriation. Mystery is transformed into fable and marvel. The neophyte, all uprooted, is rendered incapable of the act of assuming his or her worldly being—and of perhaps recognizing the "gift of God" (John 4:10) there.

Consequence: Belief Estranged

Just as the praxis of evangelization is the suppression of one's "sense of situation," and the evasion of the obligation to take oneself in one's own charge, so faith finds its phenomenological locus in the manifold renunciation of the process of inculturation. Faith is consciousness torn out of the worldly realities that it had taken upon itself and by which it was being mediated, so that it has become a stranger to its own self. Delivered up to a totally different world, it fixes the object of belief only as "other" to this object—as an outsider vis-à-vis its new world, its beyond, its abstraction, its reversal. The absolute appears with the traits of a Strangeness, without recognizable references. As a result it can be coined in arbitrary, predetermined material, inaccessible to examination and verification. Now faith is become authoritarian orthodoxy, and the adherence and conviction it calls for will be all the stronger and more fervent for being based altogether outside such adherence and conviction, where the subjects escape their own grasp, and forfeit the support and stay of their world—the support of concrete reality.

Subjective certitude and mass conversions scarcely militate against this description, as we have them on record. On the contrary, where there are no ill-integrated, disoriented tribes milling about in the folds, where Christianity is not perceived as a means of access to a "higher civilization," conversions do not come in crowds. In this case it is the marginalized who will be recruited to be the sheep. Here there would be nothing disreputable in Christianity's making it a point of pride and distinction to "proclaim the Good News to the poor." No, here the scandal is that the dominant religion *creates* poor in order to evangelize them, holding itself out as the means to human advancement. At the same time, the faith itself is struck a blow, rendered equivocal. Now it belongs to the order of means. As means it will be judged according to criteria of efficacity and productivity—by its ability to afford access to the enjoyment of the benefits of civilization. But the day will come when less indirect approaches will be available, later techniques will be more decisive. When that day comes—as the one-time pagan recovers his or her capacity for self-construction, for producing the conditions of his or her own existence—the techniques of the faith will be rejected, and yesterday's convert will only lose the faith, these estranged and estranging beliefs.

In the meantime, the person's "Christian life" will be marked by a structural, constitutive duplicity. Until now, religion was a metaphor of life—the acknowledgment, in the acts of living, of the movement and power by which life's self-transcendence never abates. In accepting one's determinations and conditionings, one's radication in nature, and everything by which one was mediated— the earth, sex, strength—the African human being moved into a position of relationship with Life, with God. It was one's attachment to this or that piece of earth, it was this particular mode of production, it was such-and-such a manner of life, such-and-such a manner of being a sexual creature, it was the playing of this or that role in society, belonging to this particular age-group that wove the tissue of the religion of existence. It was being born, living, and dying in the most empirical manner that ever could be, that furnished the framework, the matter, and the experience of God's sacrality and sovereign immanence. When you concentrate the divine in a holy land, a sacred book, an inaccessible, distant, absent person or subjectivity, when you transform a concrete existence into a neutral reality, or into evidence for a transcendent, distant God, you remove all possibility of attaching to God except from the outside: by intention, by invocation, by will, by dedication and consecration. Now it is voluntarism that constitutes the essence of faith. Now the testimony of the senses, the evidence for one's worldly existing, must be renounced without ceasing. Now the substance of life must be set at naught, held as nothingness. Now the only object of esteem will be something distant, absent—attainable only by aspiration, tension and intention, and misty recall. Now what one cannot see must be pronounced to be the only thing that matters, and life and living proclaimed nonessential.

All this is only "dogma." When the neophyte tires of "salvation" and begins to long for healing and physical and moral wholeness—when one begins to seek to discover a meaning in one's acts and passages, begins to testify to oneself that one's lot stands in continuity and solidarity with teeming humanity on all sides—suddenly the ancient piety is the essential thing again, and it resumes its old role of interpreter of everything, even the articles of Christian faith. But this reappropriation is always accompanied by a sense of shame. It is always clandestine, for it is contraband. Now the neophyte will lead twin lives—a cloven life, a life in twain. This exile of the divine in a realm of transcendence will permit the "new" domain of politics, economics, and the struggle for life to develop outside the compass of the divine. One will make an effort, by the power of the Word, to "offer up" this new domain from without, to moralize it by an act of will, right intention, and good conscience. In the same movement the Christian discourse will function as dilatory quietism, depreciation of the human being, and rejection of reality.

Christian discourse will now function as interdict. How so? Christian practice will be reduced to the monotonous proclamation of the difference of the divine, ceaselessly described by way of contrast with and opposition to the human being, altogether *as if* there were no gift to God not snatched from human beings, to the latter's annihilation. It will be dinned in our ears: vain are the enterprises of the human creature, and powerless to save. There is no salvation outside the Word of God, outside the action of his redemptive presence as manifested in Jesus Christ, projected into the present by and in preaching, the sacraments, and the life of obedience and piety on the part of the faithful. No, not even what the human being conceives, thinks, and wills as possible is actually possible to him or her. In each crisis, in each problem of human destiny, when humanity asks itself what it is that it must urgently do, the language of faith will refer it to the necessity of a radical renewal that can only be brought about by God. Before conversion, or in the absence of repentance and obedience to the faith, any solution will be sullied by sin—the sin of pride—and sooner or later will be blasted by the divine wrath. The language of "the faith" takes its point of departure in the dogmatic postulate that men and women *wish to suffice unto themselves*, "save" themselves, *make themselves God*. This is the absolute evil from which they must be protected, by the constant summons to a total, trusting abandonment to the salvific and all-powerful will of God.

Let men and women recognize their utter dependence. Let them disqualify in advance all they do. Let them "accuse themselves" without ceasing, and let them renounce all that presents itself as self-exaltation or the desire of self-transcendence. This discourse is addressed to men and women in their particular, concrete situations; hence, it is there precisely that the prohibition from transcending their limits will charge action with guilt, any action that innovates, that seeks to change the status quo or to rearrange the alleged limits and confines of the human being's "territory." Novelty is the badge of recalcitrance, and the covert or potential rival of eternal truths. When acts fail—when our designs for the transformation of society and the human conditions are checked—this can and should function as the occasion of a renunciation of human pride with its pretensions to clairvoyance.

But the imported novelty will abide. Its origin will be sought in the Bible or in Christianity. Quietism, fixism, and refusal to take risks will be accompanied by the conviction that one is always right—that one occupies a position that juts out over the risks and uncertainties of history and action, so that they disappear. Alienation consoles itself by forgetting itself utterly, and plays the role of monopolizer of the truth—of messenger of truth in all things to all persons everywhere and always. The only difficulty is that a like unificative truth is not of this world. Ideologized Christianity knows nothing of the eschatological not-yet. This is why it alienates.

Chapter 2

The Missionary Discourse

Christianity is heir to Greek reason and continuation and crown of the Judiac revelation. In virtue of this double qualification, it is the critic of the unreason of the other religions and the denunciation of their mythological nature. Its own proper element is language and history—not the obscure regions of the cosmos or the imagination. This is the reason for its eminent suitability to modern times. This is why it resists the corrosion of these times—the modern disenchantment with the world—better than do the other religions. Briefly stated, Christianity demonstrates its superiority by its qualities: Christianity is reason, history, and power. In this chapter we shall set forth the "missonary argumentation" and make a critical evaluation of it. Our thesis will be that this manner of presenting Christianity contains the seeds of the future discredit: its own procedures and weapons will be turned against it.

PRESENTATION

The Language of Derision

The first language addressed to the pagan is that of derision. The gods die of ridicule. Terrified by a burst of laughter, the spirits vanish like the dreams of night at the first flash of dawn. The helpless gods must fail to survive the laughers' boldness, for the bold ones are not struck dead on the spot. Thus did Elisha avenge the honor of his God and evince the divine origin of his mission by cursing the naughty boys of Bethel, who had jeered at his baldness: "Then two she-bears came out of the woods and tore forty-two of the children to pieces" (2 Kings 2:24). Elijah, on the other hand, confounded the servants of Baal by mocking their god with impunity: "When it was noon, Elijah taunted them: 'Call louder, for he is a god and may be meditating, or may have retired, or may be on a journey. Perhaps he is asleep and must be awakened' " (1 Kings 18:27). Mockery of a god must be erased by punishment, and his dignity restored by signs and wonders. Thus the dignity of the God-Man was endorsed by the prodigies at his death and by the ensuing professions of faith by the thief and the centurion—miracles of faith beyond any mere suspension of the laws of nature.

The persistence of this theme, through many metamorphoses, suggests its importance in the scheme of revelation. This is a central concept of the Bible, and there will be no exceptions: sin contains its own punishment. It visits human beings in their earthly life in various forms—misfortune, disease, and sudden death. Malefactors and persecutors are its most frequent victims. The teaching of the prophets combats a belief in the automatism of this sanction, in its blind descent upon innocent generations. Each one bears a burden of guilt and undergoes the penalty of his or her sin. True, Jesus will renounce the quest for a one-to-one correspondence between misfortune and discoverable fault. But no one will ever untangle the ancient bond between sin and death in all its forms and figures, any malady or calamity visited upon individuals and groups. You do not defy God and his laws and fail to pay the consequences. The impious laugh is too direct a provocation to escape appropriate response. Ridicule of the divinity has something Luciferian about it: surely it will cause the good angels and nature itself to convulse in indignation. Immobility and silence? Now, that would be intolerable. Idols alone are dumb, have no voice, make no response, give no sign of attention. The true God speaks. The jeering laugh is the best lie detector where false gods are concerned. Laughable gods are killed off by laughter, and their faithful slink away amid ridicule. A god who permits himself to be snubbed without protesting—be it only by the heroism of his devotees in the face of death or by a spectacular increase in their number—is evidently an unreal god.

This is what the missionary discourse dwells upon, generation after generation. The pagan gods are not only absurd, they are downright mirth-provoking. They deserve nothing but sarcasm. The adorers of these gods resemble them, so that they, too, call down upon themselves that supreme humiliation held in store by the one true God for their prideful self-sufficiency—ridicule.

The gods love to wrap themselves in night. Strong light is most unflattering. The mysteries, unmasked, become childishness, and the loudness of our laughter today only matches our earnest adherence of yesterday. The Christian will lay the mysteries bare for the uninitiate to gaze upon in total assurance and confidence. Indeed the ardor of the missionary will transform these verbal desecrations into iconoclastic raids. Whole expeditions will be undertaken for the purpose of profanation. The missionary will stride forth to beard idolatry in its very den: in the shadow of the temple, in the glade of the sacred wood, in the dark of the caves of initiation. There shall the missionary dash the statues to earth, overturn the altars. The gods will be mute. Thus raillery, invective, and direct action all join together to create a syntax of derision. As we may expect—the exercise of colonial power scarcely entailing any risk of martyrdom or other form of reprisal—the language we are here describing has been applied without stay or stint.

The Language of Refutation

Derision is itself refutation—perhaps the best there may be. But it appeals to a sense of shame: it has recourse to defiance, to provocation. Refutation properly so called is addressed to the intelligence. It moves its discussion along lines of causality, origin, and finality.

Pagan beliefs are an outgrowth of unbridled silliness. They are the turning of one's back on the basic evidences of good sense and the first principles of reason. The veneration of idols is pure foolishness. The mind reels in the face of such obtuse materialism and anthropomorphism.

Side by side with the foolishness of the motley herd, of course, is the canny swindle of the few: the wizards, the witch doctors, the members of the secret societies, the elders—all who know how to make use of their status and function for the arrogation of special privileges, exemption from arduous tasks, and the reservation to themselves of the good things of life by means of religion and belief. How many prohibitions, taboos, and rituals have all-too-transparent a finality: that of an instrument of domination, through the abuse of the general credulity of the masses.

But there is something even worse than charlatanry, namely, self-deception. We provide ourselves with models and archetypes of misbehavior the better to gorge our passions, the better to abandon ourselves to our evil tendencies. What we desire, that we believe in. Thus pagan religion is the sacralization of shamelessness and gives rein to the basest instincts. Of course, there is another explanation—in utilitarianism, but a very short-range utilitarianism, based on ignorance of the true causes of things.

Refutation amounts to what we might call "ideological reduction." Ideology is defined here as the projection of one's ignorances and impotencies as knowledge and power (thus turning them inside-out). But this is bare seeming, and it has its negative effects. It dissuades the devotee from an effort to grasp things as they are, from colliding with them in order to transform. Ideology is an illusion, and it immobilizes and alienates. It is also a camouflage for illegitimate interests that may not be openly avowed, a camouflage in the mists of a reversed order of causality where explanation, practice, or priority of action and thought are concerned. Ideology is mystification. Ultimately it is phantasmagoric projection. The pagan expounds fantasies as something come upon, something discovered, and takes them for things "that happened," takes them for real objects. The pagan fixates on things that hold one fast in repetitious, subhuman primitiveness. The African pagan is a prisoner of a closed universe of desire and narcissism. This new language is the best translation for all that we have seen expressed in the attitudes and behavior of the human being we have to convert—the big baby, glued to its own imagination, prey to passions and instincts, incapable of managing the self.

The Language of Demonstration

Demonstration is the exposition of the Christian faith in all its order, coherence, and transforming power. The profession of faith, even as ejaculation or acclamation, is never just cry. Discourse only manifests the articulable nature of that profession.

And its discursiveness, in turn, is distinguished by a certain historicity. Its categories—the points of view from which we are to envisage its object so as to grasp it as an organically constituted set of intelligible connections—are constituted through the mediacy of the typological events of biblical history. But biblical categories, while of course still remaining the language of obligatory reference, need to be transposed into the common language of civilization, the language of transcendence of ethnic and traditional particularities, the language of philosophy.

The missionaries, then, will be speaking the language that results from this transposition. Dogmatic language is the language of revelation and biblical categories as reworked with the help of philosophy, with a view to preserving their spirit from heretical distortions, ensuring their integral transmission, and placing them in communication with the world of civilization. Such language is not the result of mere pious meditation, but of confrontation with culture, of constant altercation among Christians in their antagonistic professions of faith. The resulting complexus—called "revelation" or the "Good News"—is now pulled within the circle of civilization and interchurch polemic and substituted for the freedom of the Word of God.

When Christianity thus becomes the object of transmission, when it is the traditional religion of everyone, and thus is no longer the object of a choice, it is transformed into a corpus of habits maintained by inculcation and the need to be integrated and to conform. The distinction between the essential and the secondary is lost. Kerygma dissolves in ecclesiality. What is presented today as the Good News is actually a church, a denomination, and the criteria of faith coincide with those of church membership. Therefore catechisms of the various confessions will devote themselves to the reproduction of this composite reality (which henceforward will hold place and title of substance of salvation), which includes many considerations of a rational, customary order, and notions proper to a middle-class society and its ethos. The catechisms will be presented as manuals of the practical knowledge of what is needful for salvation, or—and this is the same thing—what it means to be a good Christian.

The matter taught is divided into truths to be believed, commandments to be observed, and sacraments to be received. Exactness is absolutely necessary: these consecrated formulas express truths whose knowledge has a bearing on one's salvation. Their faithful commitment to memory ensures orthodoxy independently of any comprehension of what is recited. The understanding of the faith can come later. Or it can fail to come—in which case the believers, via the unfathomable words, will signify their intention to embrace *in globo* what the church professes, protesting that they understand it all in the sense in which the church understands it.

What is this church? Here the word denotes the titled professional guardians of meaning—those possessing the authority that flows from knowledge and the knowledge that flows from authority. "Faith" is the sacrifice of understanding. Understanding is given over to others for the decision as to what is the exact meaning of one's belief. One's faith is directed to a belief in the institutionalization of meaning somewhere in the Bible or in the practice of those who grasp it correctly as it is handed down in the creeds, or somewhere in the hierarchy, with the support of the science of the theologians.

This delegation of understanding will be all the more full and complete in proportion as the complexus of biblical categories, philosophical notions, polemical assertions, and testimony of the Fathers and Reformers who henceforward shall be Christianity and the message of salvation, no longer retains its kerygmatic simplicity, no longer challenges or summons. Now it is learned, handed down. Devotions, piety alone give it intuition and experience in the souls of the majority, but beyond or short of discourse. The simple of heart, who see and feel more than the savants—in fact, who precede them into the kingdom of heaven promised to children—are the constant figure and theme of preaching and spirituality. In the church they have no role but that of answering the call to humility, the role of "the exception that proves the rule." They are saved by the "obedience of faith," which gathers up in their name what they are lacking themselves. "Not many of you are wise, as men account wisdom; not many are influential; and surely not many are well-born" (1 Cor. 1:26), you African neophytes—but you will place yourselves in the wise hands of your evangelizers, who will carry to you the truth, transmit to you the deposit of faith.

Of course, this self-abandonment suffers from an intrinsic ambiguity. It is not clear whether you are here obeying God or human beings. Nor is it clear whether or not it is legitimate to commit to another your own understanding of and responsibility for the faith. This ambiguity is then driven to the point of out-and-out confusion by the syncretistic nature of the object of faith, and the manner of proposing it under the formality of membership in a confession and a culture. Thus the principal themes of the Christian demonstration in missionary discourse are the worship of the one true God, sexual and family morality, the work ethic, and private property.

The truths to be believed: These truths are the mysteries of religion, which bear on the being of God and his creative and redemptive activity. They also include an *absolute* anthropology, providing information on the origins of the human being, the genesis of the person's present condition and "end," or ultimate destiny. The human being's structure—constitution of a soul and a body as "compatible with," that is, demanded by, revelation—is among these truths to be believed. To be sure, as far as the science of salvation is concerned, rote learning, accompanied by the trustful abandonment of oneself to the church, whose understanding of the faith is full and complete, suffices. Indeed it is clear that these converts' grasp of the truths to be believed is very weak, immersed as they are in concrete reality and hence incapable of abstraction. But revelation presupposes reason. The fullness of time has come when humanity has finally arrived at a knowledge of certain basic concepts of ontology, cosmology, and philosophical anthropology. Greek philosophy is a preparation for the gospel—indeed the only preparation outside the Judaic revelation.

The concept of causality is scarcely a luxury if one is to believe in the doctrine of creation. Concepts like nature, substance, and person are scarcely optional apparatus if the doctrine of the Trinity is going to be propounded. Transcendence, immanence, spirit, incorporeality, free choice, dualism of body and spirit, and the like are concepts pertaining to the faith. Catechumens' intellects may not be able to penetrate them. Still they must carve these concepts into their memories, so as to be able to cite and recite them at least with their lips. The road to reason is inculcation. One need only adapt oneself to one's hearer, proportion one's discourse to the capacities of the native, and convince that person by so-called natural, concrete lines of reasoning, by recourse to comparisons, images, and analogy that what one teaches is true. Thus, for example, in order to discover to a person the absurdity of believing that a human being can arise from a rock or a spring, or be descended from some animal, that person need only be shown "by a thousand concrete examples" that "like produces like." Sometimes merely giving the scientific explanation will suffice to make fetishism disappear.

Theological categories, even those immediately transposed from the gospel, indeed couched in the very language of the New Testament, pertain to a science that must first be inculcated before being understood. Predestination, the opposition between the law and the gospel, between nature and grace, the divine dispositive will with its transcendent quality of the arbitrary—all of these, besides presupposing a knowledge of ancient texts replete with difficulties, presuppose as well a spirit of scholastic disputation and the admission of certain postulates concerning the divine nature (its omniscience, its omnipotence), as well as the nature of the human being as an individual. As neophytes have no preparation for these oppositions, these dichotomies, they must be taught them. Without any preparation for the gospel in their own tradition, they will now receive gifts of "nature and grace" in a single package. Access to the gospel tacitly or explicitly presupposes the possession of what has prepared for that gospel, of what constitutes its necessary, however insufficient, condition. The evangelical demonstration is simultaneously the demonstration of the reasonableness of the faith—education to the reason that the faith presupposes.

The commandments to be observed: The emphasis here will fall on sexual and familial morality. The concupiscence of the flesh, just as much and more than the pride of life, is the sign of the irresistible empire of sin. In practice, fornication is sin, and that is all there is to be said. It symbolizes sin—or better, it *is* sin par excellence. It only seems far removed from idolatry and fetishism. It is the humiliating chastisement of the ignorance of God, but only because it is already rebellion. It is unbridled liberty, and ignores the restrictions placed by God on enjoyment, which restrictions attest to his sovereignty and the right order and finality with which he has inscribed his creation and nature. Debauchery, shameless acts, and sexual license are at once the cause and the effect of ignorance of God, of disobedience. They cloud the mind and the intelligence. One becomes blind to spiritual values. They are the shortest way to insensitivity to such values and the shortest way to addiction to vice with all restraints removed. This is why they dominate and abase the life of paganism. In Africa impurity is institutionalized in license—the license of premarital sexual relations, concubinage, and polygamy.

The gospel is the inexorable, uncompromising eradication of these tares. Monogamy is part and parcel of the Good News, just as is the indissolubility of marriage. Polygamy is to be interpreted as the refusal of conversion. It is a sinful state. That it degrades the human being to the level of the beast only proves one thing: that that human being has need of grace, that cultures have need of being Christianized in order to preserve the humanity of the human being. One is not concerned to deny that institutional monogamy, the understanding of marriage as a contract between two individuals, and the doctrine concerning the ends of marriage are of non-Christian origin, the marks of a civilization. This only indicates once again the preparatory character of this civilization with respect to the gospel, by virtue of its rational, reasonable cast; but, one hastens to add, Christianity alone has provided the strength to observe and put into practice all that can be seen or known by culture or by reason.

Christianity bestows the power and the execution by grace as well as by its institutions. Hence the inevitable ambiguity of the latter. Institutions are required in order to ensure the humanity of the human being, and yet they are inconceivable, or at any rate not totally conceivable and surely not practicable, apart from the light of inspiration and revelation. This ambiguity authorizes and urges administrative and legislative measures directed to the suppression of customs and mores contrary to the gospel. The model of the family held forth by Christianity is not simply one model among many. Hence one has the right to impose it upon those with whose tutelage one is entrusted, and not only with a view to their earthly well-being and human enhancement. One must proclaim it, one must preach it as pertaining to the Good News. Is not the Christian family the church in miniature? Is it not at once the basic building-block of society and the basic community, where the faith finds its first and last radication, where the faith can reproduce and be transmitted naturally after the manner of an inheritance and legacy? Evangelization can be conceived of as the multiplication of Christian families, where the faith has become consubstantial with family traditions and customs, with parental authority and filial obedience. Social action and the transformation of the world can be conceived of as the extension to all men and women of the happiness that flowers within the Christian family. Justice will reign on the day that everyone who wishes may have a happy family, rear beautiful, numerous children, and enjoy a miniature society of mutual assistance, love, and pardon. Does not Christianity teach that, ultimately, humanity itself constitutes a single family, with the one God for a Father? Indeed, is not this God—this Trinity—himself a Family?

Work and property: Among the virtues whose crucible is the Christian family is the taste for toil. It would scarcely be too daring to assert that Christianity alone has set a positive value on manual work. Christianity has made of professional conscientiousness, of duty well done, a moral obligation, a vocation—that is, a way of religious perfection and salvation. Elsewhere, in Africa especially, the ideal is leisure and ease. Labor is held in contempt. Work is left to slaves, and to those who, without having the name of slaves, belong to that condition. It is left to children and (especially) women. One's superiority, one's status and rank are measured by the amount of free time of which one disposes. Status is inversely proportional to the sum of one's efforts to maintain oneself instead of having oneself maintained.

Societies like these condemn themselves to servitude, to decline and dissolution, founded as they are on idleness and the degradation of those whose labor sustains them. In these leisure civilizations, human beings are helplessly delivered over to the ravages of depravity and the delirium of unbridled fantasy. Here crimes against nature and the most incredible superstitions find the best climate for their proliferation. It is easy to understand why their collision with a civilization based on toil has spelled their death. Violence from without reveals the rotted foundations of their social systems and their philosophy of existence. Their salvation will be in the forced labor that will be imposed upon them as a beginning. Moral exhortation to toil will become unremitting. Earnest responsibility, regularity, a more balanced division of tasks between the sexes, cooperative exertion toward common goals, the fine savor of

a job well done, the proper care of the tools of one's occupation—
all will become the subject of Christian teaching.

Toil is the curse of sin, and the sign that we are not yet redeemed
is our distaste for and flight from work. By work the human being
reenters a state of order, taking the divine road of rehabilitation-
by-obedience. Furthermore, work, by tiring the body, causes the
easement of the passions and the softening of the instincts. It paci-
fies the desires and curbs the imagination. But God normally
blesses the virtuous life of industrialized nations and diligent individuals. Wealth is dangerous in itself, but under Christian govern-
ance, ownership is absolved by beneficence and by a gratitude that
sees the source of all its goods in God. This happy equilibrium is
broken where faith is lost and lust for lucre carries the day.

Then shall greed and thievery rage. Where fortune is no longer
the legitimate fruit of toil, where the rich renounce their role as the
providence of the poor, paganism rears its ugly head again, and riot
and social subversion are a constant menace. Right and duty are
recognized no longer. All refuse the role and place fixed for each by
the hierarchy of services and by providence. Thieving becomes the
normal thing in lazy societies. It is the all-too-convenient and generalized means of procuring what one lacks, to the point where the
distinction between "mine" and "thine" is completely clouded
over. A weakening in one's sense of responsibility supervenes.
Slothful societies ruin human dignity. They secrete a spirit of beg-
gary, obsequiousness, fawning. They prepare their members for
servitude. They develop in them a dependency complex. A sense of
the pursuit of the common weal is no longer possible, and the *res
publica* dilapidates in plums and the pork-barrel. Sloth establishes
administration by stopgaps and expediency. No, one cannot insist
too much on the virtues of hard work.

The Language of Orthodoxy

Considerations of moral excellence must not be allowed to lead
us astray however. The "Christian difference" resides elsewhere.
The Christian difference is the faith. It is this that gives morality its
truth and sense, and not the other way about. The worst of misfortunes is to be wanting in faith, not morality. Christians' superiority
lies in the fact that they know revealed truth. The first danger that

threatens the Christian privilege is ignorance of one's own religion. "Faith" is "knowing," but it is a knowing that avails unto salvation. A knowledge of the faith is imperative. If we admit that certain truths are necessary for salvation, we must also admit that ignorance of these truths entails the loss of salvation. Whatever must be believed in order to know God as he really is, as he makes himself known in revelation, must be clearly enunciated, professed, and retained.

The second danger that threatens the correctness, the rectitude of the faith takes the shape of heresy. Doctrinal error is pernicious and destructive. It is a poison, a venom that rots the soul and kills it. The terminology most apt to describe it is that of infection. The agent of the contagion is the spoken or written word. The disease enters by the ears and spreads to all parts of the defenseless soul. Prevention will consist in keeping one's medicine cabinet stocked with exact formulas, and using them on a one-to-one correspondence with whatever diseased theses one may come to hear. In order to find the corresponding label, it will be well to have a catalogue of heresies. Faith is battle for truth. Let others surpass the Christian in virtue, but to the Christian alone is entrusted the deposit of faith, the knowledge of the true God. Faith is orthodoxy or it is nothing. And since a common appeal to Jesus Christ is no guarantee against the proliferation of antagonistic churches and sects, the profession of faith will include the implicit or explicit rejection of heretical beliefs. In Christianity this polemical sighting will become direct. The fact of being Christian in and of itself means to take aim, however indirectly or obliquely. What will be handed on in missionary lands, then, will be the language of anguished orthodoxy in all the various confessions established on the principle of "Cujus regio, ejus religio," and it will be marked by controversy, protestation, and apologetics.

One last characteristic: instruction in the language of orthodoxy must overtake ignorance and error rapidly. Hence it must be accomplished early, and be complete from the very outset. It is addressed to Christianity's children; hence, as it will be exhaustive from the very first, it will be fashioned to fit an infantile universe, without rough edges and without any possibility of further development. Progress at the most will consist in living more intensely what one has known since the beginning. Even theology will not actually contribute anything new, since the scope of the catechism has been to furnish a condensed, popularized version of all its theses and concepts. Consequently, the acceptance of the faith will be less a conversion than an integration into a Christianity that bursts forth full-panoplied and rigidly fixed in the terms of its dissemination.

The Language of Conformity

Missionary practice remodels social time and space by rites and works. Its discourse explains the sense of these changes.

Rites initiate one into the time of mysteries. They teach one to relive the history of salvation, the time in which the believer's destiny has already been anticipated and effectuated by the divine initiative to save human beings gratuitously, without desert or demand on the part of the latter. Salvation's time is global. It embraces all moments of life. Its omnipresence must therefore be made sensible through signs, feasts, and a more and more conscious, more social consecration of one's individual and collective existence.

A like dedication, or consecration, is free and gratuitous, and a sign of grace—but it is not optional. Without the Christian presence, without the presence of Christian institutions, the world would regress or be destroyed, for it would remain shut up in its own baneful self-sufficiency. The world creates disorders that it is helpless to right. Christian institutions, besides serving to shield the faithful from evil and to attract any who might be touched by the devotion and charity of believers, have their prime finality in the incarnation of the unlimited charity of the divinity, in the demonstration, via the love that believers bear their fellow human beings, that God loves them all. The purpose of Christian institutions is to show forth the miracle that this divine love works in the hearts of men and women. One must first, then, establish the transcendence of God and his love, and human helplessness.

The negative function of the Christian institution is to denounce that radical indigence under which human projects suffer until such time as God himself intervenes. The perpetual failure of human undertakings guarantees the perpetuity of specific Christian institutions. Let the ideologues dream of doing away with the ancient miseries that have weighed upon humanity since the beginning of time. They are ignorant of the source of these miseries. The seat of violence is the heart of the human being. That human being's efforts all come within the category of Fall. They are all exerted during the age of the reign of sin, and they are all exerted by means of sin, so that they fail to be able to transcend sin. Perpetual disorders and evils, then, will always call for the heroism of charity, free dedication, and ingenious creations of love. Victory over evil is love and faith, which vanquish sin and human self-sufficiency. Humanity stands in need of the Christian ethos of compassion, respect for life, and free devotion in the name of Jesus Christ, in order not to destroy itself and dehumanize itself in its own brutality.

So runs the missionary discourse, in its structure and essential themes. We have respected its religious authenticity and coherence. Now let us examine its value and efficacy. Let us judge of its consequences and its sometimes unexpected results, keeping in mind that the one making this judgment is the man or woman who has actually received the missionary discourse, and who now asks what the price has been in terms of ambiguities and mistaken comprehension, so as to be able to render a personal account of his or her commitment.

CRITICAL EVALUATION

Trial by Might

The language of derision is a trial by might. It is valid because it is unanswerable. Truth coincides with might. Truth has the right and the duty to impose itself by force, but force may not licitly be used against truth. Such are the presuppositions of Christian practice.

Violence and constraint are justified if their end or consequence is to lead to the gospel those who otherwise would not have come. Force is authorized in order to remove obstacles to Christianity which at the same time are offenses to natural law and to reason.

> While it is not permitted to constrain barbarian subjects to baptism and the Christian faith, it is licit and desirable to suppress their idolatrous cults even by force, that is, to destroy their altars and their temples, and to banish their devil-

ish superstition—things which, all of them, are not only an obstacle to the grace of the Gospels, but contrary to the natural law as well. . . .

Thus formulated by Acosta in the sixteenth century, in a context of the Spanish evangelization and *conquista* of the New World, this doctrine rose again, or was reinvented, at the moment of the colonial expansion of Christianity into Africa. Indirect constraint, or force, is licit, for it only imposes on savages a manner of life in conformity with civilization and the demands of the gospel. As we have shown, this violence is equivalent to a disorientation, a disarray, which delivers the indigenous to an alienated and alienating belief, and to global submission to those who have power of constraint and whose ethnic religion is Christianity.

In that citation from Acosta we hear the distant rumblings of a threat. Anyone who opposes Christianity or seems to be about to turn it to derision can and should be destroyed. The scoffed-at pagan may not retort in kind. Legitimate violence is a one-way street. Violence is at the service of revealed truth.

Such premises will couple the lot of Christianity with victorious Western expansion. To clear the ground for sowing the gospel, missionaries will collaborate with the praetors and proconsuls. To escape the reaction of the pagans in the form of counterviolence, they will take shelter under "grants and privileges," embassies, and the armed protection of their countries of origin.

The decline or ebb of imperialism, provisional though it may be, is the refutation-in-practice of trial by might. One of the reasons for the loss of credibility of African Christianity is its dangerous alliance with might and force. And yet, is not the perduring attitude that underlies a like alliance in turn linked to a certain inability of revealed religions, and of the laicized ideologies that fall heir to their pretensions, to accept the diversity of the manners of being a human being and acknowledging the absolute? Is it not linked to their inability to renounce their monopoly over "truth," over the sense and the direction of history? Doubtless it is too early to debate these questions. We shall have to return to them in the next chapter.

The asymmetry just observed in "one-way violence" is based on "theology." As we have indicated, trial by might establishes the inanity of the gods by their helplessness to express their ire in the face of sacrilege. The God of the Christians, on the contrary, is a strong God, with vigorous passions. He experiences anger. He feels jealousy. He speaks. He reacts to prayer, crime, and defiance. To be sure, he is slow to anger and prompt to forgive, but one must repent, and acknowledge him in truth—acknowledge him as he reveals himself. Obdurate enemies of the name of God and of his elect are punished in the life to come, but they are punished in this life as well.

The history of Christianity is shot through with this ancient Judaic belief, and it will crop up again and again. The godless one, the persecutor, will never prosper on this earth. The godless one will surely meet with some misfortune, know terrible interior torments, and die a violent death. The tragic end of the enemies and persecutors of Israel, the tragic end of evil people proved of old the glory and fearful power of God and bore witness that the Jews were still his chosen people. It is only too well known how the church, the New Israel, appropriated this dogma and turned it on the Jews themselves, those "murderers of the God-man," whose manner of life and existence was to refuse salvation and to contest the realization of the biblical promises in Jesus Christ. The destruction of the Jewish nation, their Diaspora, their misfortunes now passed for the underside of the triumphs and prosperity of Christianity, passed for the proof of its truth and of the untruth of Judaism. This is the doctrine that will be exported to the missions. We shall hear it expressed more or less in the same terms as those of Segneri, in the seventeenth century, who, in chapter 14 of his *Unbeliever with No Excuse: An Apologia for the Christian Religion*, wrote these terrible words:

> The ancients had the singular custom of writing on their slaves' shoulders and sending them as living letters to distant friends. This, I should surmise, is what God has done with the Hebrews, a people who, having been utterly free of the spirit of rebellion in the beginning, became rebellious with time. He has carved, deep in their shoulders, letters of misery, of lethal reprobation, to the end that, in the chastisement of this unhappy nation, we may read the truth of the church of Christ and the power of its Founder. And he has done so not in

mysterious signs and symbols, but in letters so legible that no one can mistake them, even at first glance—except that very people who, having their sentence on their backs, cannot cast their eyes upon it.

Thus the trial by might is trial by the failure, misfortune, or humiliation of another. You can see, painted there on the face of Africans, the curse of God. Their misfortunes, their miseries proceed from their abandonment by God for their depravity or for some original fault proper to their race. They are the living proof of the divine puissance, and the *e contrario* proof of the truth of Christianity. Woe to those who know not the Christian God! Woe upon woe to those who persecute Christians! God is patient with them, yes, and waits for them at the turn of the road *in articulo mortis*.

Lactantius had already described their fate in his pamphlet *De mortibus persecutorum* ("How Persecutors Die"), in which he relates the horrible end of the Christian-baiting emperors, from Nero to Diocletian. Other authors continued the series, depicting the tragic historiography of the unhappy death as God's last word. In the unhappy death the immanent justice, which God has been working deep down in the darkness of the heart and the tortured conscience, beneath the bare façade of "success" and the appearances of triumphal power, suddenly bursts forth like a thunderbolt, and the persecutor dies a violent, sudden, horrible, and ignominious death, visibly struck down by the hand of God.

The manner of death of the heresiarch—that murderer and poisoner of pious Christian souls—is surely proof both of the divine assistance to the "true Church" and of the truth this wretch has dared to assail.

Thus Christianity has an arsenal at its disposal, well calculated to dissuade the potential vengeful spirit from reprisals. The fear of the mighty God who rewards good and punishes evil will be the beginning of faith. Deep at the heart of alienated belief will be the doctrine of a divine interventionism, by miracles and prodigies, in favor of the chosen people and to the rue of those who resist them. This supernatural terrorism will make its impression. It will bear fruit. But it will orient minds toward the legendary, and present Christianity in terms of power. One will look for its secret then, and judge it in terms of its efficacity. And when the Christian God too, challenged and defied, keeps silent, when the lands that persecute prosper, the absurdity of the proof by might will be recognized by those who have until now confounded Western capitalist expansion with the Christian propagation of the faith.

Behind all this there is a principle animating the attitude we are here criticizing. More exactly, there is a question tormenting the conscience of the believer. Just what is the Christian privilege? Surely Christianity's originality and superiority should make their appearance in some fashion. The fact of election ought to be marked by a recognizable divine signature. If Christianity is the supreme revelation of truth, the true religion, does not the principle of perfection demand that in its most empirical expression it should be the best that can be? But then how is this excellence to be conceived? Its Founder's life is marked by weakness and failure, but these do not seem to apply to the work he founded; at least it does not seem that they should, since he promised it would prevail over all powers and fill the earth.

Then what is the proper force of "truth"? If Christianity is that by which one becomes superior in some way, is it not thereby degraded to the order of means? It becomes the best means to have peace, a good conscience, and confidence of salvation. It becomes the best means of building a happy, prosperous, and just society. But if you say that it is the purest religion, the most reasonable religion, you are measuring it by a norm not identified with it, a norm to be found outside it—and it becomes a possession, which can be had in a greater or less degree. Evaluations on the basis of criteria of efficacity are never conclusive. Do Christians commit fewer crimes than others? If we examine Western Christian history, it gives us no answer to such a question. Is the Christian more perspicacious, wiser than the rest? If the answer is Yes, again we have Christianity as a means—the best means of using one's reason correctly for the purpose of possessing one's senses and possessing oneself. But there is no intrinsically superior means. All means depend on the end pursued and on the opportunities, place, and time of the occasion presented. There is no absolute means—even, and especially, to an absolute end.

Thus the faith lives in this ambivalence of a Christianity that holds itself out, now as the revelation of God as he is in himself, now as the best (or only) means of being a human being, of attaining happiness and of having sufficient spiritual resources for resolving the problems of life. Now God enters the system of means-to-end. One abuses his name in order to dominate, that is, to evade one's responsibilities. A Christianity that presents itself as the best means of humanizing the human being can only face a crisis and lose its credibility with the arrival on the scene of real independence—when the Muntu regain control over their own destiny, and begin to seek out the best possible means to ensure their "development." In the best hypothesis, Christianity will continue to appear as a factor favorable to development. In the worst, it will appear as an obstacle and a curb. Christianity will become "privatized." In either case it will become the best means whereby certain individuals will "have principles," will "behave themselves," will have certain "convictions." A Christianity of empire will strive to "get itself going again" by proclaiming the struggle for justice and integral human promotion for all, seeking to translate the content of the faith in terms of liberation, that is, revolution.

This immediate identification of the faith with human emancipation and revolution is too sudden not to shock. The language smacks of opportunism. This new phraseology is totally lacking in verisimilitude in the context of neocolonial Christianity. We are showered with massive, lyrical assertions, but not favored with a theoretical presentation of the practice actually under way. The juxtaposition of these new goals and proclamations with the hoary data of tradition is lacking in any attempt to demonstrate the coherence and continuity of old and new—and surely lacking the courage to make any clarifying, liberating breaks with the old.

The Refutation and Its Consequence: Rationalism

We could present the critical argument under this head in the following terms. In availing itself, against the religion of others, of dialectical, formal refutation, of ideologic reduction, or of historicizing or materialistic explanation, Christianity invites retort—the turning of this same kind of critique against itself. It narrows its own self-comprehension to the confines of "reason" and "history."

Formal logic and ontology: Both logic and ontology have been invoked against indigenous belief. The incoherencies of the latter have been "demonstrated." It has been an easy matter to show up their contradictions, their loose ends, their violations of the principle of identity, and their transgressions of the boundaries of separation that demarcate the areas of the human spirit.

The metaphysics serving as infrastructure for the missionary discourse on revelation—the "natural reason" that revelation presupposes—is self-evident to the evangelizer. Its factitious, constructed, "non-natural" character is easily overlooked by the evangelizer. And yet it will be there, demonstrable by the difficulty of grasping its categories without long acculturation. A lack of agreement on its premises, or the absence of a common experience of the "evidence" of "first principles," will serve only to inaugurate a dialogue of the deaf. The refutation will be purely formal. It will throw everything into confusion, like the old sophism that jostled and jerked, disturbing "common sense" and ridiculing it but never convincing or persuading anyone.

The missionary argumentation taken in itself will be the art of being right and showing the neophyte to be wrong, by dint of imposing upon the latter all the terms of the discussion, the questions, and the answers. The neophyte will acquiesce, but without understanding. It is not to the argument itself that the neophyte will yield, but to the person who is refuting the neophyte's manner of life, not in words, but in reality, by virtue of organizations, equipment, and effective techniques. This general effectiveness "rubs off" on the religion being proposed. But once the neophyte comes to perceive the bases and character of this effectiveness, the Christian religion begins to appear as the result of a *rationalization*, marching along in step with the rationalization of Western society in its totality.

In itself, Christianity's content is no more rational than that of any other religion, but its formalization is superior. When cultures meet and clash, this is what conditions survival. There is a certain process of formalization that makes the weak strong by disengaging the essential form of one's traditions, by rationalizing them, making them agree with themselves and with one another in view of their respective premises, anticipating objections, interpreting *dubia*, and dissipating apparent inconsistencies.

Thus does the rationalization process, extending itself even to matters of religion, promote itself to religion's safeguard and strength. Religion now dismantles the partitions around itself, transcends itself, and enters into horizontal dialogue with the other areas of existence and society.

Ideological, materialistic reduction: It is ironical to observe that Christianity has taken up, against indigenous religions, the demystifying *reductio ad absurdum* of its own enemies, the "philosophers." "Silliness" is a Voltairian word. Religion is said to be based in the credulity of an ignorant people of imbeciles. There will always be crafty persons to group together to exploit this inexhaustible mine of wealth and power: we call them seers, sorcerers, shamans, or priests. Religion is one enormous swindle. Further, it serves as a cloak for the base intent of its manipulators; it will cloud people's minds, the better to serve these base intents. Finally, it is a technique of impotence, which supplies, for lack of objective knowledge by beliefs, that "knowledge" of weak minds who "think" only by association of images, as children do.

Christianity itself has been subjected to this same description. Indeed it was the first to be so characterized. It defended itself against these accusations in two ways. First, it took care to exorcise itself of its own troubling doubt. Criticisms of this kind will disturb the hearts of the believers themselves. The most effective way to overcome them is to project them upon other religions. Christianity they do not fit. Other religions they fit very well indeed—those of the pagans. Second, it revaluated its own rationality. Now it has neither myths nor symbols. It knows only "historical events," occurring in the homogeneous time of the stars and the calendar. It has allegories, but only the most transparent allegories, which let the light of the Logos shine through very easily. Other than the immediate datum or figuration representing reason—reason of a superior order—there is nothing in the deposit of this religion.

In refusing to understand its own mythic and symbolic dimension, Christianity has forged an illusory consciousness of history. The things that actually ought to found empirical events, or "happenings," are themselves transformed into things that have "happened" historically. This positivism has spawned a supernatural materialism, in which the religious sphere is presented as a world like ours, but paralleling it—an invisible world with its own times, its own events, its own places, and of course its invisible, spiritual population. The supernatural world is a parallel, or twin, of the one "here below." How do we pass from one to the other? By the bridge of the miracle. A miracle is a historical event, a material datum produced in this world by the inhabitants of the other, invisible world. Without participating in the framework of causality, it has the worldly, mundane characteristics of all that falls within the purview of the senses, all that is situated at the intersection of homogeneous space and time. It is the trace, as it were, the imprint, the material proof of the supernatural. It is an event like the others, but it bears the divine signature. And that signature is visible, discernible. It sends us back to the Author. How? By characteristics whose forms will necessarily be of this world? Yes, but we *know* they come from God, thanks to the Word—thanks to the authority of revelation.

The Bible as a whole poses the question of the meaning of an empirical event produced by God that can *appear* different from those produced in his creation. Events produced by human beings, or which happen to human beings, take place in the framework of creation. The Bible is the very incarnation of the contradiction involved in a material proof of the divine—proof of a "descending relationship" of God to the human being, as if the latter could be his direct correlate, as if there could be *relatio* in God.

Supernatural materialism denies all value in an experience devoid of the material element, lacking in prodigy, occurring on the level of meaning, on the level of word offered and received, on the level of the spirit's presence to itself as it "becomes world" via collective creation. What we have here is "a nominalism of the Holy Spirit."[1] The resulting impasse and crisis is only too well known: the demythologization of a pseudo-history, via a most limited, topical rationalism. As measured by the criteria of history and reason with which it has been identified, Christianity is nothing but shameful mythology plus ill-disguised rationalism. Furthermore, it is a horrible corruption of language, which calls "history" what everyone else calls "mythology"—what Christianity itself calls mythology when it finds it in other religions. Now the believer, with back to the wall, is forced to admit that faith creates its own events, that certain things which escape all ordinary cognizance have actually happened; faith alone knows them—and knows them with a knowledge that can rightfully be made the object of scientific investigation, for these events have occurred in human time, as the

Scriptures attest (although in fact this is of course impossible, since God reserves the beholding and the memory of these events to the privileged, such as our fathers in faith).

Such is the vicious circle of "bad faith." Illustrations would be easy to cite. Myth is transformed into history, and demands of the believer not faith, but credence in the unverifiable, that is, demands an adoration of God in his irreducibility, as he is in himself, which by definition can have no relationship to anything else. Mystery does not oblige one to sacrifice one's intelligence, but credence imposes contradiction under the name of "paradox." Thus, for example, in the pseudo-history of Adam, the first human being "disobeys" before he has acquired a knowledge of good and evil, before he knows what is permitted or forbidden. This knowledge comes to him only after he has eaten of the forbidden fruit. The mode of transmission of the "fault," committed before the acquisition of the sense of prohibition, condemns us all to the unverifiable hypothesis of our preformation in Adam, our common descent from a first human pair, and so on. Other dogmas will give rise to similar paradoxes, and will oblige us to a series of psychological presuppositions that we shall be called upon to believe in. The mystery of God will be pulverized into mini-mysteries, and faith will place its subjects in a Pavlovian "paradoxical situation," to issue in neurosis or schizophrenia.

The following dogmatic line of reasoning scarcely does anything to resolve the contradiction: "The sense of these images is a rational one, for it stands in relationship to the Incarnate Word, who is the principle and source of all reason. Other myths, on the contrary, cannot be rational, for they have no relationship to the Word." Entirely apart from the fact that the argument begs the question, it is to be remarked that a transcendent Principle is utterly other from its derivatives. There can be no isomorphism between them. Furthermore, how can one assert that other myths have no relationship to the Incarnate Word, while simultaneously teaching that *all things* have their crown and perfection in this Word? There is nothing to prevent one avowing that the Word is Logos and Mythos all at the same time. On the contrary, there is everything to suggest it. The divine is beyond the oppositions of human understanding. The Word became incarnate *in history*—which is at once the homogeneous time of the calendars and the mythical time of human existence enveloped in the enigma of the Beginning and the End.

Denial of myth and de-Christianization: When you deny myth, you have to substitute pretend facts and allegories. On a deeper level the denial of myth is the loss of the sense of God's immanence. It is called desacralization, secularization. Once relegated without, once resituated in the exteriority of transcendence, God can no longer be present to the world and to the human being except by violent irruption, "breaking and entering." Miracle, prodigy, prophecy—those white-hot, intermittent signs that pierce the dark of night and the absence of God—become necessity. Myth repulsed, refused, and rejected induces at once rationalism and the marvels of fideism to balance the rationalism. The world deserted by God, who is now concentrated in particular events and revelations, is delivered to blind, anonymous forces—the forces of *things*—which faith can now take into account only from without in the helpless rage of voluntarism and moralism as religion turns to drama, and the divine and grace come only with sound and fury, to condemn, to justify, and to upset. A relationship with God is now conceived of only in the modality of a violence against nature. The shredded Christian conscience now oscillates pathetically from agnosticism, to a naively anthropocentric rationalism, to fideism or credence in the marvelous, to bad faith.

Thus Christianity has laid the groundwork for its own ruin. True, Christian exegesis has demonstrated a belated repentance vis-à-vis the myths, but too little and too late. It continues dogmatically to maintain the phantasm of the *possibility* of a historical kernel in the Christian myths, so as to be able to continue to believe in its *reality*. In doing so, exegesis continues to seek some distinguishing trait, some *thing*, whose exclusive possession will mark Christianity as being of a supernatural exceptionality, and hence superior.

We call these divine *things* "fetishes" or "idols." It is true that revealed religions are only a sacralization and supernaturalization of the distinctive characteristics that mark them off from the others, the elements that constitute their singularity. This singularity is thereupon erected into the measure of all things and the source of all things. All else beside is reduced to its negation, its caricature or sketch. The violence that a like principle inflicts, on texts and reality, is all too well known. The bad faith and fanaticism it engenders is proverbial. It is maintained only at the price of a formal, empty explanation, slapped across reality in order to hold together, in some kind of abstract unity, what is actually irreducible diversity.

Thus, we shall be told, in the Bible the human being stands before the sovereignty of a God who takes the initiative in calling him or her to communion with himself in a promise that he makes and keeps. God strikes in wrath and restores with tenderness. Biblical history oscillates between these two poles as it oscillates between sin and grace, but it is ever God's love that has the initiative and the last word: mercy and grace always have the final victory over sin. This is a theology custom-made for the totalization of history in its reduction to a drama of sin and grace. A like totalization is legitimate, of course, if it is understood as a view of things from the standpoint of their last end—if it is understood as eschatology. But it fails to provide the necessary element for the integration of history. It is merely hope and is a long way from divesting events of either their opacity or their historical signification. This totalization is not one whit different from what other cultures do when they totalize history, translating everything in terms of a combat between life and death, where at last the victory falls to life. This is the dimension, the element of myth.

Thus Christianity, boasting in its rationality, has been altogether too prompt to clip the wings of mystery, to station angels armed with flaming swords at the portals of certain "sanctuaries" lest anyone approach too near. For example, Christianity has sought to secure the Bible from criticism—chronological criticism, first, then cosmological, then mythological and sociological. Defeats in these areas are always followed by belated protests of we-knew-it-all-along. Thus resistance has withdrawn to the fortress of dogma. But a state of siege is in effect. Surely by now it is clear that the central doctrines of Christianity are riddled with unacknowledged anthropomorphisms as well as an animism that the discursive language of theology has managed to rationalize but not surmount. The notions of Word, Person, Divine Will, and so on fail to elude the "psychological equivocal." They make God an imaginary center of attribution, a unity of faculties. Is not the case the same with creation, so external to its demiurge, so consonant with the psychological picture of God as a person?

Faith is called upon to avow the oneness of revelation as something that goes without saying *because* the God who reveals himself there is "one." And where, pray tell, does the cardinal numerical unity of the Judeo-Christian revelation correspond to the oneness of God? If God is above number, beyond the worldly opposition of the one and the many, how can the manifestation of his ipseity be adequately expressed in mere cardinal unity? Why are we unwilling to admit that unity and uniqueness are but halting human representations, the product of a polemical moment in the religious experience when it had become urgent to set some human concept in relief in order to safeguard the authenticity of human reference to God? If on the contrary we absolutize these relative needs and moments, with their conditioned protestations along the lines of orthodoxy, we are condemned to remain caught in the snares of a mythology which is not content to signify the *incomprehensible* presence of God, but which pretends to furnish an adequate description and knowledge of him in virtue of these or those particular privileged words or images!

Criticism knows no self-circumscription. Either it is universal or it is nothing. Nor is it limited from without, for it automatically goes beyond itself just by doing all it can. When we pretend to resolve the question of myth in Christianity merely by jettisoning a few mythical matters of secondary importance like Adam, the demons, and the angels, while continuing to discourse upon the Word of God, his ways, the incarnation, a revelation which comes to human beings from the great beyond, God's acts of judgment whereby he condemns human beings and transforms their history—in other words, while continuing to speak of God in terms of vertical relationship with human beings and the world, in terms of a metaphysical and cosmological dualism—we have not only *not* resolved this question, we have not even broached it.

The partial denial of myth does nothing for reason. Reason is still prevented from going the whole way. Reason blocked generates a narrow, stupid rationalism and an irrationality as well, sublimated into a supernatural wisdom capable of judging all things by wafting above all mediations, and economizing its own toil, when what is in order is the toil of painstaking and painful research—research that learns by groping, and finds truth by creating it.

Now we see why those who have been subjected to Christianity's assaults on their own traditions will never be content with half-measures and half-truths. Christianity will never recover its credibility, at least in the eyes of some. It will suffer from inadaptation to an Africa on the move until such time as the deepest, most radical questions are no longer handled by preterition and evasion. African Christianity will always be suspect as a mere religion of the herd, a theatricalization of the continuing subordination of Africa to the West in the neocolonial context of a shameful, cowardly dependency in all areas—social, political, economic, and scientific.

Hence we must take the measure of the obstacles that an authentic Christianity will have to surmount. It may be that a Christianity to which the African can respond in soul and conscience will be born only from the ashes of so-called middle-class Christianity.

Chapter 3

African Resistance to Middle-Class Christianity

BOURGEOIS CHRISTIANITY

It is not hard to see why Christianity of a certain tone could offend the sensibilities of Christians belonging to another cultural tradition. Italian devotions, for instance, will repel a sober Anglican piety. We accept the notion that the mentality of whole civilizations may, temporarily at least, be impermeable to Christianity because some of its dogmas and usages shock them—China and Japan, for example. But it is taken for granted that when Christianity learns to speak to their "soul" these same peoples will hasten to embrace it and will translate it into a language in accord with their sensibilities and culture. This is the notion at the origin of the discourse on the necessity of the indigenization of Christianity, of its incarnation in new cultures. This discourse, these programs are usually reducible to a criticism of what is referred to as Western Christianity. Rarely do they sketch the form to be substituted for this Western Christianity, and when they do, the sketch consists mostly of a disquisition on local curiosities, folklore, or peculiarities of lifestyle that have indeed disappeared or are barely surviving.

Thus these appeals for indigenization only call forth skepticism. Their sterility and monotony engender an overwhelming lassitude, and common sense tells us that the only way out of the impasse will be by way of an exact determination of what these programs are rejecting, and a clear vision of what they seek to have instead. We do not reject the abstraction they vaguely denominate as "Western Christianity," and we do not reject its "mentality." The only Christianity these peoples have ever encountered is the one the missionaries brought from a middle-class society. What we reject is bourgeois Christianity. We seek not a pristine restoration of ancient customs or traditional ways of living. We seek the transformation of existing relationships. From our past, the only things we "jealously guard" are our models and principles of being-together, and only in order to transpose them for modernity. Nor does the project we are setting afoot have any vested a priori of its own. No, we mean to build a tomorrow *in function of what is occurring today*—build it out of what has been produced by these mechanisms of resistance to Christianity and a middle-class world.

Ideology and Superstructure

Let us describe the middle-class Christian that the African sees and resists. The bourgeois Christian appears under the double aspect of colonist and missionary. The distinction between religious and profane, between faith and politics represented by these two figures appears to us as a contradiction only in the abstract—a contradiction capable of being lived all the same. To our way of seeing, it is a purely verbal distinction. Converts will perceive the unity of a civilization and its mode of living all in a batch, and will be wary of setting up "colonist" and "missionary" in contraposition. Converts will accept in principle the recommendation that they distinguish these persons along the lines of the distinction of the dualist categories of body and soul: the colonist will be concerned with the affairs of the body, the missioner with those of the soul. But in real life, the convert will see these roles overlap and even trade places, or at any rate pursue the same end and be exercised upon the same subject. Colonist and missioner will both agree to stamp on other people the image of themselves and their world. For the neophyte, the West is the West because of its religion. Religion, technology, and social life are all of a Western piece. All form a whole, all subsist in solidarity. Baptism appears to the neophyte as a rite of integration into this community with a view to sharing its secrets and advantages, with a view to becoming the brother or sister, becoming the equal of those who offer him or her their "Holy" to share.

But worship of the same God and profession of identical ideals do not necessarily imply effective solidarity. The middle-class world is dualistic. It speaks a forked language. There is the ideology of practice, and then there is discourse on that practice. The ideology professes abstract ideals: the unity of the human race, the equality of all men and women before God, a universal communion of sisters and brothers. In religious terms, men and women are the sons and daughters of God, called to be such by faith and baptism, called to form a single "body." The middle-class Christian repeats these formulas, but gives them a mystical meaning. This unity, this communion are realized only in the invisible no-place where souls gather, whether here below or in the other world. Faith is a community of beliefs in the same truths, a communion of adherence to the same values. Faith is a moral community of sentiments and minds. It is not that the minds will be encountering one another by exchange and dialogue. Their oneness arises only from their orientation in the same direction, from the single object at which they aim. In faith, their unity is hidden in God. It is in Jesus Christ, who has returned to his Father, or who is present in word and sacrament in his church.

Consequently faith can be dissociated from charity. Charity is not the content of faith. Faith enjoys a merely extrinsic relation to love. Love is the power that creates new human beings by transcending the ancient divisions caused by sin in concrete life. Love is the constitutive force of communities, where each person is the gift of the other, and in himself or herself is the means of nothing and of no one. Charity has become alms and beneficence. Charity distances and separates. Charity is likewise the means of leading souls to the faith, the means to attract proselytes in order to be able to share with them the same beliefs, the same image of oneself—not, surely, for letting them *be* as oneself. Zeal for the faith does not exclude contempt for the person whom one has rallied under one's banner, nor does it exclude slavery or racial discrimination.

The autonomy of the religious sphere frees one for the game of competition and acquisition, for individualism, for another language. The higher the ideals the less they come in contact with daily life. One wishes them high precisely in proportion as one wishes to exile them from relationships of work, commerce, and industry. Christianity's abstraction adjusts it to the bourgeois world. Its spiritualism gives it a good conscience and a high ideal of itself. After a few hyperbolic assertions about gratuity, human helplessness, and the primacy of charity, things come down to merit, money, and competition among interest groups that are more real than the communities of faith.

The missionary shares this scale of values. As we have seen, the missioner is closer to the colonists, even bad colonists, than to the sheep of his or her flock. The Christian mysteries are often "legends" for missionaries, things to be preached and professed, things whose being actually consists in this preaching and this profession. They will be prompt to drop them and pass to the teaching of morality, the virtues that make one respectable, and toil. The ethics thereby proposed will be no whit different from a middle-class ethics.

The neophyte encounters a society where religion can function as ideology. Ideology serves to propagate the ideal image of oneself. Ideology is the sharing of the sacred, but nothing so sacred as material goods. In ideology, the offer of what is declared to be the most precious thing of all can go hand in hand with the refusal of what is most elementary. In a class society, founded on individualism and profit, religion is transformed into a superstructure. Its transcendence places it at zero degrees longitude and latitude, from whence it can arrange to fit all situations, and accompany either pole of a contradiction without modifying it, indeed by serving it as metaphor or camouflage if need be. It is no longer a matter of astonishment that, in the presence of positions other than dogmatic—in the presence of this tautological insistence on Christianity's irreducibility and identity, just as of its pretension to superiority and universality—Christian thought and practice should be diluted and fragmented into contradictory opinions and actions. Faith, like Hegelian Being, will be the poorest of concepts, while being asserted to be the first and the "All" to the point where, in a given Christian assembly, one may see persons united more on the basis of their profane ideologies than on that of their common belief.

Middle-class Christianity will never, anywhere, surmount the antagonisms of race, class, age, sex, or nation. It will necessarily be lived according to the spirit and culture of each people, in the sense that what unites or differentiates a people, the motive force of its action and reactions, will not be religion. In mission lands, nationalism, which is constituted of racial and cultural elements as well as the battle for material goods and prestige, place the missionary in solidarity with the colonist more efficaciously than religion places him or her in solidarity with the indigenous person. And the legionnaires may sometimes march in the missionary name.

Individualism and Dissociations

At bottom, the middle-class Christian is a creature free of all natural ties, one who has broken with the tribe—the great family— and is before all else an individual, a closed subjectivity, finished and perfect in itself, maintaining no purely extrinsic relationships with society. Such, at any rate, is the goal and representation that bourgeois Christians conceive for and of themselves. The first and last reality is individuals. They preexist and survive all else. Society is the result, at times even the voluntary result, of the interaction of individuals in the pursuit of their self-realization. Institutions, then, are but means that are exterior to each individual. The expansion of the individual comes before all else. This is the absolute value. All other things shall pass—individuals alone shall abide, in immortal individuality, in their souls. The aim of faith is to save those souls, to immortalize that individuality.

Here we have the source of the dissociations that characterize bourgeois Christianity and its impasses. At the moment of its triumph, it erects its dissociations on principle, and makes of individualism the very condition and sign of Christian authenticity.

The first breach demanded, and transformed into a precondition of adherence to the faith, is a renunciation of the texture of relationships with the dead and the living that makes the traditional human being a person, a being-oneself-with-the-others. In modern times, confessionalism and sacralized nationalism are the return with a vengeance of the very thing that is here being denied. The individual, self-centered, obsessed with continuity, obsessed with self, now oscillates between raving self-affirmation and self-sacrifice to collective idols. Faith is confounded with certitude, with a manner of assigning oneself to oneself in one's incommunicable individuality. But one will have to balance this interiorization with the reinforcement of institutional and dogmatic criteria of Christian membership, and ethnic and regional contingencies will furnish the matter and form for the expression of community: "Cujus regio, ejus religio."

By taking the individual in isolation, by separating the individual from what constitutes him or her a part of reality, one creates insurmountable problems of passage, together with an obsessional hypertrophy of the human being. These transitional problems come down to questions like: How does what is not the individual come to be added to him or her? How, and how far, can foreign elements come together in unity? What sort of unity do they form? What is the common element, the intermediary of passage from one to the other? And what is the precise nature and quality of this element? Answers will be forthcoming in terms of the relationship between God and the human being, of the human being with creation, of law with the gospel, of nature with grace, of faith with the sacraments, of conscience with the institution, and so on.

The problems involved in bridging the gaps are those of individuals-in-isolation, individuals who do not think of self in their being-together-with-others, who are not content with starting out with what they actually are: one with the one world. It is important to understand the processes by which this oneness is realized and maintained, the processes by which the individual is a person-member-of-a-community, one of the "faithful." Instead of centering one's attention on the acts that establish the co-membership, the co-belonging, of human beings and institutions, the individual stands in isolation, and seeks after external norms ("necessary means").

Human beings are obsessed with themselves. Their aloneness is their guilt and torment. Even their avowal of their nothingness and their corruption only leads them painfully back to themselves. Faith is psychologized, just as sin is psychologized. Bourgeois Christians no longer recognize the originating, constitutive relationships of human existence: they no longer see that these are given and are anterior to every act of the individual, that they are the conditions which make possible the rise of the latter as concrete reality, as culturalized nature, historicized and socialized from the start.

Such a Christianity can only be disintegrating, as it is itself disintegrated Christianity. Theological activity will exhaust itself in overcoming antinomies by establishing verbal gangways between them. Confessions will collide as antithetical unilaterals, stock and issue of this dislocation of the unity of existence. Middle-class Christianity has thus become the growing disintegration and unintelligibility of "mystery," of the unity of life. Whether it ontologizes or subjectivizes, it only creates dualisms, stacks of worlds, and dilemmas like "Either the individual is everything or it is nothing," or again, "Either the individual forces himself or herself on others in virtue of some institutional mark, or is the equal of others in virtue of sheer lack of functional difference or title of personal vocation." Examples could be multiplied. Every subject of theology could be reconsidered under this revealing formality. But perhaps we shall do better to contemplate these antinomies and internal contradictions of bourgeois Christianity via the reaction of the sects—the African Independent Churches.

AFRICAN RESISTANCE
TO MIDDLE-CLASS CHRISTIANITY

Were it not for the context of acculturation, the vast movement at the origin of the numberless Independent Churches and dissident Christian sects in Africa would be incomprehensible. The whole phenomenon is a response to a certain situation in the sense that it is both the reflection of this situation and a protest against it. The dissidence is determined in respect to missionary, middle-class Christianity. The dissidents interiorize certain aspects of this Christianity and are content with mimicking other aspects, either as they are or by setting them on their heads; and finally, they react to still other aspects, or even to the whole ensemble, via an "initiating breach" consisting of resumption and transposition, on the level of faith, of the real, social, political, and economic conditionings of the African man and woman today. Our own purpose will best be served by tarrying on the positive, innovative side of the resistance, yet without forgetting its polemical tenor. The polemics must not be allowed to conceal the essential intentionality of the movement, which is to save the tribal man and woman—in their solidarity, their relationships, and their person—in this confrontation with the bourgeois, industrial, and scientific world. The tribal person must be "renewed," integrally. Hence the characteristic traits of the various forms of "black Christianity."

The Tribal Condition in a Situation of Acculturation: Taking This Condition Seriously

First and foremost, and most often, the opposition between membership in the tribe and incorporation into the church is ignored or surmounted by simply identifying the two. The "necessary break" theory is refuted by practice, by a *probo ambulando*. Instead, what must be broken with and rejected is evil, symbolized by sorcery. There is no need to break with one's solicitude for the dead or any other ancestral traditions. The message of Christ is not in competition with them. On the contrary, this message has come to fulfill the dream of a life in all its fullness, a life destined to triumph even in the collapse of the framework of a way of life that had been consecrated from time immemorial.

Hence the coming of Christ bears on the lot of the group as such, and it transposes itself into, passes into a church. The continuity is there—the continuity of a life undergoing a metamorphosis in depth. The continuity is not from without, via a power or a legitimacy passed down from hand to hand or church to church, in an uninterrupted spatio-temporal chain. It is not a matter of the rediscovery of a lost meaning in the Scriptures by a bookish return to the founts. Here the one who "rises up" in the name of God is not a church reformer but a prophet—and indeed "another Christ," or at very least the personal, black emissary of the Founder, and thus someone vested with a power of initiative and decision, and not merely of witness, commentary, and the preservation of an intangible deposit of faith. This person has the mission to do for this particular African community what Jesus did for his own people when he came to fulfill the Scriptures. This new prophet is to reeffectuate—keeping in mind the particularities of the concrete situation—an initiatory deed of the fullness of time. This deed, which is now so busy determining conditions, has been hidden by theologies and schools of exegesis. The exegesis of the sects is neither philological nor historical-critical. It is not situated in a hermeneutical tradition that is forever resuming and elaborating the meaning of an already completed event. It is a creative interpretation or, better, a prophetic actualization, a fulfillment: what the Scriptures tell, what Jesus did, is being reactualized here and now. Once again "something is afoot" on the face of the earth, and that earth trembles. The world changes. It is the coming of the kingdom of God, and not the spread of a Christianity or the reproduction of foreign national churches and squabbling denominations.

A Christianity of Mystery and Healing

Christianity is a celebration of life in its victory over death. Its core is the Paschal mystery. The prophets, these "other Christs," receive their mission and investiture only after passing through death and resurrection themselves. The content of the message is the everlasting victory of life over death in every one of our lives. Liturgy and daily existence alike actualize this drama in ongoing fashion. One enters into the mystery with all one's being, to receive there the meaning of life, life in all its gratuity and superabundant measure, pressed down and overflowing. Even death puts no end to life. This is a festive Christianity. It sings, it dances all the way to the Passion. Death is not explained by fall or fault—death is explained by life. The Paschal mystery is joy, not because it solaces human beings languishing under the weight of their guilt, but because it shows forth life in the midst of death. The imputation of guilt, the sense of fault as offense against God need not precede, is not the necessary, universal condition for entry into the understanding of Easter. Sins are forgiven because the kingdom of God is here, antecedently to any psychological conscientization of sin, independently of any anguish, remorse, or torment of conscience. The tears will come, but *after* one has been forgiven because one has loved much. It is not a matter of being saved so much as it is of taking part in life in its fullness. Faith becomes jubilation in the deed of divine power. The redemption that is sought after is the redemption that bestows fullness of reality on all the conditions of human life.

The whole is a quest for healing, for health—the only real refutation of disease and the forces of death. The withdrawal of all the powers of evil signals the presence of the kingdom of God or its imminent coming. The unbridled reign of death is the work of the forces of sorcery, forces that stop life in its tracks by denying it, by assigning it an end outside itself, by utilizing it as a means for something other than itself: as a means of the acquisition of wealth, or power, or any other individual, solitary affirmation. Sin, then, is indeed an "assault on God," on God's (transcendent) immanence in life. How else may we understand that a human being could wound the Utterly Other, the invulnerable Absolute? Anthropomorphisms are of no help to anyone when it comes to taking guilt, sin, and redemption seriously. Beware the Christian *pathétique*—a great hindrance to arriving at the virile maturity that accepts life in and by death.

Love as the Content of Faith

The decisive religious factor in African disenchantment with the missionary churches of middle-class Christianity is the lack of love it has discovered in their heart. Many groups detaching themselves from the imported churches to constitute themselves Independent Churches do so in order to have a church that will be a communion, a community of brothers and sisters expressed not only by participation in the same rights and adherence to the same dogmas, but by mutual aid and acknowledgment.

Conversions have created not a people, but crowds of people, each appealing to the doctrine it has been brought and to the authority of those who have brought it. The bond among these believers is their subjection to the message and to the envoys. Their being-with is produced and maintained from without. There is no common, shared experience among them, nor could there be, since faith as a subjective, individual position with a particular, exterior, absolute content eludes each one of them. In this abstract objectivization, converts only elude themselves, along with the reality of their concrete world. Further, since the world of the converts' common experience is exiled in the utterly other universe of faith, they lose, when they adhere to the new beliefs, the communication space that has subsisted among them; they lose the necessary material basis and condition of the relationships of human beings with one another. Deprived of the platform of realities that constitute it as a person and as a being-in-the-world, consciousness all in disarray "reflects" until it catapults into the empty heavens of credence and

belief. It gives its assent to enunciations that have no possible referent in its experience, asseverations imposed upon it under the
form of a normative, extrinsic orthodoxy.

Believers of this cloth and cut are genuinely taking on neither
doctrine nor institution. They have nothing in common but their
submission. Become strangers to themselves, they are strangers to
one another. Thus the moment the external pressure is removed,
the pitch of fervor plummets. Beliefs and institutions are tacitly
deserted and left without any internal support. Only their façade is
still erect and intact. The believers have discharged their mutual
responsibility. No interior norm, no pact holds them under any
obligation with respect to one another. Back they go, either to their
preconversion solidarities or to relationships they have created
more recently in their struggle for life, power, prestige, and wealth.
The new authorities, lacking any ties with their own kind other than
a relationship of domination and subordination, forfeit all acceptance and recognition. Thus we have the infamous "authority crisis" of the decolonialized lands, along with the new churches,
where power without legitimacy is either transformed into authoritarianism or maintained only by intimidation, brute force, and
laissez-faire all at once. Thus we have a general institutional strike,
at least in latent form. The established churches suffer an exodus.
Everything is still upright and in place—but only ghosts and phan-
toms live there.

None of the dissidence, desertion, and debacle is anything to be
surprised at. Being-with will have to be based on something else
now, something beyond nominalism and colonial imposition. Before all else, the "bond of charity" will have to be established.

*The dissociation of faith and love is the reason for the discomfi-
ture of the Christianizing enterprise today.* The divorce is lethal for
both virtues. Faith degenerates into legends, truths to be believed,
rites to be observed, and the canonization of middle-class morality.
Faith as certitude of salvation in and by Jesus Christ alone, faith as
assent to revealed event and doctrine *qua* revealed becomes the be-
all and end-all. Faith absorbs charity. Charity becomes interior to
faith, becomes one of its attributes. It becomes the benevolence and
beneficence that adorn the holy or pious life of God-fearing
Christians—the faithful. Faith is required in order to be able to love
with the love of charity.

In missionary practice, this reversal of right order in the relationship of faith and charity under the supervision of bourgeois Christianity has disastrous consequences. When faith is no longer a moment in a process—the process of creative love—it succumbs to a bigoted particularism bound to singular events, places, things, and persons. It is transformed into a sect, be the number of its adherents ever so massive. Cut off from its soul, faith begins to draw its value from orthodoxy, from mystery, from miracle, from a system of wonders, from human corruption and the arbitrary divine will. Yet only charity abides, bursting out of all limitations, shaping faith on its own authority and with its own signs and symbols of a superabundant, uncontainable effusion that crashes through all barriers. Where on the contrary this charity is characteristically in default, the grandest commitments turn into acts of condescension, means of individual salvation, and propaganda. Thus will they never arouse perduring gratitude, for they are devoid of mutual recognition. Without charity, an evangelizing zeal will take on the guise of a will to power, a desire to universalize one's self-image. Some will live this zeal as the perfunctory execution of the divine ordinance decreeing the proclamation of the gospel to every creature. The very essence of evangelization will then be seen as obedience to the command to lead others to the obedience of the faith and so obtain one's own soul's salvation and an "eternal reward."

This is true charity, the true love revealed in faith: to will the salvation of others in such a way as to love what is imperishable in those persons, to love them as they will be in God, to love with the love of a God who wills to save them along with the whole world. A like fashion of loving, which is properly Christian and which it is altogether correct to call "charity," is incommensurable with human love. Charity is of another order, the order of faith. Thus it is not in the least affected by the social exclusivisms of believers. Where human love is wanting, charity alone abides. Where slavery and racism reign, there charity is. It is altogether possible, then, to condemn neophytes while yet bearing them a radical love—the love of charity—because one is seeking their "salvation by faith." It suffices to vanquish one's repugnance merely to the extent of showing them an "objective love," the love of beneficence. This is how human beings acquire merit, how they obey God, how they save their souls. At the same time they dispose the object of their beneficence to gratitude toward themselves, and via this acknowledgment of the motives inspiring the benefactor, to gratitude toward the Source of all charity. Beneficence and benefaction, then, are a means of leading persons to the knowledge of the true God and to the obedience of the faith.

A like charity, of course, establishes no solidarity between evangelizers and evangelized in a community of shared lot. It is not a power that creates persons, that is, it is not a force for rendering persons autonomous beings existing for and by themselves. When all is said and done, it is offensive, and it will be rejected as the very caricature of love, as love's exact opposite. Membership in the established churches will be experienced and felt as an institutionalized denial of oneself and a source of continual humiliation. Faith will be made equivalent to the sacrifice of oneself to the cold and arrogant sacred monsters. The independent and dissident churches are the expression of the contemptuous rejection of this association, this caricature of *philadelphía* which calls forth such sarcasm and "ridicule by the infidel." ("See how they love one another!") The dissident churches have sought to be places where a human being "feels at home," where one has a face and a name no matter who one is.

Such is the evangelical project reinvented by the sects in their reaction to bourgeois Christianity. It comprises liberation in one's condition of life, the healing of body and spirit, and the permanent celebration in one's life of the Paschal mystery as it aims at a community of brothers and sisters as a total and effective transposition of tribal solidarity into the modern world. We are not endorsing the opinion expressed by some that true Christianity is to be found today in African religious movements. We are not even suggesting that the traits composing this way are to be found all together in any one particular church. Rather, these traits form an ideal model, or type, which affords us a better view of what the force of this dissidence consists in, of what is at work here, even if its full expresssion and clear formulation is lacking in the actual churches. Indeed this very factor creates both dissatisfaction in these new churches and the dissolution of strict morphological and dogmatic conformity behind the façade of "uprightness."

Meanwhile these key ideas, for want of being energetically thought and willed for themselves, fail to maintain for long the groups they originally animate. A number rapidly become side-tracked, stagnate, or regress. Those that survive seem quick to adopt the norms of the established churches and minutely copy their rituals, their hierarchies, and their dogmatic structures. The intuitions we have set in relief are most often awash in a filigree of polemics and purely superficial identifying symbols and will be contradicted by the adventitious, out-of-place elements brought in and juxtaposed with them. Thus it eventuates that the African religious movements do not actually improve on middle-class Christianity—especially if they merely invert the latter's values, which of course they have had ample time duly to ingest and assimilate. But there is a lesson here, too. As we have said, these movements constitute protest and reflection simultaneously.

Syncretisms

Syncretism (together with schism) has been the bane of the missionary churches and the justification of their continued tutelage under the churches of the North. The message should have been transmitted in its purity, it is felt, without any compromise with paganism, and that duty remains. One can "give them every-thing," these neophytes, trust them with all manner of responsibility except responsibilty for the gospel and the preservation of its integrity and purity. They could not have been entrusted with the safeguarding of the authenticity of their own faith. The risks would have been too great. Separatism and confusion threatened at every turn. The gift of discernment and the charism of orthodoxy remain the appanage of the evangelizer and the founding Western church. After all, both are the product of two thousand years of habitua-tion to Christianity, two millennia of Christianity in Northern bones and blood—hence the wisdom of proceeding slowly. The end of the mission, and its flowering into a truly indigenous church, is beyond the foreseeable future, somewhere over the horizon. Hence the necessity of delimiting the Christian initiative of yesterday's converts, still immersed as they are in paganism. The faith would undergo a grave adulteration if one let them do with it as they wished.

This is precisely the rub. You have syncretism precisely where you have assimilated the notion that Christianity is hereditary. By "syncretism" here we mean that quality of religious phenomena by which they have not yet become adequately conscious of their historicity, and so remain the prisoner of a substantialist conception of their own reality and that of others, to the point of seeking a solution for problems arising from acculturation, domination, and the collision of cultures of unequal strength, in some kind of mixture, in symbiosis, in grafting on, in adaptation, or in synthesis. Religious phenomena look upon themselves as if they were mere natural processes, like chemical or biological processes. They seek to exempt themselves from history and fail to see themselves as human products in the area of meaning, fail to see themselves as products of culture via language, toil, desire and gamble, risk and power. They seek to exempt themselves from the possibility of conflict, of tragic option, of blockage, failure, and death.

Syncretism occurs where collections of objects, rites, or institutions are transmitted—where the future is rejected in the name of a settled acquisition, which one has no desire to modify or lose. Syncretism accumulates things, juxtaposes things, without transfiguring them in accordance with the exigencies of form, figure, and locus. Syncretism is the formless, the amorphous, that which is compatible with whatever one pleases because it has no organizing structure of its own, no concern for internal consistency. Syncretism is an emulsion of trifles and vacuities.

The remedy will not be found in conservative purism. Meaning riveted to the Scriptures, tradition, the writings of the Reformers, or hoary constitutions does not abide intact. It decomposes. Syncretism most surely appears when Christianity contents itself with commemorating, glossing, and repeating. It will be avoided where revelation is received not after the fashion of a content or deposit, but as a project, as a model of re-creation and renewal of the face of the earth and itself into the bargain. What is received by way of legacy can be received only by inserting it into new dynamics, by giving it a point of departure in that which already is, by refashioning conditions and planting it there. What is impossible to do without distortion and syncretism is to reproduce forms and shapes forged somewhere else. The simple transfer of belief and already constituted institutions in response to questions and tasks of another age and situation will be syncretistic every time.

Any criticism of missionary evangelization as the transplantation of middle-class, bourgeois Christianity to Africa must include a consideration of the result of that operation as syncretism, and must include its forthright denomination as such. For want of radicalism, Christianity's reappropriations in Africa make up a collection of heteroclytic characteristics, gathered from the Bible and various Western Christianities, with a few elements of the "African genius" thrown in by way of anecdote, curiosity, and folklore. The sectarians, or indigenists, fall into the same anachronism and syncretism as the missionaries whom they oppose, for, at bottom, syncretism is the rejection of the essential principle of conversion whereby one gains by "losing." Syncretism recoils before the Paschal requirement of losing all in order to save one's life, of dying in order to rise again and enter into glory.

Regressive Particularism

Regressive particularism is a denomination of syncretism from its inevitable result. Syncretism fails correctly to take up and assume the past. It undertakes a return to the sources, a return to the tribal heritage and Judeo-Christian origins simultaneously—and the "find," of course, is nothing but old treasure, where one can dig out a few "new" ready-to-wear truths for all circumstances. The ancient founts are ever a-bubbling—all we need do is bend down and steep ourselves, quench our thirst for truth and justice. These facile quests for the founts neglect the *distance* that separates us from times gone by. Our own cares and concerns did not yet exist, and there could have been no way for those times to anticipate our situation, our position, and our responsibility, and so be able to manufacture truth for us. When we find fixed content there, analogies with today, and a preestablished harmony with our own situation, we evade the present. We are searching in the past for a refuge from "future shock."

One after another, the sects have discovered the height of novelty in the service of the old, and in a service not of vivification but of preservation. The gospel is reduced to a series of "basic evidences," and invoked to lend stability and legitimacy to the ancient system of privilege and discrimination—the ancient inhumaneness. It "modernizes" this system and this inhumanity, and confers respectability upon them. Now they are *koine*, and enjoy an equivocal coexistence with the other cultures encountered. But nothing has really changed. The old rivalries live again, the ancient alienations are transposed to the present. Christianity becomes an ideology of conservation, camouflaging a helplessness in the face of profound changes. Christianity becomes a veil for a cowardly, fogbound mentality.

The most characteristic trait of this unrecognized particularism is the recovery of the group's primitive certitude of being the whole of humanity. This certitude now becomes "faith." The "others" are not human beings in the proper sense. Legitimate differences do not exist. Difference is something to be indicted and discredited, ascribed to obstinacy, bad faith, and diabolical malice. This particularism is not grasped as a perspective, which would suppose other perspectives.

Doubtless it was necessary for Christianity to be regionalized, localized, and tribalized in order to be really a Christianity for those of this region, this place, and this tribe. Christianity is not absolute. It is always the Christianity of the one professing it, it always exists relatively to these or those human groups. But it is a contradiction that each of these expressions should proclaim itself unique and exclusive, that each should claim to be universal, while in fact it is the very principle of Christianity that it is linked to a past that is never more to be repeated, a very particular past of a very particular place, time, person, and death. The sects take up the pretension of each confession to be universal, to have a monopoly of the truth, and multiply it to infinity. This proliferation is their own best refutation. But it does not exorcise them of the demon of intolerence and the fund of violence it has built up.

Imaginary Praxis

Imaginary praxis is praxis operating with a network of symbols that fail to correspond to the infrastructure of real relationships among persons, whether it be in the production and distribution of goods or in the acquisition and distribution of knowledge and power. As we have said, when alienated belief finds its platform withdrawn, it shoots into outer space; it floats free. All activity issuing from this alienated belief now unfolds in a total ignoring of the relationships among the forces and conditions of historical efficacity. Its mode of action has an affinity with that of magic, which identifies the relationship between signifier and signified with that between cause and effect. By seizing control of signs and manipulating them, one believes one has seized control of the realities they symbolize. In attacking superstructures, one thinks to have grasped the infrastructures as well. Religion and culture have been taken to be the secret power of the West. They have been the symbol of the totality of its social and historical being, the precise instances of its absolute legitimation and validation. Thus they appear as the reality-of-its-reality, its quintessence. Appropriate its symbolic universe and you have grasped the whole—science, technology, everything. To make these one's own it suffices to mimic their possessors—their manner of worshiping, of drinking, of eating, of making love. A simple substitution of black "colonials" for white ones, black "missionaries" for white ones, has been the primordial act. There is something of the carnival about the Africanization of the colonies. It is the inauguration of a playful, imaginary, cruel, tragic praxis. The inability to face up to the real turns to resentment against those whom one can caricature but can neither equal nor do without. Hence one demonizes them, makes them the alibi, the scapegoat, the cause of all one's miscarriages.

More often, however, the resentment is directed against oneself. The natives have by now introjected the norms of their masters and mistresses, along with all their censures and distastes. This teaching has inculcated in them the notion that the pitiful lot of their people has been due to their superstitions, depravity, and paganism. Ignorance of the true God and of God's revelation has been the real cause of their poverty and the curse that has weighed upon them. In order to regenerate indigenous society, missionaries wielded certain superstructures, a certain symbolic apparatus. Their African successor will do the same. The latter will not rest content with reinstatement of the dowry, superstitions, and polygamy, but will subjoin exhortations to hard work and appeals to "development," thus duly sacrificing both to the gods and to the slogans of the day.

This facile recourse to the reigning ideology betrays the fragility of the African churches. They turn promptly to conformism, they hasten to place themselves at the service of new princes and new chauvinisms with the same spirit with which yesterday's missionaries placed themselves at the service of their own national idols.

We have cited the merits of a festive communion of brothers and sisters. But when celebration is a simple parenthesis in life's daily round, an escape that fails to fill one with courage and a taste for living once the liturgy is over, it can fall prey to the imaginary. Liturgy, with its music, dances, and incantations, puts one in a euphoria, a spell, a trance. One's personhood drowns in the collective emotion, and one escapes the daily prison of censure, injustice, and humiliation. The sparkling exaltation finally dies away, however, and the person must return to the misery of daily relationships—to the routine of scheme, graft, contempt for human life, and scorn of the spirit to which one is accustomed. What a contrast! The need for numbness becomes desperate. Celebration is on its way to becoming an opiate, delivering and consoling human beings in a realm of the imagination alone.

Thus we have the lights and shadows of the resistance to bourgeois Christianity. We have considered it both as a criticism of the latter and as an attempt to transcend it. We have scrutinized it with a view to discerning, from a point of departure in their varying degrees of success, the conditions for the possibility of an adherence to Christianity in spite of the equivocal or negative circumstances of its transmittal and first acceptance. It has come to light that what the "black churches" refuse is the misery of middle-class Christianity. They break with the collaboration and connivance that maintains the status quo of native subordination and devaluation stamped on all their institutions, discourses, and practices. They strive to emerge from that sublime resignation, that twilight slumber, which distills an abstract understanding of the transcendence and universality of Christianity by reducing it to a demand for acquiescence, self-sacrifice, and the pious preservation of a "deposit" as intangible as it is opaque and meaningless. They likewise renounce a syncretism or scholasticism of adaptation, indigenization, and inculturation.

These rejections provide us with a sketch of just what is needed for an authentic Christianity. We could express this as follows:

1. A positive self-determination vis-à-vis Christianity is possible only via a return to the first introduction of Christianity into Africa, approaching it as a fresh opportunity in a historical situa-

tion characterized by specific needs, sufferings, and tasks in a general framework of domination and an anxiety to survive biologically and historically.

2. We may expect this proper perspective to lead to the formation of particular communities conditioned by circumstances of locale, moment in time, and ethnic group, communities willing to limit themselves to verifiable conditions of judgment and action in the world.

3. This limited perspective and verification, marked by the cultural, historical, and economico-political condition of Africa, will occur by way of the birth and expansion of Easter communities, joyfully celebrating the triumph of life over death as they experience that triumph in their daily existence.

4. This verification, again, will occur by way of the working reality of an effective communion of brothers and sisters, in and by the recognition of the reciprocal gift of life and hope through the sharing of goods and power.

5. This limited perspective and verification will receive its constant legitimation in the unlimited quality of love via an ongoing, active relationship with other Christian formations in the name of their common origin, with a view to a welcoming acceptance, assistance, and mutual "fraternal correction" through the ongoing and constant explanation of the content of the faith in terms of the creative power of beings endowed with liberty and their design of enhancement of the condition of all human beings as human beings. Doubtless there will be more to be learned from today's African religious movements. But if so, account will have to be taken of the requirements here listed.

STRUCTURE OF RESISTANCE

There is one more demand that will have to be heard as we bring to a close this description of the African resistance to bourgeois Christianity. The question arises as to who or what, indeed, is doing the resisting. And of course the answer will be forthcoming: "The African man and woman." But who are they? An abstraction? Not exactly. What is here meant by "African man and woman" is a certain manner of understanding oneself, of living one's relationships with the earth, the living, and the dead. The resistance is organized around certain principles. It demands a certain cohesiveness, it has its own self-consistency. We have to call it something in order to be able to talk about it. For our part, we prefer to call it "African spirituality." Describing it negatively, we might say that African spirituality is a logic that organizes attitudes of resistance to alienation or estrangement. This negative description will suggest a positive one as well, inasmuch as the polemical point of departure is of decisive methodological importance, for a pair of reasons that we shall now briefly note.

First, let us "ambush" African spirituality and actually catch it in the act of resisting. In this way we shall be able to seize it as "subject," instead of merely as an object of interpretation. Unfortunately, this spirituality is generally reconstructed of disparate elements lacking in any unified direction. This, however, is because the people doing the reconstructing do not know what to look for. False objectivity and naïve subjectivity alike, which, respectively, make lists of traits and come up with a robot portrait of traditional religion, or which think they are obviating appeal to philosophical or religions systems, end either in projecting categories of Western discourse into their portrait, by turning them inside-out, or in "finding them here as well," as such, underlying the African cultural data.

If we fail to explicate our point of departure, if we fail consciously to include in this analysis this conditioning of which we have been speaking, if we fail to take account in this methodology of what is at stake and interest in what we are studying, then we shall not know what we are researching. The result will be amorphous and syncretistic. Generally speaking, works on African religions and traditions are either high-floating rhapsodies or solemn, conventional collections of banalities. But we are not piecing together a fossil; we are dealing with something living, something that reacts, mobilizes, and creates antibodies to resist aggression from without. Our point of departure is a situation of violence. We cannot, then, allow ourselves to rest content with a rehabilitation that proceeds via a dilettante, culturalist relativism that proclaims all religions and all cultures equally valid and equally respectable just as all "races" are equal. Inescapably, in actual practice some cultures succumb to the blows of others and perish, just as some races dominate others. Let persons' certitude waver or be subjugated, be it only for an instant, and they have discovered that it is not an eternal truth after all. Those persons will not succeed in avoiding the axiological question of the potential decision to return to it as something by which to live.

It is easy to proclaim the vacuous consistency of what one does not see. It is easy to wax lyrical about "the beauty of death" when one is not caught in the grip of death. But no one desires to dwell in the kingdom of shadows. Not only are they inconsistent, but paeans and exaltations of African religion, culture, and traditions are under suspicion of being either ideologies of mystification or pure entertainment.

Second, the point of departure demands that to one self-consistent system we oppose another self-consistent system only if it is a living one. We have spoken of logic and system. It is false, unjust, and dishonest to oppose the ethno-religious rhapsodies attributed to the Africans to the mighty conceptual architecture of the Summas. It is not the same game or the same rules, and the victories will be illusory: they will be simple misunderstandings. The Summas and tractates are not the first expression of faith. Lived, spontaneous religion has loose ends—it is fragmentary, it is a set of habits and dispositions in a state of mutual adjustment, without benefit of a unifying theory, without being "objectively" suited to their goal as if they were a system of means-to-end. Lived religion, Christianity included, is made up of propositions, stories, legends, rites, laws—in short, of a content whose unifying authority is tradition alone, the imperative of things to be done or not to be done because "it has ever been thus from the beginning," because "this is not done in Israel," because "thus saith the Lord . . . the Word of the Lord."

The case is no different with the African traditional religions. Rationalization and reflection emerge slowly. They emerge in response to heretical contestation, contestation from without. It is collision with imperial whims that obliges human beings to justify their Holy, to put some order in it, to reconcile the diversity of its heteroclytic elements. The self-consciousness of a practical system comes by polemics. It modifies itself, constructs itself under pressure from something "other," something it perceives as "its other." Challenge and response only have meaning among equals. As long as it dominates, the West does not enter into confrontation with anyone. There was a time when Christianity itself had to explain itself to Hellenism on the basis of common premises. It had to justify itself, defend itself as a minority religion. Christianity could never have won out except by "rationalizing" itself, by "refuting" the irrationality of the Pantheon and its olden syncretisms.

This, then, is the challenge and struggle of Africa today, as it takes up its own traditions and unifies them, reflects upon them, "bends back" upon them. The logic that must result from a like initiative is not the lifeless combination of the associative properties of inert things. It is not going to be a matter of reducing African data to formal structures of mathematical logic, but of "demonstrating" the dialectical logic of a living spirit, which is becoming world by surmounting contradictories, by transforming itself in the very becoming and surmounting. This emergence is in no way random. In its very process it manifests its organizing principles, and these principles have the capability of producing their system of practices that will be cohesive among themselves and with objective conditions.

Such are the observations that must be made preliminary to our presentation of African spirituality. They can be summed up in a single proposition: "African spirituality does not 'go without saying.' " An active speech or discourse on the part of a living, locally situated subject is part and parcel of that subject's content, part of its reality. That reality demands justification and, if it is to survive, must raise itself to the level of a reality-that-*ought*-to-be, and a deed-that-*ought*-to-be. It must subject itself to such address as may enable it to "learn itself" and "regain control of itself" in the face of and because of adversity. Discourse can become a strategy of resistance in the second degree, in which case it is the language of reflex practices.

We shall not attempt to furnish a complete sketch of African spirituality. We shall indicate the organizing principles of this spirituality—the principles that will govern our reading of the gospel and our understanding of what could be one of the forms of authentic Christian existence in the African condition. We shall observe these principles in their functioning in the integrative notion of "person" as a being-in-plenitude, for which we enunciate the principle of the "included third." This principle may be stated this way: A relation between two beings can obtain only if an invisible third "thing" is interposed under the species of a material referent—human being or thing—to represent that third "thing." But the formative principle of African spirituality, the principle permitting the construction of the "concept" of that spirituality by situating itself within the movement of its effectuation, will be formulated as follows: it is possible to have one's identity in something other than oneself. This principle is detailed in the others, particularly the one referring to the "person."

The spiritual is attribute. It is a given, a datum of experience, just as the spirits themselves are given in and by the realities through which human beings grasp their position in the world, that is, their co-membership with these realities in this world. The spiritual manifests itself as the order into which human beings insert and lose themselves that they may understand and possess themselves, that they may be-in-truth. We are not responsible for our place of birth or ancestors, and it is in reference to these that the inaccessible origin of our life is unveiled and snatched up—for this origin is anticipated outside us, in the radical exteriority of its constitutive elements, and yet its authority is that of fundament, and not of the fruit of the tension of an individual. Still, this exteriority is not altogether "other" from the human being. It is no stranger to this being, not something foreign to one. Human beings see themselves within it—within their most concrete existence, that of a "natural" being, a being of nature, and yet not that of a simple animal, a mere searcher after nourishment to digest and shelter for sleep, but as the issue of what the human being has already transcended: the cycle of the seasons, the rhythms of life, and the being-together with earth, sky, and the dead. Work, rites, and symbols are means of standing apart from oneself, of leaving off from oneself and coming into tune with all these, to the point of having one's defining being by them and in them. Thus human beings become what they are— become "persons"—only by conforming to the "conditionings" of their existence, only by inserting this existence into the framework proper to all life, only by liberating within themselves the necessary power to act contained within this life, and so taking up and accepting the law of all fecundity.

Thus all life has its roots in death and feeds on death. All "coming alive," all creation, and all passage to another order are obtained only at the price of death and demise. Hence the set of schemata, images, and archetypes whose actualization and effectuation integrate existence into being, by submitting the human being to the latter's laws. Such existence can be characterized as "spiritual," or indeed as "just." Justice, here, is just-ness, or correct insertion and reciprocity, in respect for and obligation toward what is "ourselves otherwise." We must leave everything in its place. There is a time for each thing. We must repair every breach of harmony, every wound and lesion. We must demand reparation for ourselves because we are not merely ourselves, and for others because they are also ourselves, the what-and-who of our preexistence and survival, the what or who of some manner of our "presupposing" ourselves.

In this total responsibility there is no vicarious satisfaction because the others are not strangers to us. They are selves-other-than ourselves. Their sins are the others', and vice versa. Thus there is neither guilty party nor scapegoat. The essential is that order be reestablished, by all and for all. Indeed there is no culpability or guilt in the Christian or Western sense, no sin as an offense against a lawgiver above and beyond life, "with sufficient reflection and full consent of the will." Ignorance and inadvertence do not suspend the structures and laws of what is. Every transgression, conscious or not, is disorder, and demands a restoration of order. Disorder is not only in the spirit wide-awake and fully aware; disorder is also in the body and its mutism. And because he or she is "total part," the individual is not the only one concerned. Failing, fault, is the intrusion of a strangeness that isolates human beings from one another, that dislocates them, makes monads of them when their genuine being is being-oneself-together with others. Fault is evil. It is the failure that cuts off and isolates; it is the shortcoming, the want, the lack, which engulfs individuals in their own whirlwind of night. What is important is the reestablishment of community, the reestablishment of the circulation of life, so that life can go on transcending itself, go on bursting the barriers, or the intervals, of nothingness, go on being superabundant.

Thus generosity is the virtue par excellence, the supreme expression of life. Generosity destroys all greed and acquisitiveness and puts products and goods into perpetual, festive circulation. Generosity and largess insert death itself into the circuit of trade and communication—under the species of gladness and symbolic compensations and substitutions. Death is the source of innumerable sayings and proverbs.

Death, after all, leaves a legacy in the form of the "word." It is "the word in the place of death" that opens up communication space among the living—by providing them with the mediation of the "absent third"—absent indeed, but included thanks to covenant, genealogical tradition, and memory, in which life finds the witness of its ongoing, unquenchable being, and death finds the element of its own peculiar presence: a presence that is real and personal, but mediated by those who speak of it, by it, and for it. Dying, human beings are born to that which they have been. Dying, human beings are part of the universal dynamics of presence; they are present to each and all, without the distance implied in the space and time of the living. Now they are all to all. Death has meaning, and death with meaning is durable, lasting word—ongoing form, informing the life of the living. The dead become spirits, and these spirits are the instructors and guardians of the living.

A world like that is one. Its population is constantly passing from one group to another by birth, death, initiation, and the art of the seer. It is the quality of life that is essential, for this is what permits exchange, communication, and joy.

This is a coherence, a cohesiveness to be affirmed, to be strengthened still further. Christianity must accept and welcome a confrontation with this manner of thinking and existing. It has been avoided by artificially inculcating an anxiety about salvation, a sense of guilt, the isolation of individuals, and a metaphysical and cosmological dualism. But in spite of the onslaughts of Christianity, African spirituality abides, as human beings' conscientization of their position in the world through the cycle of tasks and seasons and ages of life and social roles, through the bond among the generations, through healing and festival. It abides as the permanent, regulatory metaphor of the structures and basic activities of existence, by which are accomplished the genesis of human beings, the conditions of their being, and their access to their humanity until death comes and is accepted as necessary to the truth of life, and as source of solidarity, communication, and reciprocity among the living. African spirtuality is a spirituality in which the afterlife is in the hands of others. *My* survival is other people's problem, not mine. The important thing is to exist really, without ever seeming to have discharged one's obligations toward others, living or dead. True life is never absent.

African Christians have the intellectual and moral obligation to experience the solidity of this spirituality, and not to be too hasty to exclude it from the quest for wisdom, truth, and happiness. They should demand that their Christianity not turn its backs on this spirituality, but confront it. For it summons Christians to abandon the security of the status quo and begin to take their own measure by the experience that is unique—the experience of being a human person, the experience of taking the initiative in the transformation of life and the genesis of oneself and one's truth in the world.

Part Two

THE CHRISTIC MODEL

To emerge from alienated belief is to experience the transfiguring power of Christ upstream, as it were, from where dogmas begin. Dogmas, with all their coherence and consistency, do not constitute a closed system. The articles of faith make up a "relational" being: they all come together in God. They all converge on his mystery, and on the complexus of operations and modes of behavior to which the recognition of God gives rise, and by which that recognition is signified. Cut off from this double referent, the articles of faith may seem to remain intact, but now they are compatible with anything at all, and they can enter a system in which they are not true, in which their intentionality and their aim deviates from its true course. Now the dogmas become "legends" demanded by conformism. They dissimulate themselves, but even in their dissimulation they are not to be believed. They become incredible.

Faith doubtless begins with the personal and collective verification of something that has transcended missionary rumor and hearsay. ("No longer does our faith depend on your story. We have heard for ourselves, and we know that this really is the Savior of the world"—John 4:42.) A "word" like this issues from one's *experience*, one's *situation*. "Words" too are a kind of "Scripture"— the "Scripture" of each person's own formation and set of historical and cultural moments, in which Christ must be crucified, die, and rise anew in each person. Only then has one passed from a foreign belief to a hearing and *knowing* of one's own. For we can relate to God only through the mediations and processes that really constitute us as persons. It is not sufficient to "work on ourselves." Autosuggestion is not enough, whatever the stories told, whatever the inspirational techniques invoked. These only make silence and absence fairly shout. We must not attempt an imaginary straddling of the distance, the abyss, that separates us despite the letter of the gospel, despite death absent and silent, despite this faraway, foreign Jesus of Nazareth who has gone back to the "Father." An immediate, "personal" rapport with Jesus and God by psychic acts transpiring within our intentionality is what we rightly call paganism, fetishism. "Personal" contact with God and Jesus can only mean a relationship expressed through and by human determination, effectuated through work done with the materials of nature, through an encounter with other persons and with things. Here the gospel will speak to us in the horizontality of historical and cultural existence, provided two conditions are present: (1) that the questions, strivings, aspirations, and tasks of the time of Jesus still be our own "in a certain way"; (2) that the gospel furnish us not with specific, singular content, but with a model of self-restructuring in and by history.

By way of explanation of these two conditions, let us explicate the principles, or hypotheses, or our "appropriate reinterpretation" of the Christic phenomenon. Regarding the first: How can a response to questions rising out of a particular situation in an age long past still be valid for us who belong to another era and another situation? The solution will be found to lie in our determination of the nature of these questions, so as to be able to isolate the originality of the response made to them, and its permanent value, or lack thereof, when it comes to our own situation and questions. Our thesis, or rather, hypothesis is the following: "Questions of a singular community of a bygone age are still ours today insofar as they have been conditioned (determined) by the occurrence of a 'problematic of the universal,' which calls upon the particular, the singular, to understand itself and to exist from a point of departure in a 'world' perceived as having become one world—which calls upon it to transcend itself in the unprecedented novelty of a community with no one on the inside and no one on the outside." The Israel of Jesus' time was a small nation, whose identity and physical survival were at stake as invincible military, political, and cultural empires raged and stormed around it. It must redefine its relation to itself and to others, it must retrace the boundaries between its "within" and "without," it must invent a new way of living in the world. The appearance of (actual and potential) universal models, which claim to explain everything to everyone, will call into question the principles according to which particularisms have been constituted as singular totalities. They will not spare the personhood that becomes incomprehensible to itself in the blinding flash of a collective destiny, or "vocation."

Christianity arose in response to just such a situation. Hence its original, and originating problematic is open to repetition—not in the form of a reiteration of "the same thing as back then," but in its reinvention.

With regard to the second condition: reiteration would be vain in any case. The model is not a stack of recipes, a package of "things," a "deposit." Nor, at the other extreme, is it a form without a content, ready to slap down on uninformed matter. The demand and the structure of self-transcendence, of going beyond one's limits, do not arise from without, but from the working action of the particular upon itself. This demand and this structure are the fruit of the toil and patience of this particular singularity. It was by its conscientization with respect to its own history that Judaism judged and restructured itself with a view to producing a new, concrete universality. It did not judge itself by some external norm—detachable from its intrinsic constitution, detachable from its own genesis and its own experiences—in spite of the fact that its (internal) norm did permit it to orient itself in time and then transcend itself in history.

Such a model, the product of history with a view to the transformation of history (or the transformation of something in history) is a "model that has become." Its production is bound up with the singularity of a particular locality and temporality. It has a local habitation and a name. In the transverse dimension of a history that retains a memory of its genesis, of its "having become," such a model is unthinkable without a Christic reference.

There we have our premises, or perhaps we should call them our hopes, our expectations. They arise out of the experience of our pilgrimage in alienation, as we wandered far from home. With these in hand, let us now approach the gospel—the Christic phenomenon.

Chapter 4

The Fullness of Time:
Religious Movements and Currents

Jesus lived, acted, and spoke in the midst of his own and for his own. His actions, his words, in order to have meaning, presuppose a shared field of communication, made up of what everyone believed, hoped, or feared, and marked by the problems, events, and forces that conditioned everyone's life and dictated the collective future. In order to grasp the import of what Jesus said and did, one must be able to discern what he accepted and what he rejected of this common fund, what he retained as such and what he transposed, and, finally, what he invented. Thereby one will understand the sense of his choices and the originality of his innovations. The adequate context of his activity extends beyond the limits of the time from his birth (or the beginning of his public life) to the death of the last apostle. Jesus' context is a whole *era* in the history of the Jews.

What is an era? An era is characterized by two things. First, it is characterized or defined by what "goes without saying" for those who live in it. This is what procures everyone's cohesion and certitude; this is the framework within which one thinks, acts, and protests. This is the authority by which institutions carry out their ordinary functions, and by which beliefs enjoy their effectiveness. Second, an era is distinguished by the nonsubdued, the nonrepulsed, the nonrepressed—as expressed in tension and violence, or need, or vague aspiration in search of formulation and satisfaction.

89

One era has ended and another has begun when "underground" aspirations and needs are perceived and clarified, and ways and means of satisfying them defined. A new era is heralded by the appearance of effective counterforces, legitimations that enjoy more credibility than the old ones, theories that explain the effective practices currently in vogue. Now the fullness of time has come, and a new beginning may be invented.

Thus by situating the Christian phenomenon in its proper era, we shall be able to see the newborn Christian sect as an original response to common questions and aspirations. We shall see it as the offer of a "new coherence."

The era in which the Christian phenomenon is rooted extends from the time of the Maccabees (175 B.C.) to the revolt of Bar Kochba and the destruction of the Jewish nation-state (A.D. 135). Here Judaism encounters limit-situations and learns how to survive persecution and preserve its identity in the midst of an irresistible, hostile civilization and empire. Here Judaism undergoes its greatest and most lasting mutations. Various religious movements and currents arise in response to this situation of unprecedented gravity. Furthermore, long before the final dispersion, a continuous emigration, now forced, now free, swells the Jewish colonies already disseminated throughout the Mediterranean basin. Already there are more Jews in the Diaspora than in Palestine, which, with its "Zion," remains the mother (cf. Ps. 87), the spiritual center of this immense periphery. The unity of Judaism, stretched between two poles, enters a dialectic. Palestine and the Diaspora fertilize and maintain one another. What occurs in the interior is understood to be valid and pertinent for those afar, and their eyes are ever turned toward Jerusalem, where they come on pilgrimage with their gifts for the Temple treasury.

What indeed is it that thus "occurs in the interior"? The era is pregnant with challenges and contradictions. How can this be the chosen people when it is such a minority, sometimes "hateful" in the eyes of others, and so ill integrated into "civilization"? How can the Jews be God's favorites when they form a colonial, subjugated nation? How can they be redefined, how can they preserve their identity, their "mission," their vocation and calling, without risking their biological survival? The religious movements and currents make an effort to respond to these questions.

MOVEMENTS

The word "movement" here is not to be understood in a narrow sense. We are merely opposing it to a "current." A "movement" is formed around a totem-personage. It is organized. A "current" is diffuse and spans various groups at once. Josephus calls the movements "heresies," that is, "sects," in order to stress their optative character. He lists the Pharisees, the Sadducees, and the Essenes. Perhaps "Zelotism" and "Baptism" are "currents" in his eyes; at any rate they do not figure in his list of heresies. Taken all together, these movements and currents make up living Judaism in the time of Jesus, and this is what conditions his teaching. He makes his declarations and takes his positions with respect to these movements and currents. When the New Testament declares that Jesus died "according to the Scriptures," that he rose "according to the Scriptures," it is referring to a manner of reading and interpreting the Bible that was in vogue in a milieu charged with apocalyptic currents. It is indispensable, then, to be acquainted with this milieu in order to be able to perceive the ties and the divergences between its various elements and the new Christian "sect."

The Sadducees

Israel is developing strategies of survival in the face of subjugation and the danger of destruction. The establishment of the Hellenistic monarchies is decisive in this regard. In the course of the struggle against these, the Sadducees and Pharisees make their appearance. The Sadducees form a part of the nobility. This nobility is at once lay and clerical. From John Hyrcanus to Ishmael ben Phiabi, by way of one "Joseph, surnamed Caiaphas," the high priests are generally of Sadducean origin and persuasion. The mass of their partisans is composed of patrician families and landholders. Via this aristocracy, Sadduceeism plays a considerable role in Jewish life. The material bases of its effectiveness and power consist in real property: the city-state of Jerusalem with its Temple, which is both a place of worship and a treasury maintained by world Judaism. The great Sadducean preoccupation is to ensure the continuity of this possession and its institutions. These are the foundation upon which rest the "traditions" of the Fathers, and the law in its literal integrity. The one thing necessary is to safeguard the Jewish national entity and religion, in the genealogical bond and the relationship with the Promised Land—in other words, to safeguard that by which Israel is the People of God. The rest is subject to compromise, so long as the Abrahamic descendancy may be assured of its permanence on the land promised and granted by the Eternal.

The destruction of the Temple and the nation-state is the death of Sadduceeism. Of course, it has already begun to be superseded, by Pharisaism in the religious area, and politically by the radicalism of the Zealots.

The Pharisees

After the fall of the second Temple, Pharisaism and Judaism will be coextensive. For now, however, Pharisaism is but one sect among others: an association, or ensemble of associations, with its own particular rules and usages. The Pharisaical movement is a lay movement, recruited from the middle class. Its authorities are the scribes, versed in the science of the Scriptures, for the Torah is more to the Pharisees than life itself. In meditating on it, and commenting on it, one draws out something useful for anything and everything. It has more than six hundred prescriptions, forming a closed network over all of life, down to the least details and trivia of daily living. It contains the law, the tithe, and ritual purity. With Pharisaism the center of religion moves from the Temple and public worship toward ethical observances, the science of the Scriptures, and the synagogue. Meditation—that "sacrifice of the lips"—and the practice of the commandments replace holocausts. No longer is it in the blood of heifers and the smoke of victims, but in the verses of the Bible that the divine intentions will be scrutinized.

What separates this people from the others, what sets it apart and signifies irreducible election is this "hedge" of observances drawn from the very words of sacred Scripture. Provided the essential be guaranteed, the Pharisees are broad-minded and tolerant. They welcome foreign influences, and these determine the development of their dogmas. Thus, for example, they confront the traditionalistic Sadducees with the resurrection of the dead, the inauguration of a Messianic era, the existence of angels, and so on. The pagan power finds them a more reliable support than the other groups. The reign of the Gentiles even has the happy side-effect of putting an end to the catastrophic confusion of politics and religion maintained by the Hasmonean dynasty. Political independence is not redemption. By an unfathomable disposition of the wisdom of God, the ways of salvation pass tortuously through misery, suffering, persecution, and exile.

By their rigorous praxis the Pharisees affirm Jewish identity. Their great flexibility of mind and spirit is joined to an immense capacity for endurance as they gather around the Torah to await indefinitely the Messianic age.

The Essenes

The Maccabees were supported in their war of resistance to the "pagans" by the band of Hasidim, or "pious ones," the valiant, "holy" men and women whose heart was attached to the law. These are seen as the ancestors of the Pharisees, and especially of the sect of the Essenes. The Essenes live in monastic, ascetical communities, whose rule prescribes a life of chastity, poverty, and obedience. It prescribes the times of work, repose, prayer, and meals. It determines the number of ablutions. It defines the Essenes' beliefs, their use of their goods, and their attitude toward outsiders.

What does such a manner of life mean? First, it means that the entire Jewish nation is sullied and spoiled. Second, it means that the Essenes are the "faithful remnant," the healthy kernel reserved for a future restoration. The regime of the Hasmoneans, who have captured both throne and sovereign pontificate, now in its corruption has lost its title of legitimacy to both. The worship over which they and their successors preside at Jerusalem is a simple abomination. As for the masses, they are impure and without piety. They are ignorant of the law, negligent of its observances, and soil themselves a thousand times a day, even by contact with foreigners, and foreigners are everywhere these days. The Essenes' self-sequestration has for its purpose the preservation of a little remnant from this generalized evil, and its training for combat against the powers of darkness. Their reclusive life is a long vigil of arms, in which, by continence, purifications, and contempt for a perverse world, they prepare for the final struggle—the battle that will open the way for the legitimate High Priest of the last days, the Messiah King. The Essenes are so conscious of their legitimacy, so aware of being Israel in its totality that they appropriate for themselves Scripture itself. They "update" Scripture by applying it integrally to their own group, whose tribulations and glorious destiny it prophesies. Indeed they pursue the creative process themselves, and add products of their own making to the sacred canon.

These are the Essenes. With them the struggle acquires both interiorization and apocalyptic breadth. The need for a New Israel begins to take the shape of a marginal group, far from the epicenters of dominant society and tradition.

The Zealots

These are not the *sicarii*, the armed guerrillas of mountain and desert, the raiders of the roads and cities and murderers of the forces of occupation and their collaborators. Nor are the Zealots the bandits and highwaymen, the desperadoes sprung of the misery and distress of the economy. The Zealots are associates of the clergy, perhaps the lower clergy, and are characterized by their "zeal for the House of God" (Ps. 69:10). They seek to be worthy sons of the Levites who, on Moses' order, went through the camp from tent to tent, massacring brother, friend, and neighbor after the Israelites had delivered themselves up to the worship of the golden calf. Their patron is one Zadok, whose descendant Phinehas will transfix with his lance a man who has dared to marry a Midianite, a pagan (cf. Num. 25:6–14). The Zealots continue to pursue this tradition of safeguarding the Jewish identity or calling, demanding purity of race, the exclusive worship of a jealous God, respect for the sanctity of the Temple, and the legitimate priestly succession. Their objective is the restoration of all these values, with their culmination in a worship to be presided over by the sons of Zadok, who alone may approach the Lord, to serve him in the "new Temple" announced by the prophets. The affinity of the Zealots to the *sicarii* consists in their rejection of everything foreign and their refusal to submit to a pagan authority in the land of Israel. They give their protestations a "theological" basis—a basis in the nature of God's relations with Israel.

Judas Maccabeus reproaches his compatriots with cowardice and infidelity to God in paying the tribute to the Romans, that is, in accepting other masters than Yahweh alone. Theirs is the sin of idolatry. Furthermore, according to the Zealots, resignation to the pagan reign for reason of military inferiority is an archetypical manifestation of lack of faith. God's support is altogether sure, guaranteed in advance, for the victory of his people and their hegemony are his own victory and hegemony. They bear witness that he is the One, the Strong, and the True. With the Zealots, the spirit of revenge and conquest, of violence and temerity bids fair to become the supreme form of piety, and of faith in the omnipotence of God—*their* God.

CURRENTS

Currents are "movements" that are less individualized. They reveal the themes, the spirit of an age. They manifest its need and wants, its aspirations, under the form of a mentality, an intellectual and spiritual atmosphere, and popular practices.

Baptism

Lustrations are a common symbol of renewal, and regeneration. Pharisees and Essenes make considerable use of purifications and ablutions. Judaism is familiar with sacred baths in the Jordan and imposes on its proselytes not only circumcision, but baptism by immersion. The meaning of baptism at the time of Jesus is altogether original and special. The Jews have become collectively unclean. They are no better than the pagans in respect of purity. In order to belong to the new, genuine Israel, they must be reborn by penitence and the ritual plunge into the water that authenticates that penitence. The baptismal rite is the safe-conduct pass permitting the penitent to enter into the kingdom of the Spirit and of justice, which is to presage the inauguration of the reign of the Messiah. A sentiment of collective unworthiness and general defilement along with the expectation of the imminent and purifying coming of the Messiah are the powerful catapults of a movement that will survive, in Christianity and in the sect of the Mandaeans.

This discussion of the baptismal current must not omit mention of exorcism, baptism's companion-current. Defilement takes on the shape of illness and possession. Jesus is not the only exorcist-healer of his time. ("If I expel demons with Beelzebul's help, with whose help do your people expel them?"—Matt. 12:27.) Exorcism and healing signal extreme distress: the prodigious combat against the empire of the Evil One and the imminence of its happy resolution.

Apocalyptic

The expectation of the Messiah is now carried to the highest pitch of intensity. The return from the exile has been followed by an almost uninterrupted foreign occupation. A grave institutional crisis has brought discredit on priesthood and royal estate alike. Internal divisions are ripping the nation apart. The loss of identity, or "apostasy," that threatens everyone is already an actuality for a great many. The measure of danger and humiliation is brimful. The situation can only reverse. God alone can accomplish it. Therefore he will intervene. Nothing is impossible with God. Now one can brave death and failure. The impossible has become probable, and the probable certain: death will be followed by resurrection, and failure can only be provisional and apparent.

This imperious prophecy takes the form of apocalyptic. It is a hallucinatory form, and replete with detail. Apocalyptic says: Just as the past has unfolded in accordance with a preestablished plan of God, so the liberation to come will be accomplished with the same necessity, the same implacable rigor. The present is already heavy with the future, for one who knows how to read the code. We know in advance that God's intervention on the side of his people will be punctuated by the following events: the return of the tribes, the last agony of the powers hostile to Israel, the final victory of the just, the conversion of the Gentiles who survive, the new Jerusalem, the Messianic benefits, the resurrection, the judgment of individuals, the final lot of the good and the evil, the final destiny of the world. This sequence is not without its variations, for a number of its points are the subject of controversy—the resurrection, for example, or the particular judgement, or the lot of the Gentiles who are now annihilated, now only partially destroyed, now subjected to Israel or first subjected and then saved after Israel and out of regard for Israel. Sometimes the horizon of this canon of eschatological events is nationalistic and ethical, sometimes it is heavenly and universal, but apocalyptic always announces a new start, and an ineluctable one.

Hellenistic Judaism

The Diaspora is a periphery that is growing more and more active. With the destruction of the center, it becomes all. The geographical dispersion is a school of the transcendence of particularism—indeed its material basis. Judaism is constrained to open up to other cultures and adjust to them.

Popular Judaism is the least impermeable. It is borrowed from the folklore and mythology of others. Its strong point is magic, and its trump card here is its marginality and its affinity for the Chaldeans with their Book of books with the strange writing in it. The Jews are devoted to astrological computations and circulate magic formulas to pronounce or carry in talismans.

The Jews are adopting the Hellenistic world's framework of material life. Their techniques, their architecture, their decorative arts, even their discipline and habits, are becoming Hellenized. The Bible has been translated into Greek now, in case one no longer understands Hebrew, and the Hellenized Jew subjects it to the methods of interpretation in vogue among Stoics and Pythagoreans. This is no game, no pagan exercise. Greek has taken root in the Jew's heart. The Bible is as shocking as Homer and his mythology—on first reading—and so, in order to save appearances, one must go beyond appearances and apply an allegorical interpretation. The Hellenized Jew will bequeath to the Christian the doctrine of the "four senses of Scripture." The first sense, or meaning, of the sacred page is the literal one, the one in the words themselves. Because this first meaning is opaque, it must be progressively illuminated by the other three meanings, or senses: This Book is allegory, for it speaks of Another. It is ethics, tropology, for one's individual life. Finally, it is analogy, accessible to the wise and the initiate alone, a flash in the night, "black light" full of mystical, eschatological truth. Scripture speaks the language of reason, indeed. But it can bedazzle and transport that reason, too.

In order to be acceptable in its particularity, to itself as well as to others, Hellenized Judaism invents apologetic discourse, which ap-

peals to discussion, to the adversary's spirit of investigation and
good faith, and refers to some common standard under the presidency of reason.

Finally, the *oikoumenē* becomes, for the Hellenized Jew, the seat
of universality, a special framework for thought and religious
imagination. The empire is providential, pacified, unified space.
The Name of the one true God resounds from end to end within it.
The empire-builders are his instruments, his toys. It is for him that
they are building.

THE NEW SECT

In order to emerge and exist alongside the others, the new sect
must establish, practically and effectively, its nonredundancy and
historical necessity. Its viewpoint sketches similarities and differences. The other sects lack this, and this lack justifies the new
sect in its immanence. It reveals the others' limits after the fact and
judges them by the very fact of its own existence. It *is* judgment.

Conflict with Sadduceeism

The new sect is in head-on, mortal collision with Sadduceeism—
be it the Sadduceeism of the prominent, of the Zealots, or of the
sicarii. Jesus' activity and teaching seem subversive to the Sadducees, and the priests will kill him for it. His message, whose horizon
is the imminence of the reign of God, proclaims that that reign has
placed itself within reach of all, without the obligatory intermediary of a place, a corpus of prescriptions, or specialists in the sacred. Its proximity means that it does not delegate its sovereignty
part and parcel to its representatives or some symbolic apparatus.
It means that its freedom and its generosity receive neither determination nor restriction from the fact of choices or gifts in the past.
Finally, privileges of birth, religion, wealth, or knowledge are no
infallible sign of the favor or presence of God. In themselves they
are not the best means of reaching him.

Jesus' message, then, is not centered on the Temple, liturgical
life, the preservation of the holy places, ethnic purity, or the maintenance of a sacral order centered around the ancient gifts of God:
the land and Abrahamic descendancy (the race). Jesus' message is

turned toward the future, where no one can have staked a claim, for the future is God's alone. It is addressed to all, and proclaims the annulment of the sacralized oppositions by which human beings organize and exploit inequality and weakness. More precisely, its practice and teaching involve the termination of the priestly mediation, which lives on exploitation and guilt, and on the fear of defilement and death. Sadduceeism is national religion—or better, territorial, ethnic, and cultic religion—and lacks the prophetic dimension of hope and justice, which could preserve it from self-installation and make it a "consolation" for the "people of the land," for all the ignorant, and for people with doubtful pedigrees. In Sadduceeism, all these are without a future, earthly or heavenly, for there is neither belief in the immortality of the soul nor expectation of the resurrection and the kingdom of God. Sadduceeism is a satisfying religion only for the rich, the powerful, and the well-born.

Conflict with Essenism

Essenism is still a form of Sadduceeism, even after its breach with it, even after its self-imposed exile from Jerusalem and its abstention from public worship, power, and wealth. Its sole pursuit, and the heart of its religion, is the restoration of a renewed Temple and monarchy. But Essenism is situated in the future: it is the expectation of God. Hence it is adventism. The waiting will be active: one must prepare for the hour of God by a holy life. The combat is an interior one: the battle of Light and Darkness. The struggle is cosmic and eschatological. Present times are the last times, and God is busy shaping his "perfect people," his true Israel. All these ascetical and eschatological traits will lend Essenism an affinity for the new sect: the new sect will borrow them along with many others. Meanwhile, Jesus has taken the opposite position on certain essential points. The Essenes are simply consistent Zealots, who have fled Jerusalem until at last there be a high priest of the stock of Aaron, to the image of the great Zadok. They scarcely look for any radical novelty. They do not refuse institutionalized mediations, but they keep to themselves. They are an exclusive salvation-group, hostile to all outsiders. They practice spiritual segregation. According to their *Manual of Discipline*, the novice, "in undertaking this holy association, will thus pledge to cut himself off from all men of perversity, who advance by the paths of impiety. . . ." All but the members of their own sect are to be avoided like the plague: "Let them not descend to the waters of purification, lest they sully the men of holiness. . . . Let no one in the community take account of their advice on anything concerning doctrine or judgment. And let none drink or eat what is theirs." The Essenes are prisoners of an obsession with defilement, and they seek to escape its guilt by the rigors of asceticism, purification, and isolationism. They count themselves among that "little number of the elect" who are to escape the universal deluge.

For Jesus, God's mercy is abounding and gratuitous. God takes the initiative with human beings. His grace surprises them wherever it finds them. Even before they realize it, "their sins are forgiven them." Finally, believers are delivered from what they have become a slave to: the law, rules for purity, and prohibitions. Obligations must be reconstructed from a point of departure in the twin commandments of love of God and of neighbor. There is no longer any such thing as "unclean persons," be they tax collectors, lepers, or Samaritans. It is useless to isolate oneself in the desert in order to avoid evil and "meet God" by deeds of ascetical prowess. Such deeds only nurture a consciousness of belonging to a predestined elite, and feed a sweetish, cloying self-exaltation and sense of moral superiority, which in turn instills obstinacy, insensitivity, rash judgment, and resentment.

Conflict with Pharisaism

The violence of Jesus' confrontation with Pharisaism is a matter of record. Pharisaism is a historical success in its own line, just as Christianity is in its line. It has ensured the survival of Judaism. It is a religious revolution, whose originality must be recognized if we are to appreciate the Christian vehemence it will arouse. Here are its main traits:

1. *Pharisaism is a "laicization" of religion.* In Pharisaism, what distinguishes the priests and forms the basis of their privileges is their submission to certain obligations of purity—not their birth. To constitute a "priestly people," it will suffice to extend these

obligations and their observance to all. Pharisaism is a democratization of religion, tempered by merit, knowledge, and the strict observance of the prescriptions.

2. *Pharisaism inserts religion into life.* What matters is no longer liturgy, but ethical comportment: what one must do all day long to please God. It is by one's good works that one proclaims and signifies the holiness of God, the respect due him. By these good works one lays the groundwork for the redemption. All the dogmatic and ritual content of Judaism is invested in rules, prescriptions, and usages.

3. *Scripture becomes central.* It absorbs the sacrality of worship and Temple. Soon it will absorb the sacrality of the land. It "substitutes" for them: it is lived in, it is celebrated, and it is scrutinized to discern the divine intentions. Pharisaism makes Judaism a religion of the Book. Its readers, the scribes, are the new "priests." They explain it, interpret it, and meditate over it. They draw from it the rules for behavior, for what must be done to be pleasing to God— for every situation and all cases. The age of the scribe is the age of the closure of the Book in upon itself, the time of the end of the prophets—the time of casuistry, often balanced by mysticism and enlivened with the hope of the resurrection and the expectation of the hour of God.

Christianity's critique of Pharisaism can be reduced to the following points:

1. *The ritualization of ethics ends in the sacralization of usages and precepts.* These are invested with an intangible form, and this is injurious to human beings. The law, instead of being for human beings, places the latter in its service, sacrifices them to it. The ritualization of ethics is a principle of bondage: it multiplies prescriptions, and thereby multiplies the occasions and possibilities for transgression. Multiple prescriptions increase one's obsession with impurity and defilement. Success in the minute observance of numerous rules lends a false security and assigns merit to difficult performance. It locks one up in one's good conscience, self-complacency, and self-justification by works.

2. *Hypocrisy and self-dissimulation are the lethal danger of a religion of the Book.* An interpretation or code adequate to the changing reality of actual events is drawn from the very words of

Holy Writ only at the price of allegorical exegesis and subtle casuistry—that is, by artificial means, which translate a materially bad faith and develop a false conscience. Scripture becomes a screen between oneself and God or one's neighbor, between oneself and the real. It serves to evade their impact and the obligations they impose. This is the essence of Pharisaism. There is no escaping the manipulation of Scripture, except Scripture be interpreted by the rule of the First Commandment, and the Second, which is like unto it. For on these depend "the law and the prophets."

3. *Pharisaism places the whole content of revelation in a corpus of usages, precepts, formulas, dispositions, and habits, which it identifies immediately with the will of God.* It inculcates these as such, thereby sacralizing its own society, its own way of life. That way of life is now the adequate response to the divine Truth—the expression of God's holy will and its solitary earthly projection. It is the sacrament of the encounter of God with the human being. Apart from this mode of living, which is the "one" mode of living because God himself is "one," there is no revelation and no salvation. Pharisaism culturalizes the faith, and makes of salvation a worldly matter.

4. *The Bible, become part of a Talmud, now becomes a determinant of the "culture of difference" into which rabbinical Judaism is being transformed.* Believers must build a hedge around themselves in order to be safe in their being and "calling." The defense system has certainly been effective. Henceforward in Judaism, ethnicity and religion will be inseparable. Its claim to universality is now expressed in a form and language that give it the lie: that of processes of ethno-cultural assimilation. Here we see a paradoxical situation indeed, which seeks to "pass off" the particular for the universal and the universal for the particular, just as if God had created the entire world with all its peoples for the service and glory of the Chosen People. The opposition between Jews and others has become eternal, for it has been transferred to God by establishing it in his immovable, arbitrary choice. With Christ, the Person of the Future, there is no longer "Jew or Greek." The Judaic equivocation of the "carnal" and the "spiritual" is dissipated, and no longer signifies anything but the irreducible singularity of a particular historical society.

In Summary

Let us sum up these findings concerning the new sect. It bathes in an atmosphere of the apocalyptic. Its members await the imminent "consolation of Israel": they believe that Israel's reestablishment and the inauguration of the kingdom of God are in the offing. The new sect is part of the baptism current. It will keep baptism as its rite of conversion, purification, and entry into the kingdom, which has now been inaugurated with the death and resurrection of Jesus, and which is present by his Spirit. The new sect has been the heir presumptive of Hellenistic Judaism from the very start. It will prolong the latter's openness and become the religion of the empire, while Judaism will close in upon itself to the point of repudiating even its ancient Hellenistic liaisons.

The new sect's confrontation with the Sadduceean, Essenian, and Pharisaical movements has permitted it to sketch the shape of something called "Christianity." Through its protests, we begin to see what it is. In fact, its protest is actually its self-definition, for it comprises the actions and deeds by which it posits itself in its specific difference. These primitive refusals and rejections reveal the sort of ongoing obstacles it will have to surmount in order to be itself. It will have to stand fast against the will of the theocratic power, against cultualism and ritualism, and against the sacralization of mediations. It will have to get beyond the territorial principle, the ethnic principle: it will have to burst through the exclusive logic of membership in a group, even (and especially) a religious group. No way of life can become the obligatory path to God. Christianity, then, will legitimate none of the systems of opposition in which human beings arrange one another in "hierarchies," in which human beings determine one another's degree of being and degree of nearness to God. Thereby Christianity will bestow on human beings the capability of recognizing God in himself and for himself, in his mystery, and the capability of being-for-themselves as well, in God's image and likeness.

Chapter 5

The Work of Jesus

What we have just described, by way of contrast with other sects, is Jesus' message. The term "message," however, runs the risk of being misunderstood if it is taken in the sense of a teaching or a doctrine, a corpus of truths to believe. The message has been delivered to us in the form of a creative action: the birth of a group in confrontation with other groups around it. The message is the description of concrete action, of the realization of a destiny. This is why we are about to consider Jesus' teaching under the formality of his work, his action, his deed. This is also why the present chapter will be followed by a consideration of the person of Jesus. The realization of Jesus' particular lot and destiny will be interpreted here as the form and content of that of which his verbal message and his conscious and voluntary activity are but moments, albeit privileged ones. The personal model is the one for making history, for integrating historical conditions into one's own lot, for receiving oneself from others. The personal model is the manner in which the principle of illimitation becomes the actual, realistic horizon of collective and individual life.

It will not be paradoxical, then, if we present what is usually called doctrine and teaching as action and deed. What Jesus says, he first performs. He acts before he speaks. Teaching is the fomulation of an *operari*, of a work performed upon oneself and others in order to bring things, and oneself as well, to actualization—in order to give the principle of illimitation an operationalism in a finite world.

104

THE ESCHATOLOGICAL PRINCIPLE

The principle of illimitation will take the form of the eschatological principle. What do we mean by this?

It will be inadequate merely to observe that Jesus, like so many of his Jewish contemporaries, shares the expectation of an imminent end of the world, and that his message bears the mark of a sense of urgency. There is something else that can and must be said. Determining the form and content of what Jesus proclaims is the "eschatological principle," and Jesus actually applies this principle; he does not simply draw conclusions and implications from it. To be sure, Jesus is awaiting the Parousia. He talks about it. His preaching is shot through with words like "near," "soon," "sudden," "unexpectedly." He exhorts his hearers to watchfulness, to haste. There is no time to lose.

His speech is also judgment. It pronounces, expresses a set of transformations, a complexus of effects to be produced in the area of behavior, attitudes, and institutions. This judgment is the irruption into thought, word, and deed, of the end of history—of the perishability of the world as human beings have made it. Human beings have erected their world on the basis of the opposition and struggle between man and woman, master and slave, rich and poor, instructed and ignorant, saint and sinner. The proclamation and practice of the end unveil the provisional character of the hierarchies, institutions, and values, which sin—the overestimation or fear of oneself and of what *is*—transforms into ultimate, final realities.

Eschatological activity is an operation of deconstruction and deconditioning. It relativizes ideologies and institutions in order to place them in correlation with the desires and interests which have given rise to them and which ensure their vigor and durability. It also places them in relation with one another, thereby demonstrating that they are defined in relation with one another, and that the system or totality which they constitute must be transcended if one seeks "salvation"—if one seeks that leap out beyond the impasses and contradictions of today toward another world. The ferment and the sense of urgency have the effect of revealing the possibilities, aspirations, and needs that the dominant systems ignore, censure, or disqualify through the conditioning they exert on human minds. This qualitative change will not take place through recourse to the forces of the past, which have a name, but only by recourse to that anonymous, indeterminate force that surges up from the future and is manifested by the displacement of frontiers and the inversion of hierarchies. The transgression of limits is one of the means of eschatological practice. The cleft between life and death is minimal and closing so rapidly that human persons now pass from the one to the other with ease. The dead are among the living, who will soon be dead. Elijah, John the Baptist, and then Jesus himself will all be here again. Transcendence is so near now that its sparks are flashing, now here, now there, bright signals in the night of immanence. There are signs and prodigies. The distance is short from promise to fulfillment, from means to end. The indiscernible means to the end is symbol, and the end, inseparable from its means, is pure act and expression. Eschatological practice does away with these reduplications, these divisions. It joins contraries. It turns the "signs" upside-down. Prostitutes go before the "just" into the kingdom. Those who exalt themselves shall be humbled, and those who humble themselves shall be exalted. Blessed are the poor.

Jesus accomplishes deeds, posits acts that effect these inversions and these transgressions. He sups with sinners; their company is not defilement, for they are the sons and daughters of Abraham too, and salvation has come to their house. They are nearer the kingdom than many "saints" who have not loved much. He heals on the Sabbath, and allows his disciples to gather a few fallen spikes of grain on that day. "The sabbath," after all, "was made for man, not man for the sabbath" (Mark 2:27). Though a Jew, he does not eschew the Samaritan: to be sure, salvation is from the Jews, but the day will come, and has already come, when God will have worshipers in spirit and in truth, worshipers who will no longer have their holy places in Jerusalem or on Mount Gerizim. There will no longer be Jew or Samaritan. The latter can be the former's neighbor by title of the compassion and the love that dismantles walls of separation. The nearness of compassion and love will be stronger than the bonds of blood: Who is my mother? Who are my brothers and sisters? Those who hear the Word of God and obey it. The principle of heredity will not strike root in the community of those who are born not of blood or of the will of the flesh or of "man," but of "God."

These transgressions and inversions acquire their full meaning when considered as alternative solutions to the system of responses in vogue at the time. They take charge of what is left out, neglected, and devalued by that system. They concentrate intensely on what is near, everyday, and elementary—the things that occur short of where the consecrated divisions begin. But they do so in concrete, immediate operations, which lend content to the force of illimitation, or love, or God. This content and meaning can be postponed no longer. It is carved on everything one does, on the least of one's acts, as if it were the last, the ultimate act. The urgency with which it is invested forbids evasion in the far climes of proselytism, parallel worlds, and superstructures. Now human beings must save the lost sheep of Israel and not traverse the length and breadth of the Diaspora in search of converts upon whom to lay crushing burdens. Now they must love the neighbor they see, they must succor their parents, and not flee to the divine alibi. Now they must look reality in the face and accept their responsibilities and not deform everything by the prism of commentaries and citations from Scripture.

At bottom, the eschatological principle signifies that there are no more intermediaries. God is present right here, referring men and women to the divine mystery by referring them to their own proper reality. The presence of God makes reality the only possible mediation. Reality as mediatrix becomes sacrament. God is no longer in the rites whereby a group identifies with itself; God is no longer the possession of a society that takes its holy name as the standard or totem around which to rally. God anticipates us everywhere: indeed, God is already there, under the form of concrete demand, under the form of the imperative of self-transcendence by which God is the God of each and all, and stands in no need of any alienating, estranging procurement by anyone or anything else.

GOD'S PARENTHOOD

The "fatherhood" of God is not a question of a new principle. It is a matter of "naming" the eschatological principle, the force of illimitation. Here God refers us to ourselves, by the concrete exigencies written on the solid tablets of all things and addressed to the human being as human being. This referral of oneself to oneself is an eschatological revelation of God in the most real sense of the terms and not merely in the chronographic sense. Further, it signifies that the human being lacks adequate means to make response to God as such. When God is real, human beings find themselves confronted not with a face-to-face vision of him as he is in himself, but with the only "image" that can represent him: they find themselves confronted with themselves, as responsibility and word. Word and responsibility are the active, real representation of God as acknowledgment and commitment, as "profession of faith."

The eschatological God is mediated by the humanity of human beings in act and exercise. He is mediated by humanity in its source, which, in all roles—in the arrangements of life in society, in work and the relationships of production—is itself presupposed as spontaneity and gratuity. It is by the exercise of their humanity in the real conditioning of this creative gratuity that human beings emerge as the image of God, that they become the sons and daughters of God. One is not born a child of God, one is not God's daughter or son by the simple fact of belonging to a chosen group or people. Being God's son or daughter is an event, a happening—the materialization in history of a relationship of freedom. We must emphasize the nature of this filiation and this parenthood.

The filiation of the new human being is not to be posited "behind" that human being, but "before." He and she are the active contemporary of their commitment. They are sons or daughters at the term or center of a deed of liberation, in and by the process by which they are images of God, by which God takes up his being in them in representation. Thus the God who "begets" is the God who arrives, who supervenes. He is not the Ancestor, out of all reach, disincarnate and reduced to the state of a principle, not even the First and Highest. He is not the primordial Artisan, who modeled the human being and organized the world in harmony. This ancient God dies now, in the clash of cultures and civilizations, in the violence of a history that has never declared the glory of God to everyone the way the heavens do, with their seasons and their astral revolutions. He dies right along with his violence, along with gods who act *a tergo*, and particular divinities who die and vanish.

Some of these gods are simply swallowed up in their indeterminate immanence, for when you are everything you are nothing. Others evaporate in their distant, idle transcendence—the affirmation of their existence is as idle as they are, and compatible with whatever one pleases. Such an affirmation can even become murderous, a dehumanizing machine, a derealizing machine. Particular divinities die off as so many contradictory absolutes, one another's enemies via their interposed worshipers as they cast the latter against one another in inexorable combat. They are ambiguous to the point of equivocation. Are they ancestors? Are they civilizing heroes? Are they the totem of some ethnic group? Even the God of Abraham is not exempt from this ambiguity. As we have seen, Judaism never succeeded in delivering its God from his ambiguity. These divinities are among the elements that differentiate one group from another—where God, when all is said and done, is a principle of exclusion, and is transformed, in conflict or competition, into a principle of intolerance and elimination. These gods of town or tribe are imposed on those outside only by violence, by the victory of the expansion of their standard-bearers. When peaceful coexistence is inaugurated, when the tribes and cities disintegrate and swirl together into "tolerant" empires, the gods are joined together in a syncretistic Pantheon, or else transformed into ideas, "hypostases," aspects of a superior, integrative unity or totality.

It would appear that this theism is too empty for human beings to strike an accord by, at least not an accord of any consequence for them—too abstract to indicate a way, a direction. It cannot serve as point of departure or motive force for injecting meaning into a conflictual, opaque history. The gods of the past are disqualified—bound as they are to the implacable law of death and destiny, against which they are helpless. Human destiny has been fixed once and for all, and the gods are either accomplices or impotent witnesses of this fact, this fatality. Jesus, on the other hand, declares that the "children of God" are born neither of blood, nor of the will of the flesh, nor of "man," but of a God who is acknowledged, recognized, and thereby authentically discovered by human beings in response to a demand. One becomes daughter or son of God by free, personal achievements, in virtue of which one assumes in truth the gratuity of a new beginning, built on the ruins of the divinities of earth and fertility, of blood and power. Human beings are no longer predetermined by their original nature, their genealogy, their chance membership in a chosen people. The being they now acquire forever is the one they will have developed and exercised during the "time of salvation"—the being that will have produced their self-determination as "image" of God, as representation of him as end, as gratuity, within a network of concrete relationships and practices.

A profession of faith is not the recitation of articles of belief. Faith is but the process by which human beings are constituted as beings of word, responsible, spontaneous, and gratuitous subjects who cannot be the "means of" anything, as they are in the likeness of God. Faith is the effectuation of this creative autonomy of the human being as gift, as real sharing in the Spirit who works in, "works on," the world and renews its face, a real sharing in the force of illimitation that creates the shoreless universe.

Thus ends the time of the stars, the "powers," and the "elements of the world"—the age of the occult forces that piece together human beings' destiny without them, without their deepest consent, without their fulfillment as capacity for self-determination—capacity for free and creative spontaneity. We may even make bold to say that this is the end of the God of the Jews, that equivocal God of Abraham, for "God can raise up children to Abraham from these very stones" (Matt. 3:9), children of faith, not those of simple credence or "circumcision." The God we call "Father" metaphorically is the determination of the principle of illimitation, as force, as Spirit addressing itself to human beings in their responsibility, in their humanity. Humanity, effectively realized, is the true manifestation of this force, and entry into its dynamism, into its insertion into the world. The process of this realization, this actualization, can be called conversion, and its anticipated "result," faith. "God's fatherhood," God's parenthood, properly understood, will thus be the formal principle of the Christic revolution. It will not be an article of doctrine side by side with eschatology and charity. It is a name for both—beyond substantialist or psychological ambiguities. The parenthood of God comprises the rules according to which God can really be called "Father" in the context of the relationships of human beings with one another, of the institutions that preside over these relationships, and of specific behavior.

THE COMMUNITY IN THE FORM OF LOVE

God's denomination as Father is what the logicians call a "performative." It is an assertion that performs what it asserts. Calling God "Father" involves a certain manner of binding together relationships, of behaving, of forming a community. Calling God "Father" is not a simple allusion to an eternal subject, but an act that engages and involves the human beings performing it, and imposes on them certain rules of conduct: an original way of being-with-the-world, of being in society, of creating a community—the community of the "sons and daughters of God." It is a matter of the principle of illimitation (called God-who-is-Father, or God-who-is-Love) becoming the structuring principle of a community of human beings. This community must be a real one, located in the conditions of place and time and yet it must not be exclusive, but an openness, a self-implementing negation of its own closing. How is this possible?

1. *Conversion is at the basis of this society.* The community in the form of love must be such that the men and women who belong to it may be capable of, and ready for, a profession of faith. This presupposes not only liberation from physical and spiritual constraint, but also that special "availability" that consists of, and is characterized by, a self-transcendence together with a self-limitation to the actual, true conditions of action in the world. Thus, for example, in order to be able to say that we love God, whom we do not see, it is necessary that God not be "the best means" of having some effect or other upon ourselves—the best means of seeking peace, of escaping ourselves, or of affirming ourselves. He must be willed for himself, as the one toward whom we turn in the very movement of our own becoming and self-creation, as that which gives both "the power and the performance" in creative generosity.

This acknowledgment is genuine and true only to the extent to which we treat our neighbor as the presentation of this God-who-is-End in the affairs of every day. Conversion is this twofold movement, of self-transcendence and of self-limitation to the verifiable. "Be converted, for the kingdom of God is near; it is among you." Conversion, then, is marked by the change of mentality that disposes us to accept divine surprises—the reversal of our scale of the most sure values when God comes near, when he inaugurates a new creation. But in order to seek first the kingdom of God and his justice, one must be delivered from the seduction of Mammon, of Money. We must be delivered from the will to power that we find in heads of state who pass for benefactors of nations, so that we become as "the one who serves" (Matt. 23:11). We shall have to be delivered from the cares and concerns that keep us in these chains of ours, the chains of anxiety, the chains of the fear of risk, confrontation, and death. Where entry into the kingdom is concerned, anger and the spirit of vengeance are diriment impediments. The required metamorphosis is not a surface one. It aims for the depths of our personhood, our center, our "heart." Here is the locus of the essential orientation. Here is the source of sense and meaning. Pure hearts will see God, for theirs is welling, surging creativity, released to a pitch that bids fair to launch them forth beyond themselves toward the other, the elsewhere, and show them what is not themselves, nor in function of themselves, but something given in a free initiative, coming upon them as a grace.

We might express the same thing in other language: human beings are under the obligation to deliver themselves from the dictatorship of the "flesh" and the dictatorship of the "world," and so to discover their original self and calling. The "flesh" is the alienated expression of self—a self locked in the prison of needs and desires, a self given over wholly and entirely to the objects of these needs and desires, so that it makes fetishes of them. Human beings decay in the midst of their possessions, swallowed up in a "having" that masks them from themselves and blocks their desire for what is to come, for what is gratuitously given, blocks them off from that which can only be the object of recognition, acknowledgment, and gratitude. In service and self-dispossession, human beings show forth what they are by renouncing what they have, by "desisting" from themselves, by standing off from themselves, withdrawing from themselves. Instead of gathering all things to themselves, they allow their own being to burst forth in a flash of light—this being of theirs which has its measureless measure in what justifies itself and thereby justifies all things besides.

The world is likewise the alienated expression of self, a self lost in its fabrications, its works, its "languages," and its institutions.

These become idols, to which human beings sacrifice themselves and subject others. These become destiny; they impose their own course, mechanisms, and fatality upon human beings. Structures of violence inaugurate "the banality of evil" and oppression. One must die to the old self, then, and achieve a second childhood. Then the axiom "Nothing is impossible with God" will be real and effective.

2. *This community is a communion of brothers and sisters and friends.* It is in God that we find the measure of love and pardon—in his mercy that cares for the little ones, that makes the rain to fall on just and unjust alike, that is ever disposed to bestow good things, and that watches over the sparrows and the lilies of the field. This is the model of gratuity and liberality on which one may build a society that will not rest on the sand of debt and obligation, but on permanent solvency, thanks to genuine interchange, communication, and collective creation. As we have seen, a relationship compatible with the equality of all before God rejects discriminatory hierarchies, which set up priests and laity, rich and poor, instructed and ignorant, saints and sinners in mutual opposition. This relationship is called "fraternity," a communion of sisters and brothers. "As to you, avoid the title 'Rabbi.' One among you is your teacher, the rest are learners" (Matt. 23:8) and are one another's brothers and sisters. "Do not call anyone on earth your father. Only one is your father, the One in heaven. . . . The greatest among you will be the one who serves the rest" (Matt. 23:9,11). We are to effect the inversion, the reversal of the general practice. Authority is to be understood as power placed at the service of fraternity and love, without the perquisites of honors and advantages. "Earthly kings lord it over their people. Those who exercise authority over them are called their benefactors. Yet it cannot be that way with you. Let the greater among you be as the junior, the leader as the servant" (Luke 22:25-26).

What is this space, when is this time, in which nothing will be as elsewhere or before? Only the place and time of worship? Or in the imagination, the "invisible kingdom"? Men and women in trouble must be given an absolute future, a community where solvency reigns. The profession of faith, the acknowledgment of God as God is not compatible with just *any* exercise of power. It may not be allowed to let the walls of separation stand. The "message" is not content with revealing its sense and meaning. It must set the whole human scene on its ear and remake it. As creative force and drive, the message seeks to structure a space where law and the Sabbath are made for human beings, and not human beings for law and the Sabbath—where human beings have a greater value than observances and practices.

Love is the name of the driving force that invents organizations and institutions with a view to making new life possible. Love is the constitutive principle of the eschatological community, for this community will no longer be founded on violence in the form of all kinds of privileges—knowledge, fortune, power—or on the confiscation and free disposition on the part of a few of what belongs to each and all, of what is necessary to each one's humanity in order to be "plenary humanity." Love is not opposed to order. It poses the principle that validates all order, all law—the creative principle of the human community of the future, where there will be no more male or female, Jew or Greek, slave or free human being. "I no longer speak of you as slaves. . . . Instead, I call you friends" (John 15:15). A friendship can be struck only among equals, persons who are free of all obligations toward each other. It is founded on gratuity, liberated from the need for, dependence on, or fear of the other. It seeks solely to enjoy the other as other.

If a like program seems utopian, this is only because of the degree of alienation of the one who judges it, and the power of those who impose themselves as invincible. The faith that moves mountains counts on the improbable, and knows how to read the signs of the times that announce the possibility of a "new game"—a new tune instead of the old refrain of violence. Next, however, it knows the "imperative of limited realization," limited but urgent and indispensable for battering a breach in the ancient ramparts, for calling into question the false finalities that maintain themselves at the expense of human beings' self-determination, at the expense of their availability for unhesitating acceptance of the gift of life. Finally, this faith is not euphoric. It lives on hope, that dream of the waker. Indeed, it knows nothing of the immediate. Mediations demand an endurance to the death. The possession of oneself, one's "soul," is a long exercise in patience. For ours is not a combat against mere flesh and blood, but against those frigid monsters, the principalities and powers. It would behoove us to prepare ourselves for the day when they will break free and unleash their warriors and their apocalyptic dragons against the elect. The eschatological horizon includes the trial, the test; and it will be the height of perspicacity to take account of this on the most individual, most concrete, most everyday level we can.

3. *The community's first self-limitation is simultaneously its radical openness.* This community of converts is part of Jewish society. Born in its bosom, it shares its aspirations, its needs, yes, and its faults and ills. It is from Jewish tradition that Jesus borrows his models, his images, his arguments. He sends Israel back to its own resources, he calls upon it to listen to Moses and the prophets all over again. In a sense, everything is already there in the Scriptures. "You shall love the Lord your God with all your heart, with all your soul, with all your mind, and with all your strength . . . [and] your neighbor as yourself" (Mark 10:30–31), a scribe with his wits about him managed to rattle off. The Good News is tradition understood and grasped. It is tradition's reconquest, its recovery from forgetfulness, routine, conformism, and betrayal. It is tradition rediscovered as constitutive spontaneity, as a gushing spring.

"My mission is only to the lost sheep of the house of Israel" (Matt. 15:24). It is to this society, and it alone, that Jesus addresses his message of restructuring. He refuses to transgress the limits of Palestinian Judaism. At a time when Jewish proselytism is intense, he forbids his disciples to engage in it. When Greeks seek him out, he refers them to their own grand rite of initiation:

> Unless the grain of wheat falls to the earth and dies,
> it remains just a grain of wheat.
> But if it dies,
> it produces much fruit [John 12:24].

Except in particular cases, preaching to non-Jews would be to "take the food of sons and daughters and throw it to the dogs" (Matt. 15:26). One does not remake society from the outside. Effective protest comes only from within, for then one is not denying one's heritage, but seeking to lead it to its highest fulfillment. Then universality is actualized in history. It is particularity, but particularity that transcends itself. How so? This new community must surmount, in its own interior, the divisions and discrimination that are tearing Israel apart. It must base itself on some principle other than convergence of might. It must realize a society of brothers and sisters and friends, where authority is service without compensation.

The new community must attack, within itself, society's most concrete evils. Thus it is to change this society from within, for it is a "segment," a "total part" of that society. Thereby it does not erect itself into an end in itself. It does not close in upon itself. In this practice, so radical, however limited in time and space, this community encounters human beings beyond their social and cultural roles and masks. The Samaritan and the pagan are then accepted and welcomed beyond the point where convention and prejudice end. The erstwhile stranger is now within. One is now equal to the task of confronting the variety and diversity of the world. To dispose Israel for the coming of the reign of God is to posit the consequence foreseen by a number of the prophets: the incorporation of the pagans into the People of God as a decisive act of God's power. It is God himself who gathers the scattered and brings home those who are far from the land. It is he himself who places a term to the era of the mediators and special intermediaries.

As we can now see from the manner in which Jesus' deed declares itself, its importance resides less in its content than in the model it proposes. This model comprises three inseparable, mutually implied elements: *(a)* Conversion, which is constant review of oneself in respect of one's desires, possessions, and activity, in such wise as to remain open to the novelty of God. Liberation from the trammels within—deliverance from the passions—goes hand in hand with a change in mentality that unveils chained, repressed possibilities, namely those manufactured impossibilities that are imposed as fate on the cowardice and resignation of human beings. *(b)* A community of converts, which is one that actualizes these ultimate demands and demonstrates their concrete possibility, indeed their vital, ineluctable necessity. Its task is to produce outside itself what God is realizing within it: a life altogether contrary to the "laws" that subject the human being to idols. *(c)* A particular society that is reworked from within by the community of those who are converted. Salvation is tradition, placed in a perspective of the end of history and the nearness of the God who comes. Salvation is in these ancient relationships, rebaptized in the fire of the creative

Spirit, and retranslated into the language of the emancipation of all destiny.

This, then, is our model. It is not an abstraction, but the implementation of what a fulfilled person is: God's "image," God's re-presentation—"God by participation." "Person" implies society, and exists only via the instituting action of the latter. Finally, a particular society is justified only in its self-transcendence and only insofar as it places itself both in a world perspective and in the perspective of the end of history. The emergence of this model is bound up with the singular event that is Jesus of Nazareth, with the singular events of his life, death, and posthumous lot. This model will be exact if it is also given by Jesus' actual existence, and this is something we must look at in another chapter. Meanwhile, we shall devote some brief remarks to what might seem a flagrant omission in a treatment of Jesus' works: his miracles.

Chapter 6

On Miracles

The gospel calls the miracles, very precisely, the "works Christ was performing" (Matt. 11:2). They cannot be treated indirectly or bypassed without an explanation. It will not be enough to designate them as eschatological phenomena, as signs and prodigies marking history's great turning point, when the unheard-of new things to come are anticipated in surprising, extraordinary events, in which one discerns the presence of God at work as he inaugurates his reign. No, there is more. The final combat begins in Jesus. He challenges Satan and dislodges him from his strongest positions. Satan's empire, the empire of sin, is on the retreat now, and this is manifested by exorcisms and cures. The miracles bear witness to the mission of Jesus: the finger of God is visible in them. God is with Jesus.

Such language, for some, does not outstrip the capacities of good faith. But we would be speaking from another position than our own were we to enter into the old apologetic on miracles, whose argumentation runs as follows. The miracles form an integral part of the framework of the gospel, which is God's revelation in history. The miracles cannot be fictitious, for it is by them that Jesus "demonstrates," proves the redemptive power he incarnates in history. Furthermore, textual and historical criticism as well as the science of hermeneutics have never managed to discover any other intentionality in the gospel accounts of the miracles than that of declaring the salvific meaning of certain extraordinary things Jesus did. In Judaism especially, it is impossible to separate fact and

118

meaning. One can and should admit that there are elements of legend in the Bible in general and the New Testament in particular, but these are always embellishments or amplifications of an irreducible factual core. Science has never ceased to confirm the depth of the New Testament's radication in history. The evangelists should have the benefit of the doubt here. We should presume the veracity of their accounts. The burden of proof rests with the doubter, who must proceed without any metaphysical a priori militating against the possibility of miracles, for the evangelists are reporting them as actual occurrences. It would not be scientific to exclude the possibility of miracles beforehand: we would be caught in the fallacy called begging the question, the vicious circle, since by definition a miracle is that which does not conform to known or knowable rules. A miracle *is* singularity, situated in the order of a nonreiterative event.

Our own purposes will be better served, however, from a point of departure in certain very simple propositions based on the logic of belief and our experience. The *first proposition* will be enunciated as follows: "It is not miracles that arouse faith, it is faith that works miracles." The power of doing miracles is not the private property of the thaumaturge. He or she has need of the excited expectation of a large number of people, and of their acknowledgment of a divine activity capable of giving life, saving life, and actually and presently intervening. Miracles do not happen where no one expects anything like one. Here it will be appropriate to appeal to modern scientific knowledge of Jesus' milieu and observe that it was one in which people believed in miracles, one in which Jesus was neither the first thaumaturge nor the last. Miracles could not have come as a complete surprise; they were scarcely something unheard-of or astonishing. Jesus' milieu is familiar with exorcism. The demons are spirits, often the spirits of the dead endowed with superhuman powers. The spirits frequent out-of-the-way places, and yet they are also everywhere in the air around us. They are the cause of calamities, disease, and strange or terrifying occurrences. But one can appease them, control them by appropriate means. Since disease and epidemics are the deed of the evil spirits, the techniques of healing will be those of exorcism, and many diseases occur in the form of possession. This society also believes that the vices and the passions are the result of the sway that the unclean spirits hold over human beings. Moral fault, or sin, is committed at the instigation of the devil. Deliverance from disease and liberation from the passions are operations of the religious war against the powers of evil. Exorcism and healing are institutions. They constitute a reciprocal social relationship with expectable results, provided certain conditions are fulfilled. It is within the context of this "pact" that miracles are produced. They are products of a shared faith, of the delegation to one or a few persons of the expectations of all. The miraculous fact, then, is never pure fact. Its witnesses, even its "unbelieving" witnesses, belong to the number of its producers. Jesus' enemies never reject the "fact" of his miracles, they only attribute them to Beelzebul. They assign them a negative value, but a value still within the enchanted circle.

Now we may express the *second proposition*: "The thaumaturge works miracles because he or she is recognized to be a miracle-worker, and not the other way around." One does not become a miracle-worker by apprenticeship or by trial and error, but "all of a sudden." Even if one's first miracle can be dated, it has been preceded by the miraculous, and this has been appreciated as such. The transmittal of powers, initiation, and spiritual trials are themselves a prodigious contact with the powers or the Power. In the Gospel of John the first miracle occurs after Jesus' deeds of clairvoyance and supernatural authority (John 1:47) in the manner in which he gathers his first disciples. Further, he has already been "rendered sacred" by John on the banks of the Jordan. The power of miracles is one of the attributes of the eschatological prophets, and consists in the power of exorcism and healing. Show me a prophet and I shall show you a person who has always worked miracles from the moment of his or her birth.

At this point we can add a corollary, the *third proposition*: "An acknowledged thaumaturge always works miracles." The recognition and acknowledgment of a prophet is in the attribution and conferral of the power of miracles. The impostor is the one who endeavors to "acquire" that which is the gift of all to one (or to a few). The impostor is the individualist, the "self-made person." Popular consecration is essential: the consecration of rumor, a current of opinion crystallizing around a name, a person. *Vox populi, vox Dei*: once the people have spoken there *have* to be miracles, for sincere witnesses are ever ready-to-hand. There will always be eyewitnesses to present themselves who have seen what everyone believes. Indeed there are always those who live within themselves what others see and believe—beginning with the actual prophet and those the prophet heals. Instantly a chain of *testimonia* forms, detailing deed, time, and place. The space and time of the miracle are precise; they are circumscribed by the circle of faith. The community of "believers" reports its own faith, the verification of that faith, and its confirmation and reinforcement. The prophet recounts the story of God's call and its confirmation by signs and prodigies, or this task can be carried out by the prophet's disciples, who recall their leader's birth and childhood.

What is essential here is to realize that we are not confronted with those infamous alternatives, fact-or-fiction, veracity-or-lie, reality-or-illusion, truth-or-error. Here, fiction or illusion has a reality. It is time to abandon the theory of the "historical kernel," which is so resistant to, and unknowable by, received historical methods. From start to finish the miracle is the product of faith. One does not begin with a neutral fact and then interpret it as miraculous; nor does one begin with a miracle that can later be considered as either a miracle or a neutral fact.

When we are confronted with a miracle, we "cannot believe our eyes." We see with the "eyes of faith," that is, with the eyes of everyone. The individual point of view is precisely nonfaith, the aberration of unbelief, possession by an evil spirit: the spirit of blindness, the spirit of faulty judgment. Miracles can be rejected indeed, but it will be a collective rejection, which will attribute them to "another spirit." Expertise and scientific investigation belong to another age, and perhaps another credence. Even in case of doubt, even in the hypothesis of an act of fraud, no one proposes a neutral verification. One would fear to disturb, surely to one's rue, a power thus rudely approached and indelicately called to account. What is beheld with the eyes of the body generally encounters *only* "faithful witnesses," people who have no reason to suspect imposture or deceit. One's degree of mental balance or moral excellence is no indicator of neutrality and objectivity, and does not imply a presumption of historicity in the modern sense of the term. These qualities, as such, leave the circle of faith out of consideration: they have all their meaning in the individual, "abstract" domains of ethics and psychology. Thus it is that miracles, attested by these "faithful witnesses," do not bring us into "testimonial contact" either with themselves or with the thaumaturge. They bring us in contact with the culture of the latter, with a unique era. We meet this culture and era in the form of an account, a story, a recital.

This brings us to the *fourth proposition*: "Miracles, once they have become account by way of testimony, are first and foremost the object of culture and knowledge, and not of credence in the testimony of the witnesses or the thaumaturge." We may not leap over mediations. We have to take into account all the operations through which we must pass before a "miracle" can have any interest or meaning for us. We should notice certain elements, obvious in themselves but often omitted from a consideration of miracles, to the detriment of a balanced and lucid view of the same. First, the thaumaturge does not work miracles for the absent, but only for those he or she can "touch," for those within hearing. Second, a miracle has a limited radius. It must fall within human measures. It must be limited to small cultural communities. Finally, a miracle presupposes a *personal* relationship. It refers us to the time in which the thaumaturge actually lived or, mediately, to the time of his or her "successors." A miracle *recounted* recalls an absence. Hence the necessity of mediations. A simple, immediate account is out of the question. Thus, in the case of Jesus, the miracle accounts enter into a complexus of elements that we call the gospel. Here they take on new functions and meanings, with multiple applications and uses. The experience canonized in the written Gospels has been located on precise coordinates. It has been made into the sacred Book of an imperial and imperious religion. It has thus been dislocated from its context. Accordingly, its content will be displaced as well, both in function and in meaning, and it will acquire an immediacy and universality that are purely specious. It will have forgotten its origins. The phenomenon will be reinforced when Christianity becomes the traditional religion of Europe. Now the text, with its accounts, will be read as "gospel truth," and received as part of the certitude of the religion of the dominator, or of custom and usage—for this is the matrix in which this Book has been preserved, transmitted, meditated, and commented upon. This is now the historical context in which it has been the object of the devotion of the faithful, the source of the artistic representations much admired by an elite, and the subject of inexhaustible exercises of intellect on the part of the savants and the erudite in all manner of prestigious disciplines: archeology, epigraphy, textual criticism, exegesis, and the like.

The association of all these elements of culture and usage with the Book can change its "looks," that is, can change *our* outlook, and thereby the way the Book looks to us. We run the risk of forgetting about distances and mediations. The Book can acquire a different sense and meaning in this "immediacy," which makes it the cultural possession of a civilization. It can serve to characterize this civilization in its specificity, for now one will search it for the seeds or roots of what distinguishes this civilization from the rest of humanity: rationality, for example, or historicity. The whole content of the Bible, including, of course, the miracles, will become the vehicles of reason and historical objectivity. The Bible's myths and legends will be such only in appearances. Parallel worlds will be invoked in biblical interpretation. Promote the exceptional character of the Bible in this fashion, and you only court rejection on the part of a conscienticized liberty. A like privilege consecrates the radical exclusion of the other by projecting the pressures of modern forces into the past and into God, at the price of anachronism erected into a principle of intelligibility.

When all is said and done, we no longer have any choice whether to see Jesus' miracles as a cultural phenomenon or not. As we have said, the accounts refer us to a culture. The convergence of prophetic vocation, eschatological horizon, and the power of miracles is a reality still accessible to contemporary observation, especially in Africa. It is a reality that sheds light on the past. We are not dealing with literary genres here, but with the social logic of credence and belief, the logic at work between the founder or charismatic religious leader and the throng of his devotees. We are confronted with an object of knowledge that calls for the application of a manner of reasoning analogous to, if not identical with, that of today. The differences arise from a well-defined cultural content, from the historical position occupied in society by its protagonists—in short, from the irreducible singularity of its situation in time and space. The combinations and variations are infinite and unforeseeable, but their profound logic abides. The basic elements at play are finite in number. The forms of religious experience are not the result of some evolution or other. They are that by which change is conceivable and thinkable. Simultaneously, certian connections that dogma considers to be decisive are pertinent only in the relationship of structure to a particular event, to a locus. They are not pertinent "in general" (at all times and in all places).

The miracle accounts encompass this localization for us. They indicate for us the empty place once occupied by Jesus. They reconstruct for us his vanished singularity. What remains are the "conditionings" he took on, of which he fashions his language; the roles into which he entered in order to perform his functions, in order to acquit himself of his task and mission at the heart of a particular, absolutely unique tradition. This reference to a particular singularity, vanished forever and irreplaceable, prohibits us from reducing Jesus' miracles to atemporal, abstract generality. But we are nonetheless very far from being able to set aside indefinitely the question of our acceptance or rejection of their absolute import. We are still forced into a position in which either we consent, and invoke them, or refuse, and rebel against them. An appeal to the scientific authority of the most modern and reputable historians and exegetes, when it is not out-and-out fraudulent, at least sins by confusion of levels. Attestation to miracles is attestation to the faith of bygone witnesses and is the object of "science" for contemporary human beings. There is no longer any power of summons. The miracle is "fable," fable of the past or of a place no longer dwelt in. Henceforward the miracle exists only as object of analysis or as material for artistic or imaginative development.

These last assertions of ours, abrupt as they are, and rather too peremptory, will arouse a protest, and one long underestimated by the theologians where their arsenal of "apologetic proofs" are concerned. The miracle accounts are read in the liturgy. This is the use made of them by the generality of believers. Some of these find their reading tolerable only here. The hearing of the miracle accounts is an act of obedience by which persons are inserted into a community. It is their profession-in-practice that they are members of this group. *Lex orandi, lex credendi*: as we conduct ourselves at liturgical prayer (which is where we address ourselves to a relationship with the irreplaceable Jesus), so we believe. Here there is no question of doctrine, truth, or historicity. Liturgy is a matter of the constitution of community, of intersubjectivity in belief, of the active presentation of the basis and origin of the members of this community from which Jesus' singularity is inseparable. This singularity can only be expressed by that deed which traces in dotted lines the empty place that once belonged to Jesus. The reading of the miracle accounts is part of this deed, outlining his personal shape and figure. Here, then, the meaning of the miracles becomes clear: they are for the believing community. The believing community puts them to use in its own constitution. The believer *is* the sick person whom Jesus heals, the corpse that rises from the dead, the blind person who sees again. The multiplication of the loaves is the Eucharistic bread, distributed to the numberless throng of brothers and sisters. The object of the miracles is the church—but the church is also their subject. It is the church that breaks the bread of the Word to the multitudes, that exorcises, heals, consoles, and purifies.

Thus the miracle has come home, back to the native land of its "spiritual reality"—its reality as an expression of the profound, secret life of the community. Thus the miracle takes its place as part of that community's most intimate language, the language of its identity. It becomes part of a language that runs the risk of profanation if paraded in the marketplace. The word that enunciates the miracle can only be protected by the "discipline of the secrets" the humor of those who have been initiated into the strength there is in weakness and the weakness there is in strength, the laugh of those being reborn to a second childhood after a long, dogmatic, critical death.

Chapter 7

The Person of Jesus

We have attempted to present a picture of the "fulfilled person" in action, the person whom Saint Irenaeus called God's glory. That person's message is what that person is becoming, what he or she does, in obedience—in relationship to others and to the God who comes. Thus the model we have sketched in broad outline, the model of Jesus' activity, and bonds with his tradition and his milieu, appear as a unity of personal, communitarian, and social elements, including that of the demands made by universality in the concrete form of an ecumenism. His personhood is not given apart from society, which has lent it its real determinations, through language, through a temporality, a culture.

This society has subsisted through the instituting action of persons, which has prevented it from being transformed into an alienating destiny and fatality: this society was, or should have been, the creation of free men and women who could not be the means of anything. Institutions and ideologies, under eschatological judgment, have been justified only if they have delivered up this creative spontaneity, only if they have refused to imprison it within ethnic, political, sectarian, or self-obsessive limits. They must take a form of love, a way of according human beings a spontaneity of their own in full responsibility. Love is the power that is presupposed as efficacious strength of word. It is in the form of word, for it is manifested only in self-declaration, and is operative only along the two-way street of reciprocity, whence it emerges as "meaning" and "truth." Personal being is existence in the form of word, that is, it is arrival at self-fulfillment not only in presence to self, but in being in a being-other: in receiving self from the other.

More simply, let us say that Jesus Christ furnishes the model of a life that achieves the fullness of itself not only after having taken on its conditionings and its determinisms and integrated them into a conscious and responsible activity and commitment, but also after having undergone its destiny and receiving itself from the other. The person anticipates itself in these conditionings, and survives itself beyond its destiny. "Sur-vival" is the transcendence of former possibilities, a way of being-other. And the description of this other way involves a continuation of an attachment to the level of social and historical processes constituted of visible referents, at least in its obligatory point of departure. We are bound by rules that constrain us to take the initial critical match seriously. It goes without saying that this model is proposed only after it has been entirely developed, when it can be apprehended as a whole. The resurrection, then, is the point of departure for this understanding. The end is the beginning. The apostolic preaching proceeds from "the events of these days" (Acts 3:24), Jesus' death and glorification, that is, his definitive being. From here one can return to Jesus' public life, even to his hidden life and the mysteries of his origin.

The light that accompanies this ever more perilous pilgrimage gleams from its end and term. The direction and meaning of the itinerary is present in every stage, at every step: it gathers the vicissitudes of the road already traversed into a simple, luminous unity. Oneness of meaning is not a natural unity—the continuation of a preexisting entity, like the development of a seed. It is a self-producing activity, modified by encounters, and its destiny is in the future, hanging in the balance of options exercised by struggling liberties. The worst possible error would be to assimilate the unity of signification or meaning to a numerical or substantial unity. The moment we do so, God, Jesus, and our faith begin to refer us to a system of things-in-themselves, and the language of signification is degraded into one of "supernatural" causality. The unity of meaning of a fulfilled existence does not change into a hypostasis; it becomes a project, a "living model" for human beings. It comprises conditionings, an activity, and a destiny. Jesus reveals what each of these aspects is in relationship to the others, in a life that is perfected in receiving itself from the other.

These words complete, essentially, our consideration, throughout this book thus far, of the overall theme of activity in and for itself. However, we must still consider it apropos of two modalities of the human being under scrutiny, for it is their bond: condition and destiny.

CONDITION

We have already met "condition" under one of its many aspects. It was called "situation," and meant the political, traditional, and economic realities which one could not escape, and which, in convergence, characterized an era. Society, culture, and history not only offer possibilities, they eliminate them; they impose a framework on the accomplishments of individuals by providing them with concrete, "human" determinations. The most "natural" constraints of birth, of sex, of eating and drinking come wrapped in rules, symbols, "words," and demands. Human existence is fraught with their limits and effects. Human existence consists in what collectivities and persons do with what they receive. The person is the act of integrating these limits, of taking them on and rejecting them all at once. The person is the act of converting them into freedom and destiny.

These conditionings are but one of the moments of personal being and have reality and meaning only in and by the totality of that being. Personal being is not in a relationship of exteriority with them. It must become what it is, and what it is has its truth and meaning only in this "having become." In Jesus this metamorphosis is expressed in the following terms: Jesus fulfills the prophecies in his life and by his works and thereby proclaims and inaugurates the kingdom of God. What is "given" undergoes a mutation in Jesus: by him and in him, the given enters within the ultimate sphere of the direct reign of God. Such is the directive schema of the evangelical interpretation of the conditionings of human existence. Let us recall that, while it is ulteriorly a model capable of being "resumed," this personal schema arises from history, from a precisely determined era. The conditionings to be transcended have the cultural forms and connotations of Judaism at the time of Jesus, in confrontation with the great currents around it.

The oldest preaching of the church, as can be seen in the Letters of Paul and the Acts of the Apostles, begins with Jesus' baptism, with his public life. This is Mark's point of departure as well. The other evangelists have prologues: John on the preexistence of the Word, Matthew and Luke on Jesus' birth and childhood. It is generally admitted that these prologues were written in the light of the Paschal events, that they begin with the end, and that their purpose is to demonstrate Jesus' exceptionality from start to finish. He is a human being indeed, but by no means like others. He is God *and* a human being—and has been from the beginning. (Better, he has been God before beginning to be a human being.) What difference does this make to us? A great deal, we shall be told. Here we have the basis of his salvific power demonstrated: he is divine in his being. God alone can forgive sins, or create from nothing, or conquer death. Only God can speak all on his own authority, or manifest his holy will clearly to human beings, or bestow himself really and graciously on them.

Surely such assertions are in order, but they must be the expression of an act of faith, and not that of an initial credence. One must retrace the evangelist's steps in order to come to an understanding of their meaning. If it is possible to make an act of faith in Jesus the Risen Lord *before* hearing these accounts, or without having heard them (like Paul's Christians), then we shall have to suppose that they have nothing essential to say, or better, that they only *recount* the essential. What is important in them is not their content, but their form. The latter is their message.

The form is that of an account of beginnings, and we have learned that its efficacity is all the greater for containing no historical kernel of raw fact. What lies at the root of the expansion of faith, what forms the basis of its power is not a "fact" one can lay hands on, but something that refuses to lend its transcendence to an element of a series of facts endowed simultaneously with supernatural and tangible traits. Once again we take leave of the order of the word: we propose a self-contradictory belief. By contrast it is not surprising that we find no "historical fact" in the obvious sense of the term when there is question of the radical origin of a new manner of being: that by which something exists under a given determination does not itself exist under that determination, for a principle does not participate its own conclusion. Neither proof nor material signs are possible for the "supernatural." It is necessary that Jesus' existence have a sense for us in its integrity—that it propose to us a manner of being a human being. A treatment of his origin cannot have the function of separating us from him by designating him as "strange." It cannot be a matter of the simple manifestation of an arbitrary will commanding only obedience and submission.

Our fashion of binding ourself to this demonstration of strength is not immediate. It cannot be the result of a simple reading of the gospel books. The proclamation of the gospel is subject to risk and hazard. A "message of salvation" that pretends to be universal, even if it is proclaimed only in the history in which it appears, must have some "familiarity," some "necessity" springing from affinity, and its novelty cannot be its strangeness.

The present thesis, then, is that Jesus Christ is not come to abolish myth but to fulfill it. One may not begin by denying the existence of myth in the gospel accounts. The price of this initial, dogmatic denial is often bad exegetical faith. The exegete may willingly admit that the essential thing in the accounts of Jesus' birth and infancy is their theological meaning, into whose service the evangelist presses characteristics of tales of the genre one meets in legends of the time on the subject of the patriarchs. But then that exegete will at once add that these tales go back to a single ancient source earlier than Matthew and Luke, who therefore have not invented them. Further, we shall be assured, the evangelists had access to a tradition proceeding from Jesus' most immediate entourage, from that of his family *perhaps*. Conclusion: these accounts are not simple fiction, although the facts have been stylized.

A like conclusion surely strains its premises. The antiquity of the accounts and their proximity to Jesus' entourage have argumentative value only if myth is always the product either of bad faith and prevarication or of error arising from distance in time or space. Neither supposition is compelling. Indeed, history finds against them both. We see myths springing up during the prophets' own lifetime, coming out of their own entourage, and even originating with themselves. Myth is beyond the dilemma of good faith or bad, truth or error, veracity or falsehood. The reasons why we cannot convince the evangelists or primitive believers of fraud are exactly the same as the reasons why we cannot cite them as the devotees of historicity in the sense in which today's historian honors historicity in examining an "occurrence" at a point of intersection in homogeneous time and space. Parallel legendary motifs are well known, and it is admitted that the nature of these accounts differs in form from that of the rest of the gospel, with all their dreams and warnings, their atmosphere of the marvelous, and their continual references to the Old Testament—indeed their explicit citations to explain every event. It is scarcely evident that what we have here is an invitation to turn our backs on objectivity, on the materiality of an occurrence. It is most difficult to prove that the evangelists merely use forms that would be labeled legendary or mythical elsewhere. The a priori position that the Judeo-Christian faith is incompatible with myth does not stand up, unless we simultaneously decree that "genuine" Judaic or Christian expressions are those not blemished with myths. This is *petitio principii,* begging the question, the vicious circle.

This is not the place to go into the origin or function of a like denial. Its most striking effects are that the humanity of Jesus is rendered problematic and is rescued from evanescence only by infinite subtleties. The incarnation is a wonder now, or the theme of a dualistic morality exhorting us to humility and condescension like the humility and condescension of God or to exteriorization and expression from a point of departure in an impalpable "spirituality" of intentions and feelings of the soul. This denial issues in a contempt for the human condition, for birth, so to speak, and for sexuality. The body and place are not really taken on. Consequently neither are they transcended. They subsist as things repulsed, as obsession and aggressiveness. And because birth is not understood, neither is death—and the Paschal mystery is transformed into a creedal belief, into a dogma, into Christianity, into supernatural materialism.

The gospel begins with genealogy, however. Jesus is not an isolated individual. He is characterized by the bond that unites him to other human beings, by his solidarity with the members of his same tribe and lineage. History is a succession of generations: each falls heir to the benedictions and promises vouchsafed to its forebears, just as to their graces and shortcomings. Inserted into this continuity, human beings discover themselves as task. They receive themselves, but they must transmit themselves as well. They are at once term and commencement: sons and daughters become fathers

and mothers in their turn. Personhood is perfectly itself when it is
the presence both of what is no more and of what is not yet, when it
fulfills the former and proclaims the latter all at once. Personhood
arrives at self-realization in accordance with the ancient figures.
Better, it actualizes and renews these. It is a process of activation of
the past and invocation of the future. The ancient figures, by their
mediation, are prophecy or utopia of the ultimate world. Therefore, in order to transcend oneself, one must detach the self from
that without which one would not be.

The genealogy presents Jesus to us first as Son of David. He is
the product of a history marked by the vicissitudes of Israel, from
the first emergence of the ideal form or figure of the political entity
with which the entire people could identify because it was their
projection into their most felicitous state. Fulfilled human beings
will be those who establish the same kind of relationship between
themselves and their nation, and between that nation and history.
The Son of David must be a new David, on a regenerate land, a
being who dances the new covenant of God with his people. The
Davidic figure sets the seal of legitimacy and continuity on all political novelty, and likewise indicates the point at which the latter
begins—the threshold short of which one may not stick except at
the price of dissatisfaction, and the consciousness of distress and
loss. Jesus, Son of David, is the promise of a liberation and
restoration—better, of a recommencement.

Jesus is also Son of Abraham. He is not merely the member of
one line, consecrated to a single function, as the dynastic human
being is. His relation with Abraham is an imperative of a vaster
openness and at the same time the pledge of an older and more
pregnant promise. The patriarch opens a line, a direction, an order,
and a sense or meaning. There will be descendants, his descendants,
daughters and sons of God's blessing, and by him all peoples will be
blessed. Jesus is Son of Adam, Son of the Human Being. But he is
also the New Adam.

Thus genealogy shows us how the person of Jesus bears the destiny of his people, identifies with it in such wise as his history is the
synthesis of everyone's. He is fulfilled in proportion as he reincar-
nates the constitutive figures of his people. The identification is not
fashioned only in glory and success, but also in the test that leads to
triumph. Like the great patriarchs, he is born when the people find

themselves in a situation of crisis. His birth is preceded by dreams, by signs proclaiming who he will be. The enemy is on the watch, but the ruse will be found out, and all obstacles will be surmounted, whether of nature or of machination. Indeed, God himself intervenes to restore life to his people after "death." A special birth, announced and surrounded by prodigies, dreams, or stars, pious but childless parents, uneasy, sanguinary princes, a childhood that augurs a future marked by trial, but even more by the genius and grandeur of foundations and new beginnings—all these things are ascribed by Jewish legends to the patriarchs, to Abraham, Moses, and Jacob.

It is important here to grasp that we are dealing with a process of general applicability: successful human beings are those who are fulfilled in accordance with the Scriptures of their tradition, who resurrect its primordial images in the self at the same time as transcending them by an initiatory breach from another locus. The Scriptures of a tradition are the matrix without which they will not be able to live, but in which they will not be able to survive. They must die in order to live in another way. This "other" life is incommensurable with the first: it is not its simple prolongation. What has been merely undergone (determinism) is taken up again in history by liberty, communication, covenant, and death—a death freely accepted and exorcised by the passion of a love that gives its life for those one loves. That is to say, the determinisms are transcended—the determinisms of birth, sexuality, and a particular culture. The genealogical principle linked to biological condition is transcended by a death accepted at the very heart of life. Death in the midst of life, death as source of life is experienced by the actualization of a new paternity or maternity, founded on acquiescence and produced by creative freedom, word, and communion. The new, definitive human beings are those who create self by their choices, at the heart of a voluntary community with which they will be in reciprocity of being.

Such a life is stronger than biological conditionings. It gets beyond death by flooding it, by overflowing it, and we see that its transcendence of biological existence can only be outlined through a demonstration that human sexuality as such has had no part in it. Clearly, the accounts of the virginal birth of Jesus resume, in the light of the resurrection, the mystery of life born of death, the theme of the virgin's child who dies and is reborn—the common experience and universal question of humanity. To reproduce life, one must die. But is the life reproduced still that of the original subject. Is it of identical quality with the former? Or is it of an inferior nature? Could it indeed be of another nature, and thereby definitively escape the cycle of new beginnings of lineage and tribe? Now this universal experience and question are taken up again in a particular, special context, that of late Judaism—a Judaism that participates in the history of a vaster humanity. The response given in Jesus is accessible and comprehensible only when reinserted into this framework, from which it is all the more inseparable for being in the form of a person.

What is the theme of death-life, as treated in the theme of the virgin's child who dies and is born again? What do these themes become in the culture in which late Judaism participates as it writhes in its identity crisis? How is this myth fulfilled in Jesus? These are the questions we should like to answer more explicitly, and this is the approach that we shall now take to the central problem of the Infancy Gospels: the virginal conception. Thus we shall be seeking to restore to this theme its cosmic dimension, and to show its identity with the unique revelation or message of the gospel: the Paschal mystery, the emergence of a new life stronger than death, the emergence of a new human being who produces himself in the very act of receiving himself from others in gratuity. Here, as with the resurrection, it is faith, not credence, to which we are invited. It is not doctrine that we are called upon to accept, but divine creative Act, which rears autonomous, free beings to its likeness, rendering itself present in the very act in which persons perform the act of their own being, their being-together-with-and-by-others.

The Mother Theme

The history of religions furnishes us with abundant examples of the Virgin-Mother theme, which is identical with the Mother theme itself.[1] The latter is the key to an understanding of woman in her proper role, as well as to that of the normative structures of life in its temporal condition. She, the Mother, is that which is original, infinitely distant, timeless—but always in undiminished activity. The archetypal figure of the Mother, as we have said, is the matrix without which one cannot be, and yet without leaving which one cannot be—before returning to her "transfigured," via death.

There are three kinds of archetypal figures of Mother:

1. *The Cosmic Mother:* In this figure, the origin of all things is viewed as a parturition. The Cosmic Mother contains all, including the human being, who thus participates in the general condition. Thus tribes, couples, and individuals issue from caves and rocks. One of the characteristics of the Cosmic Mother is her virginity. She is primagravida, one who has never before given birth. Before any agriculture, antecedent to the existence of couples to reproduce their own kind, there is life, there is something alive. Sexuality comes second in the phenomenon of life. Before sexuality there are sunlight and heaven's rain to fertilize the earth. The earth is alive. The message here is that what is alive issues from what is alive, and returns to it. The human being is not necessary for the production of life. Life comes from further away, from elsewhere. One must not begin with sexuality, not even human sexuality, to explain, to understand human life. Human life is to be explained by what bases and explains sexuality, by what transcends it, which is life itself in its most universal form, in its immortal form. Those who rediscover this truth by a deeply lived experience and staunchly draw its consequences can be reborn, not of blood or of the will of the flesh or of "man," but of God; and they will be able to hold sexuality in a secondary place or as "nonexistent" in their relationships, in their quest for a communion of brothers and sisters beyond tribe and genealogical ties by the practice of continence.

2. *The Mother of agriculture and the Virgin Mother:* The Mother of cultivated plants, of the crops of agriculture is also the Virgin Mother who bears the child who dies and rises. This figure is linked to the invention of farming and to its fundamental law:

> Unless the grain of wheat falls to the earth and dies,
> it remains just a grain of wheat.
> But if it dies,
> it produces much fruit [John 12:24].

The plants that nourish human beings, that give them life, grow in the earth; but more generally they are a direct gift of God or of the Ancestors. Sometimes they are even a cutting from the tree of life, and an earnest of its return. Many myths speak of a girl, an animal, or a star that brings the gift of agriculture and then disappears as the result of some indiscretion, misunderstanding, or violation of trust. Others describe the drama of agriculture, which transforms virgin nature into a plowed field, with more detail and pathos. The Virgin must be beaten, scourged, burned to a cinder. Then will vegetation sprout from her ashes. The sacrifice may be total: the girl may be killed, sometimes cut to pieces, and buried. This burial, or holocaust, is voluntary. It does not comport the notion of original guilt or crime. The spontaneous product of earth must be given to the human being as food, it must be killed and buried, to reproduce itself and become the life of human beings. The Virgin's child dies to be reborn, and to bear much fruit.

Here we have the central core of the rites of initiation. This is their secret. That is, this schema serves to interpret life in its entirety, and the drama of human life in particular. The figure of the son of the Virgin, dead and reborn, transcends the conditions in which it emerges, and through the rites of initiation it retains its efficacity in the other forms and aspects of life. It is even capable of absorbing other symbols and synthesizing them in order to "expound," expose, make manifest the mystery of death in life, not only as it is observed around us, but also and especially as we ourselves participate in it, as it envelops us.

3. *The Mother of the hero:* Finally, there is the Mother of the hero. But first, what is a hero? The hero is not a god, sovereign in one domain or all, nor yet a mighty individual who swoops down in some idiosyncratic originality setting one apart from the common run of mortals, out beyond anything they could ever attain. The hero's reality is not to be found in historiographical determinations, not even in that imaginary central locus which is the focal point of the psychological attributions commonly called "person" but which is at the same time individuality. Individuality is of no interest. Individuality is mute. Individuality separates. Its assertion for its own sake is another name for violence. The hero is the figure of the realized person, the fulfilled person, the accomplished person—the human condition accepted integrally, made of light and darkness, success and failure, life and death. The hero is the revelation of an authentically human manner of being, by one's integration into the group, by obedience to the laws of existence in

such wise that the hero is a *repeatable* model, the object not of cult but of account. The hero's efficacity lies along the lines of "constitution," showing us the genesis of the human being and the "normative" conditions of human realization. The "passage" of suffering and death is required. The hero does not undergo them passively, but actively enters upon this path that humanizes and personalizes through the active abandonment of self, a "desisting from self," which lets the "other" be, and brings about the becoming of the deathless, immortal life of the spirit.

The hero does not live by challenge. Generally the hero ignores or resists the Promethean temptation, should it present itself. Trials endured are the necessary price to pay for a higher, more abundant life, to the benefit of humanity. Prometheus blasphemes and rebels, and not in favor of life directly experienced, but solely in an egocratic confiscation of access to personalization, as he isolates the rest of humankind and imposes his own individuality upon them as their sole, or supreme, model. Prometheus is almost an antihero, expressing the human being's disintegration.

The hero's Mother is a virgin. The virgin birth may be of the cosmic variety mentioned above. The conception may be a marvelous one. It may be astral in origin. What fecundates, the "seed," may be light, sound, or mist. The hero is conceived of fire, or the sun, or a pink cloud, and is born during the dark nights of the new moon, in the divine word of storm and thunder. The more anthropomorphic miracles are secondary elements, and their sense is derived only from the cosmic dimension.

The hero's birth is dramatic. The Mother may die in childbirth. Often she is persecuted by an ogre, a dragon, or another representation of death seeking to devour her child. The bond between life and death, as well as life's triumph over death, is violently illustrated in the birth of the hero. The hero's toils and afflictions are proclaimed from the first moment of the person's existence. Here too we have the vivid illustration of our life experience in the death of others, and our death in their life.

Myth and the Meaning of Human Existence

As has already been suggested, myths take on different shapes, according to the diversity of the experiences and the technical and social transformations that lie behind them. Symbols of death in life, when human beings are in harmony with their group and environment, are not concerned with immortality. The creedal belief in question here relates to the perpetuation of the tribe, and the lot of the individual is without interest. A guarantee of individual survival is sought when integration into the group is inadequate. In urban civilizations, where the genealogical bond is undone and vanishes, where the human being is relegated to solitude, the need for "salvation" arises. The ancient mysteries, which have been celebrations, are now transformed into mystical techniques to assure individual survival through initiation. Now the archetypal figure, the hero, can become, where sovereigns reign, a god upon whom one calls for help, worships, and supplicates in order to have life and be saved.

Where the genealogical principle is obliterated and marriage is delivered over to the fortunes of chance encounter—when the "end" of marriage is no longer the procreation of children with a meaningful future in a living, formal, "juridical," sacramental community—the sexual relationship changes, along with its role in self-realization. If heroes arise, any new figures of human personalization, it will no longer be to express the transcendence of life, unless perchance by the old symbols warmed over, remanipulated in a milieu of human relationships consisting predominantly of the urban "melting-pot" experience. The model of freedom in life will be found in freedom with respect to the determinism of human sexuality on the level of the individual, and individuals will now form "spiritual" communities of brothers and sisters, not according to the flesh but according to the spirit. Now that family has failed, now that family life has become impotent and nonsignifying, this new "family," this new community will engender the true life, the life that comes of God, at once our Sovereign and our Father. Genealogy is transferred to him who neither deceives nor is deceived. "Do not call anyone on earth your father. Only one is your father, the One in heaven" (Matt. 23:9), and the law of blood is transposed into an elective communion of brothers and sisters, and the "revealed science of salvation."

This kingdom of the "Father who is in heaven" is altogether different from that of earth. The spiritual person stands in opposition to the carnal. The human being is divided in two: the body imprisons the spirit, the dark quenches the light. One must be delivered from matter and flesh, to enter the bright sphere of the spirit. The spiritual breaks away from the empire of this corrupt world, whether by abstention from sensible pleasures through asceticism, celibacy, and continence or by the free enjoyment of a sexuality that has been desacralized and severed from every purpose and obligation through conscious transgression of taboos of tribe and lineage and rejection of the ties of blood relationship. The human being is no longer subjected to any law but one—the universal law imposed on the cosmos and the stars (the "spirits"). Now earthly, carnal human beings return to spiritual and eternal selves, which have preexisted in the pleroma. They don a spiritual body. Christianity is born in a period of human history that witnesses the appearance of a world where the genealogical principle is no longer satisfying—a period that no longer takes account of human existence, now subjected to the risk of chance encounter. Human beings are witness and victim of the decline of the gods of town and tribe. They go in quest of a meaning for a biological survival that has turned into suffering, not only as a result of the miseries of war, epidemic, and social and economic disorder, but due to the lack of any efficacious legitimation.

Judaism does not escape this great turning point in history. This people's hoary certitudes concerning its origins and destiny must undergo a renovation. Origins and destiny are problematic now, for the patriarchal family is in decline, and the "state" that assured collective survival and destiny has disappeared.

The collective crisis touches the very meaning of human existence, the meaning of human structures and basic relationships. Until now, fecundity was benediction, and the complete human being was male and female: ". . . Male and female he created them" (Gen. 1:27), joining two halves to make one flesh, the complete human being. Still, the male was first, and remained first. He was from the spirit side. Being the first, he could practice continence. Woman symbolized impulse, concupiscence, flesh, the unceasing risk of degradation of the reasonable human being, the risk of lowering him (or her) to the level of instinct and animality.

This period of history registers a change, however. By continence, woman is redeemed. She extricates herself from the morass of her carnal passions and becomes spiritual. She is raised to the level of rationality. She accedes to a sort of spiritual masculinity, thereby becoming the almost-equal of man. We cannot ignore this context surrounding the advent of the doctrines of individual immortality and salvation and the value of celibacy in an elective, spiritual community with its new birth. Nor may we ignore the context of the transposition of the genealogical principle either into a transcendent God, an Utterly Other, or into a rational, circular perfection of an eternal cosmos. We shall do well to take our position on the level of historical depth, whence we shall be able to grasp Christian singularity. For it is in the same depths of history that other forms are born, themselves destined to transcend the genealogical, ethnic principle: the gnoses and Buddhism.

However Judeo-Christianity may begin to define itself in terms of opposition to the gnoses and gnosticism, it will nevertheless be marked by them. Among the Jewish sects of the time of Jesus are the Essenes. Essenism is simply a consistent response, in the form of a separation, to a corrupt world, in purification, asceticism, and continence. Essenism is a sort of monasticism, where spiritual parenthood is the only parenthood that matters. Traces of Jewish gnosticism, formerly thought to have been just under way by the dawn of the Christian era, have been found at Qumran, and this cannot be made into an isolated phenomenon having nothing more in common with the vast gnostic movement than a name.

All the various gnoses and gnosticisms, Jewish or Gentile, shared the following emphases: *(a)* The ultimate reality is the utterly other, the negation of this present world. *(b)* The duality of soul and body, of self and its appearances is accepted even in Judaism. The soul is the higher part, nearer to the ultimate reality. The body is the lower part, far from God, and the locus of sin. *(c)* This world, this eon, is transitory and valueless. Worn out, and under condemnation, it is only appearance and weighty burden. It is contemptible, and one must aspire to escape it, toward the new world, "another" world. *(d)* The knowledge or science of salvation is a wisdom hidden from the eyes of the common ilk of mortals. It is granted by revelation alone, and only to the initiated. The constitutive realities of life in this world, the necessary structures for an existence in the carnal condition are but an allegory of the invisible—the only world that counts for anything, the only world that is lasting.

Christian Gospel and Ancient Myth

This is the atmosphere in which the Gospels resume the ancient myths. The Holy Family is a community of the continent. Jesus' virginal conception and birth occur on a level transcending this world, a world condemned to disappear. The form of life lived here is that of the members of the Christian community—enigmatic in this world, and manifest, in its true form, in the other, where there shall be no more sorrow, or death, or suffering. But there will be no more bride or bridegroom either, for all shall be even as the angels of heaven. Virginity, tending as it does to suppress the difference between man and woman, is an anticipation of the heavenly condition: it approaches the Spirit and God. Jesus' nearness to God could not but entail the absence of sexual reality; and Mary, the creature nearest God, could not but have a suspended sexuality, a sexuality in parentheses. This is the mark of the era—its "closure" —but there was nothing to prevent its resumption of the old myths of the Virgin Mother and of life in death in a new way in the figure of Jesus Christ. Are human beings the prisoners of their conditionings, of their birth, and hence of their bodies, their families, and their tribes, or can they merely assume these, deliver themselves from them, and enjoy real survival? This is the *only* question the gospel message answers, even if we admit that the answer goes far beyond the question and its boldest expectations.

Consider the following:

1. *In the Gospels, no less than elsewhere, the figure of the Virgin Mother is inseparable from the experience of life's triumph over death.* In the Gospels this connection means that it is from a point of departure in the life of the risen Christ that we speak of his birth and infancy. Life manifesting itself as resurrection is transmutation of biological conditionings. Victory over death is victory over birth as well, for birth, too, is separation—birth is death already, in seed. The end is in the beginning. Indeed, the end *is* the beginning. But risen life is in the line of sense and meaning, and not in the form of substance, as natural or biological life is. Its initial presence is absence, the vacuum of demand. This presence is accomplished by the mediation of action, of the commitment of freedom, by faith understood as the living process whereby human beings posit

themselves in the likeness of God, as his finite presence by representation. It is a life fulfilled in failure—in death, which is the disappearance of the natural *Dasein,* existence in the sense of being-there, the disappearance of that sine qua non of meaning that is at the same time the impossibility of meaning's existence-as-such, existence as universal life of the Spirit. As the life of everyone, as the Spirit of the community, it reappears. The outpouring of the Spirit that raises Jesus gives birth to the community of the Spirit, the church. Jesus himself is there, actively, personally, but in a mediated form. His presence is real, but endlessly deferred by the "others." Jesus has died to be reborn as Christ and Lord, as the community's life. He has died to be reborn in the form of community.

To be engendered by the Spirit is to be oneself, actively and personally, in mediated form. It is to exist in the form of community. The virginal conception proclaims that this mode of being is the meaning of the conditionings in which these conditionings transcend themselves, in which they are delivered from their determinism. It is the same life, but in a form fitted to its essence, an essence that is a having-become. This is the message.

The message acquires all its efficacity as fulfillment, not as denial or rejection, of the triple truth of the archetypal figure of the Virgin Mother. The cosmic dimension of the Christic revolution is perceived from a point of departure in its terminus. Mary is Mother Church, giving birth by the power of the Holy Spirit. In her, men and women are reborn to original, universal life. The power of love that makes us new is the same power that renews the face of the earth and creates the universe. It produces beings, posits them outside the creator, endows them with their own consistency, makes them autonomous, free beings—it "lets them be," and with prodigality. The doctrine of the virginal conception shrinks to shabby, paltry dimensions indeed when it is given out that it concerns a "suspension of the laws of nature" by which God manifests his sovereignty through sheer royal decree. *This is deliberate provocation to doubt* and postulates human beings so contemptible that their existence may legitimately be staked on marvel. The representation of God here is too anthromorphic, too marked by the master-slave relationship.

The Cosmic Mother constrains us to transcend "personalism"

as an absolute representation of God. In a sense, God is impersonal—in the sense that he is beyond the person and the world that he founds and creates in "withdrawing." The redemptive sense of the Christic model is precisely that this Model is *for us*: it is being-for-the-other, it is what each of us can and should be for others. Excellence consists in being integrally what one can and should be: Jesus Christ is the figure of the "plenary human being," of those human beings who release within themselves the creative force that has always seized them in advance. The Cosmic Mother places us on the road to a more correct apprehension of the doctrine of the Holy Spirit and a less animistic and anthropomorphic approach to what we call the "personal God." The denial of myth is an index of the neglect, the loss, the failure to recognize, or the fear of the experience of God as beyond the personal and the impersonal, of Love as the creative power of worlds and human beings.

2. *The Mother of cultivated vegetation speaks to us of the Virgin's child, who must die in order to bring forth much fruit and become the bread of life for the throngs, the food and drink of immortality.* The mystery of Christ is that of death-life, that of cross, resurrection, and Eucharist. The Son of man, the child of humanity, must suffer, die, and rise again in order to hand on life to others that they may have it to overflowing, that they may live eternally. The old instruction of the traditional initiations is resumed and synopsized in its entirety: it is the Good News. The gospel is life. It is initiation, not doctrine. It shows how to effectuate this instruction, known from time immemorial, in a new manner: one must exist like Jesus, one must exist according to the Christic model. The gospel is the drama of life and death. The Christic model prescribes that it is life that triumphs, through a commitment of freedom in an active expectation of the kingdom of God, through a total availability, an availability to which we attain by willing God for himself. The effect of this attitude is death to sin, to the idolatry of what is not God—and its condition is "self-desisting," a leaving-off from ourselves, a death to that without which we would not be. It is a matter of much more than "sin," then.

The gospel is not a message about sin, about human corruption and condemnation. Such a perspective is at once anthropomorphic and, paradoxically, anthropocentric, for it disparages human beings by presenting their failings as an integral part of the very mystery of life eternal. The Good News is the existing of Christ. An over-appreciation of the schema of the Word of God for translating what Christ's message is can only have developed through a failure to recognize in that message what the old vegetation myth teaches. The cry "Christ has died, Christ is risen, Christ is alive!" is not a doctrinal proclamation—a declaration according to which one adheres to an incomprehensible belief—but the acclamation of the initiated, who experience in their existence the emergence of the Christic form. Apart from this experience, apart from this vital, dramatic simplicity, Christianity succumbs to adventitious doctrines, to the proliferation of words about the Word, and to an overestimation of the Book and of interpretations purporting to extract from it what Jesus "actually wished to say." Christ ends by sinking into a morass of subjectivity. He becomes the means of having an effect on oneself, of experiencing anguish and the consolation that follows, of obtaining peace and "assurance of salvation." Everything shrivels up into the lifestyle of a culture, a social group, and their customs.

3. *The Mother of the hero likewise recalls the necessity of suffering and death for the other—and without guilt or "original sin."* The hero is not a god. Jesus Christ is not simply God and nothing more. He is the child of the Mother, the Son of man, before he is Son of the Father or Son of God. He is the figure of fulfilled humanity for us. But humanity is fulfilled only in identifying with the life of the Spirit animating the community, for the Spirit is Life. Jesus is not everything. He is not the Father. His glory, his definitive being are received by him from the Father, in an everlasting being-together with the Father. The communion of Father and Son has not yet appeared. Christ in glory is yet to come, at the consummation of the ages, according to the faith that is hope.

Here it will suffice to observe that the life of Jesus is not complete and fulfilled in itself, but in One mightier than he, mightier than the Spirit of Christ animating the church, which is to say the Spirit of God. The nature of his identification with God cannot be the possession of a human being. This identification is still a question at the heart of Jesus' existence. It has not yet *appeared* in Christ for the human being. But "the God of Jesus Christ," our access to whom and experience of whom are inseparable from the name of

Jesus, from the Christic model, is the God who brings it about that we be in his likeness, that we be his presence by re-presentation: hence our hope that nothing, not even death, will separate us from the love of God.

This means that, even in his revelation in and by his Christ, God reserves his ipseity to himself. He remains the hidden God. God is not "made common" in Christ, as if one could now possess him and make use of him. Jesus is not a substitute for God. He refers us, sends us back to God—not as a projection of ourselves (for we must receive ourselves from the Other), nor as the reflection of our needs, but as God is in himself, in that presence beyond all word and intermediary that constitutes us in ourselves. The maintenance of this difference between Jesus and God, or of this identification of Jesus with God as a process *quoad nos*, is necessary to the notion and meaning of God. Jesus receives the name of God only inasmuch as he returns to God, joins God in God's mystery and incommunicable ipseity. Faith in Jesus Christ, then, does not procure us more information about God, more "clear and distinct ideas" about him. That Jesus Christ is the Word of God still means that God, even in Jesus, refers us to his own ipseity and mystery. It does not permit us to speak of God anthropomorphically and attribute to him immediately what Jesus' temporalizing existing gives us to see and to understand. The Christic model is not a "theology of a human being," but an "anthropology of God."

Christianity dies beneath the weight of certitudes about God's nature, plans, designs, and holy will, which each Christian may multiply to suit himself or herself. Christianity is transformed into an intolerant sect when it believes it possesses the truth enclosed within the limits of Jesus' earthly life, a life become the exclusive property of his heirs and disciples. The figure of the Virgin's child furnishes us with an anthropology of God, a way of existing that opens us to the infinite, so as to be able to receive from it ceaselessly, welcoming and accepting it for what it is: the ever new. But the face-to-face vision and beatific vision are not of this world. It is possible, indeed perhaps necessary, to be a Christian in knowing what God is not, but without knowing what he is. Myth teaches us humility—but God's humility, the humility of him who is every bit as present as he is absent, and so near that he is far away.

This is Jesus' final lesson to us: human beings are fulfilled all the more completely in accepting their limits—in "realizing" that the human being is a human being and that God is God. An anthropology for God can take on the myths only as a demonstration of the human condition: a being-in-the-world and a life-for-death. A neglect of this teaching will not fail to dehumanize the human being, and will transform Christianity into a supernatural positivism or an ideology of the will-to-power. A primary demythologization leads to the violence of an arbitrary Christianity, whose complicated sense and meaning is for only a few to enjoy, or else to the counterviolence of political ideologies or liberation. In a moment antecedent to this stage, the bourgeois rejection of myth is paid for by the privitization of faith. The great symbols are reduced to mere examples of moral conformity and individual rectitude. Thus the Virgin Mother will be no more than a refuge in temptations of the flesh, outside marriage as within it. The abjuration of the myths will go hand in hand with puritanism, a religion of "interior conviction," and a moralizing Christianity of "good conscience," industriousness, self-satisfaction, and a great deal of talk.

Such are the stakes of our discussion. Jesus Christ is not come to abolish, but to fulfill. This statement is eminently valid for myth and for the human condition. For "accomplish" does not mean to preserve or to restore. It means to carry higher, further, and differently.

DESTINY

We have already anticipated the second part of this chapter in treating both of the transcendence of the conditionings and of the "mystery" of death and rebirth. The cosmic person and the hero found their plenitude outside themselves, at the price of a transfiguration. Destiny is the mode of being proper to metamorphosed beings, who have lost their individuality, their "private consciousness." Destiny is the spiritual presence of what one is henceforward: oneself indeed, but oneself in the form of community, by and in a spiritual consciousness, by and in the "spirit of the community"—the spirit that bestows structure and life on a community.

The transition to this mode of being occurs through the activity that a free being performs when it confronts its limits. The radical experience of limitation does not stop with the consciousness that one may have of it; it goes all the way to the disappearance of self-consciousness, all the way to death. What can be interpreted as annihilation, and ought to be, is experienced as self-illimitation when—and because—it is articulated as the emergence of the person, that emergence occurring as human beings transcend their conditionings and transforms their determinisms into conditions of their own possibility, in the matter and substance of their liberty and acts of creation. This power of illimitation exercised upon the human being is not at the latter's free disposition, and this non-availability takes the form of destiny, which is not an object of choice but of consent and affirmation. Destiny is that which, coming out of the past, is irreducible to the present. It is also that which the future holds in reserve, in withdrawal from the anticipations of all our possibilities. Destiny is what it issues as, as it issues from oneself in consequence of what it is and what it does. *Post hoc, ergo propter hoc.* The bond of necessity here is succession and temporality as such. But it is a matter of the temporality of others, in its articulation upon one's own, as it interrupts it, succeeds it, prolongs it. The self is an object, and as such is subjected to relationships of pure exteriority: it is mortal, it is pledged to become an object for others, in itself and altogether outside itself. To die is to succumb to the forces of exteriorization, to return to the anonymous silence of earth and stars.

This dissolution does not necessarily occur in glory—at the moment when one is "ready," at the moment when one will have attained to full "personal" autonomy. It has no discernible relationship with spiritual "growth": rarely does death come at maturation, rarely is it the ideal death of one "full of days," crowned with wisdom, holiness, and respect. For every such falling asleep in the evening of life, how many premature, abrupt, animal deaths there are! What seemingly triumphs cannot receive the name of "spirit." Human beings are submerged in a proliferation of microbes and parasites or are pulverized by mechanical forces. They are not even victims, but are merely thrown out with the garbage, an ordure rather more encumbering than the rest. For many there is no survival in the form of a name handed down or reemerging in the cycle of generations in the bosom of family or ethnic group. Families and groups are mortal, too. Besides, nominal immortality disqualifies one's reality: one occupies an empty pigeonhole that can be stuffed by someone else in perfect interchangeability. Must one admit that the success of a few will suffice for the justification of the existence of all, and for life to be transcended? Those who fail to emerge as persons will have served only for sketches—means of producing authentic human beings. It would be even more reasonable simply to speak of luck, of chance. These grand considerations upon the person, upon being-together are finally deflated. All persons are unspeakably alone, with their suffering, in their death. Is there any answer?

Discourse upon death, one should notice, is held by the living. The question of its meaning or absurdity is asked of them and by them. Death is the task of the living. Time out of mind, it is they who endeavor to provide a release, a "safety valve," for its violence, by rites, by funerals, by representations of the beyond, by all manner of things that recognize or postulate in a human being a part that is invisible and deathless. The care of the dead is the affair of the living. Human beings have ever sought to exorcise their fear of the dead—the "loathesomeness" of their dead—and magically to rid themselves of this terrifying absence become so obsessively a presence. The living give life to the dead by memorial rites, by attitudes that pretend the dead are "still there." It is a game that can entertain, but in principle the game is serious.

If there is no death but for the living, then death must be a living death, a death not yet arrived, a death that has not yet died. A living death is one that human beings can still command. They can give a meaning to this kind of death, that is, can transform it into life. Quality of life is obtained by the efficacious effort to render death human, to divest it of its arbitrary character. Death is violent when it should not have come. Death is intolerable when there is a want of human responsibility, where human beings' ignorance, rapacity, and unconsciousness triumph, where the human being is alienated, where the exploitation of human being by human being reigns. The emergence of persons is not a solitary adventure. They are saved only along with one another, in the measure that they build a community of persons where no one is the means of anything. This community of persons wages a combat against the sorcerers who live on human blood and turn others into zombies. It delivers those whom the evil spirits possess and torment, releasing them from the crushing burden of their dead and past ancestors, from a malevolent present, and from their future shock.

The struggle against disease, exploitation, alienation, and solitude can be summed up as a struggle against irresponsibility. Death can be a "happy death" only in a reconciled, responsible society where the human beings have engaged all the resources of their intelligence and heart to protect and exalt life. Human beings know they are mortal. Death indicates that life comes from further away than the individual. The absurdity this human being seeks to avoid is the "unhappy death," the death that results from human beings' violence and alienation. The sense and meaning of each one's death, then, is taken in hand by all the others who live in society. A society that attributes a value to the person in the latter's concrete being, a society organized in such wise as to serve the development, expansion, and affirmation of each of its members will care for its dead as it has given meaning to their lives.

The "empty place at table," the recognized vacuum designating the absent presence of the dead is what authorizes the free play of life. Authority is continual reference to someone absent, to one departed. In this sense the destiny of the dead certainly depends on the living. But the efficacity of the action of the living draws its strength from the enigmatic presence of the dead. The "as if" operates "more really" than spatio-temporal immediacy. The sphere of the dead, or death as imagined, acts on life in such wise as to transform it. Human beings receive their fullness from others, in the form of a sense and meaning for life. Destiny is human life perceived and lived as accomplished. Those who die in the very act of doing what is meaningful pass, by virtue of the mediation of the living, into the sphere of forces that structure the community and give it its orientation—the sphere of presences that animate the community and make existence an adventure worth living.

As long as those associated with one's deed of creativity are alive, the initiative of their departed exemplar will not yet enter the domain of anonymity. The dead one continues to haunt them, speak to them, appear to them. The dead one's personality is so intimately linked to theirs that they can themselves pronounce words their absent exemplar could have spoken. They can authoritatively interpret any ambiguous statements this model being may have made. In sum, they can be the dead one's ambassadors and envoys, for their leader is not yet really dead. Once these first followers are themselves departed, the great one may enter into anonymity. Now the great one is with the "ancestors," or the Ancestor, in a realm beyond psychological illusion, for he or she has reintegrated the origin, and been reintegrated into it. Now the exemplar is one with the Spirit, who is all in all, everything in everyone.

Here there is no speculative answer to death: there is only community in the form of love, caring in advance for its dead by giving life a meaning untouched by death; for now the latter's sting has been blunted (as far as possible) by the exercise of responsibility toward all life and by the exaltation of life served by knowledge, action, and worship. The answer to death is the multiplication of meaningful life become the daily task of the living.

This is the perspective in which we must approach the passion of Jesus; his cross, which is at the same time his exaltation; his resurrection; and the outpouring of his Spirit unto the constitution of a community of salvation.

The passion and cross are first of all violence undergone but unjustifiable. Their necessity is not a priori, but a posteriori. Their necessity supervenes only once they have been accepted and their victim has entered glory, for suffering is always singular. It is in the order of event. It is the fact of an encounter. Collisions are inevitable, but a given collision is not fated or foreseeable. Things could have turned out differently. Jesus does not wish to die; still less does he wish to hang from the tree. He is proclaiming the kingdom of God; he is calling people to conversion and repentance. Evil and sin are the deed of human beings, and so it is human beings who can and should reverse the situation, for the regenerative power of God is at work within them. They need but let that power do its work. Letting it do its work means recognizing our limits and abandoning our illusions and the lies with which we cover them up in order to dissimulate them to ourselves.

Jesus' action and word rush back upon him in contradictory echoes. Some accept them. Others, many others, reject them or are indifferent to them. What Jesus can and must do is to assume the consequences of his action and his word, including the possibility of refusal and violence. The cross is not chosen. It is imposed at the end by the fearlessness of service and the resistance of neighbor. It is backlash. It is relationship, and its proper meaning derives from relationship. It will scarcely suffice, then, to keep repeating that life issues from death, and that this was why Jesus had to suffer. To be sure, such assertions are correct provided they do not convey the impression that we are dealing with an ineluctable eternal law or decree, producing events after the manner of a staging and dramatization. The relationship is essential, but only because the meaning of the cross is manifested by those who have perceived Jesus' activity as a service of new life, the life that appears in and through the community according to the Spirit. The cross must manifest what is at stake: the characteristic obstacles preventing creative power from unfolding in action; in other words, that from which this power must detach itself in order to appear in its truth. The passion and cross of Christ are the trial, sentencing, and execution of someone defenseless, someone without recourse in the face of political power, religious interests, and the indifference or cowardice of the masses. He is sacrificed to the tranquillity of each and all. His action and teaching contribute to a ferment that threatens order and gives way to violent subversion. The risks being removed concern a situation that lends dangerous resonance to what Jesus says and does: namely, for many, "awaiting the apocalypse" means nothing less than awaiting the destruction and total renewal of the "world," as in the time of Noah. The Day of the Lord—the inauguration of the reign of God and the Saints—is first of all a day of wrath to make an end of the disorder established by force, ruse, and injustice. Whether it appeals or repels, a call to conversion is being issued by Jesus. He is proclaiming something radically different, something that calls into question the religion and power tied to the Temple and the priestly caste, the ethnic principle, and the sacralization of law. He is introducing seeds of "anarchy" by rejecting all the hallowed antitheses of social organization and "hierarchy": rich/poor, great/little, respectable/despicable, learned/ignorant, men/women, and so on. Surely this is code language for the great collapse, surely this is the call to revolution, to the reversal of the proper order of things, the inversion of certitudes. Jesus' acts and teaching are surely an aspect of the battle to establish the reign of God, the reign of justice and love. Resistance, condemnation, suffering, and death are inflicted upon him as an individual, as well as upon the values he incarnates and the power that dwells in him. Indeed this higher life is already active in those who have recognized it, in those whom it animates. As the force of the future, it triumphs, and what opposes it is disqualified. The reign of evil is not eternal. Death was not created in the beginning. One need only wait in order to see it flash forth as victory for those who suffer and die for justice and truth. Their life is hidden in God, and inseparable from him now. When God shows himself, when God comes, they are with him, they accompany him. Indeed, they are present already in their spiritual posterity. They are the spirit animating this posterity—not possessing it, to be sure, but consented to by it, as the meaning of life and of the word of its challenge and provocation, the word of its cause and generation, and hence as the self more intimate than self.

Into his Father's hands Jesus commends his spirit. He renders it up now as the Spirit of the Christ, the Spirit of Jesus-transfigured, delivered from the limitations of his singularity and capable of acting in a fashion mediate indeed, but real and personal. Now he can act via those who have his spirit, those with whom he is in communion and *circumincession*, those who re-present God in the form of a person, those who actualize the archetypal human being—the human being according to his and her beginnings. A cosmic person now, and child of the earth, Jesus the Christ can save himself only by saving the world that he recapitulates in himself, the world whose "total part" he is and with which he must live in friendship and harmony. He is the heroic human being, who takes on human existence with a passion, in its biological, historical, and cultural conditionings, accepting the risk of a higher life at the price of suffering and death—a life in transfigured form beyond self-consciousness, beyond individuality and the immediate continuities thereof. Heroic human beings revivify and fulfill their tradition and culture by causing them to explode, transmuting them, opening them up to the totality of human tradition become personal tradition. Journeys, exiles, labors, pains, are but so many initiatory rites, introducing the human being to true life, to existence in the form of community, where each is alone together with and by the others, in a mode of association and a type of relationship whose principle is neither ethnic group, nor nation, nor identity of interests or religion, but the creative spirit, the power that generates autonomies, and the rendering-present, in person, of the spirit of all, in each.

Such is the Christic model, which occurs as a process, or more simply a journey, by which, far from yielding to destiny, to the entropy of negative powers, far from yielding to death, the human being undergoes all these indeed, but transforms them into spiritual energy. Death is drawn into the circuit of interchange and communion, in such wise that the lot of each is entrusted to all.

This journey is for the individual, societies and civilizations, and finally, humanity, in indissolubility. The force that creates realities that are subsistent in themselves is the same force that gathers them together in its oneness, a force that is beyond number, beyond the one and the many. In the mutual inclusion of human beings, human society, and the world, human beings survive as "spirits." This self-transcendence, born of history, continues to be realized in history, through observable processes susceptible of being described. The being of the Risen One, his presence and activity, can be perceived mediately, through the liturgy, through his representations: in the instituting and inaugurating processes of the church, through Christian action, through a communion of sisters and brothers, through the memorial of the absent—the memory of the departed, the function of their empty place—that is, through the manner in which social reality is perceived and transformed on an eschatological basis and foundation in accordance with the mystery of death and resurrection.

God presents himself here as community, inasmuch as the community keeps its dead alive by giving meaning to the life of the living, raising them to a state of dignity, and surrounding them with a respect that nothing, not even corruption, can destroy. God is the creative force of a meaningful community, a community of persons, where, actively, in suffering and night, the totalization of humanity occurs—and in that totalization, the totalization of the world.

This God comes in the representation and configuration of society and the world, but only in personal form, only by the emergence of persons. This is why one can speak of him only in the language of "as." God is presupposed in the human being *as that which* gives him and her the power to face death, *as that which* lifts human beings above themselves—above their selfishness, their alienation, and their idolatry. At this juncture we can predicate of him a language of personal initiative, provided we translate it into the language of "as if," the language of the creative power that envelops and bases the cosmos and humanity all at once. "God sees. He judges. He condemns." This is psychological language, and is to be understood as a conversion of language calculated to convey the modality of the creative power's being-in-the-form-of-a-person. But persons, constituted in themselves, are for themselves. One does not speak of "God" and leave them out, attaining him *under* their disguise. Persons are not the means of the revelation of God, they are his real, finite re-presentation. God is "spoken" of by the totality of fulfilled human existence. It is through the latter's unfurling and deployment that God manifests himself, is manifested. The Christic model does away with anthropomorphisms and with Scriptures that rivet anthropomorphisms to a deadly literalness so that the Christic model leaves nothing but an "anthropology for God."

Finally, at this point the faith-that-is-hope begins. Working or living for the good and the true is such stuff as to enable one to vanquish death, to be reborn as spirit, to be reborn more really oneself owing to the creative, loving interference and intervention of others, including that other-par-excellence who is more intimate to us than we are to ourselves and whom we call God. Faith is the risk of hope in the resurrection, conceived in a commitment of love on the part of oneself and one's neighbor unto death and "desisting from oneself" in this world. Anything else, unless it be understood as expression of this mystery to be experienced and actualized, is but creedal belief, inveigling, alienating, estranging. Faith reveals nothing. It shows *what is* in all its nakedness: the violence at the heart of life, and the risk of hope; the chance of the improbable already characterizing biological life, and the appearance of humanity on earth; and beyond that the advent of the spirit, the coming of "life eternal." Despite this incertitude and the horror of the violence, life in its actuality today and its power, the finite spirit in the exercise of its activity and its consciousness of itself and of what transcend it are marvels that nothing can possibly reduce to commensurability with death as a biological event. Only the destruction of what makes up that which is proper to the human being, only the alienation of the human capacity to understand and to love will be the unbearable evil. The human being retains the ultimate, redemptive capacity to suffer and die in the refusal to accept this shipwreck of meaning by hoping against all hope that life will be the stronger, that life will bestow what it promises, and that God will ratify his truth by restoring life to the dead, in manner unimaginable.

Chapter 8

The Jewish Question,
or a Matter of Authenticity

The Christic model is posed as such, in its efficacity, only as power or principle of structuring in the form of the autonomous, novel community of "those who have eaten and drunk" with Jesus and believed in him. The new status and being of the Christic model are manifested and accomplished in a particular use of the Scriptures and traditions, in a manner of organizing memory and envisaging the future, a manner of dislodging and moving the boundary between the without and the within, a manner of striking a relationship with oneself and the "others." In short, the original-ity of this community is discernible in the fashion in which it es-tablishes its identity, its continuities, and its solidarities.

The "Church of the Apostles," the church of the first preaching, which produces the Gospels and fixes the "tradition of the Lord"—the churches that define the essentials of Christian liturgy, doctrine, and morality—is defined within Judaism as "the Way." "You see, brother, how many thousands of Jews have come to believe, all of them staunch defenders of the law" (Acts 21:20), we read. We find Christian communities in Samaria, Galilee, and Ju-dea, where the church of Jerusalem plays a preponderant role until the fall of the city in A.D. 67-70. This Judeo-Christianity carries with it the main tendencies of living Judaism. It contains a rabbini-cal Christianity, that of converted Pharisees of strict observance— the "staunch defenders of the law" mentioned in Acts. It hosts

Nazarenes, who are to be grouped with the baptist sects. There are
those who are hostile to the Temple and its sacrifices, and whose
affinities and ties are with Essenism and the antilegalistic current.
In sum, original, constitutive Christianity is a happy amalgam, a
true Judeo-Christianity. Its life and self-consciousness are those of
a reform of Judaism, not of a breach with it. It retains all its loyalty
for its "nation," but without excluding the Gentiles of the gospel,
and it has to battle the constantly recurring temptation to Judaize
the latter. Primitive, or original, Christianity is reconciliation in
action, visible reconciliation between Jew and Gentile by integration. Each group preserves its difference—its historical continuities, its ethnic solidarities—but relativizes them instead of
making their universalization and triumph the end and aim of history.

The breach and the opposition developed gradually. The dramatic events of the year 70—the capture of Jerusalem and the destruction of the Temple—provoked in Judeo-Christians and
Ebionites the same reaction as in the Pharisees and many others:
They too fled the city, now fallen to the dictatorship of the Zealots.
Refusing to capitulate, the Zealots struggled on, hoping for the
impossible miracle of victory. Once the war was over, a number of
Christians returned, along with the others, to a Jerusalem in ruins,
there to await the restoration of Israel and the coming of the
kingdom of God—now announced by the catastrophic sign around
them: "When you see the abominable and destructive presence
standing where it should not be. . . . Then men will see the Son of
Man coming in the clouds with great power and glory" (Mark
13:14, 26). As they sat there meditating on the causes of the disas-
ter, as other Jews were doing, being rabbis and masters in apocalyptic they saw the finger of God and a just chastisement for the sins
of the nation. Doubtless they specifically cited the great and ultimate fault: failure to recognize the Messiah, now already come
once, however incognito, in the person of Jesus. But they did not
conclude to the total condemnation and definitive rejection of
Israel. What there was most need for now was to hope and to prepare for the second coming of the Messiah "with great power and
glory."

Their loyalty will endure until the final cataclysm of A.D. 135. In
the meantime, however, their belief in the Messiah already come

will have withdrawn them from the political and dynastic dreams and megalomania of the dominant current of thought. The sense of a Jewish monopoly on God's election will have grown dull in them. Will this not surely be to have gone too far, in a time of crisis and struggle to the death, a time of all or nothing? Thus the Judeo-Christians will be accounted as traitors to their nation and allies of the enemy. Judaism will make no exception for them when its general excommunication strikes the Christians. They too will be anathematized in the synagogal liturgy, and their curse will be repeated thrice daily: "May the apostates have no hope, and may the empire of pride be promptly uprooted from our days. May the Nazarenes and the Minim perish in an instant; may they be blotted out of the Book of Life, and not be counted among the just." By this formula, the Christians were banished from the prayer assemblies and from Judaism. One could not be a Jew *and* a Christian.

The Judeo-Christians fared no better outside the pale, with the church at large. Gentile Christians were swelling its ranks now, and they were no longer content with dissociating their faith from the temporal, political destiny of Israel—refusing its pretensions of religious annexism. All too eagerly they disconnected themselves from the Jewish context altogether, closing themselves off from all the interests of Israel, among which one must number its survival, the maintenance of its continuity, and the free disposition and enjoyment of its ancestral heritage. The calamities crashing down on Jewish heads were interpreted by the Gentiles as a sign from God of their disinheritance and condemnation. Gentiles saw the ruin of the sanctuary as proof of God's exasperation with Judaic blindness and the inexpiable crime committed by the Jews against the One sent, the Son of man. The destruction of the Temple does away with rites and ceremonies that no longer have any meaning, any legitimacy, just as dispersion wipes out a people who no longer have any reason to be. Thus in destruction and dispersal alike, *jus* and *factum* coincide. Israel is dead, or can now survive only illegitimately and fraudulently. The church at large falls heir to all its goods, including the interpretation of its history. Jews are being suffocated. They are being called upon by the greater church to "dejudaize," to renounce their solidarities, preserve their identity and historical continuities in allegory alone, to be saved only at the price of becoming isolated, uprooted individuals—"souls."

Dogmatic and Christological developments are not alone in con- tributing to this separation and "estrangement," however impor- tant the consequences of effects or such developments may have been. Individual salvation apart from any collective and historical destiny, an inflated notion of the faith as exact knowledge of re- vealed truths, an exaltation of orthodoxy over "orthopraxis," the allegorizing of a Holy Book torn from its native soil, Jesus' dehu- manization or dehistoricization, the proliferation of miracle and the prodigy to the detriment of God's transcendence—all these things come gradually to form a picture, which, once completed, is unassimilable by Jewish Christians—by their mentality, their reli- gious loyalty, their tradition. Their usages and theologies are de- clared heretical by the greater church. The Judeo-Christians are excluded and banished. One cannot be a Christian and a Jew.

Henceforward the Judeo-Christian mediation will be missing, and Judaism and "pagan" Christianity will define themselves in terms of mutual opposition. Christianity will imply membership in a civilization, a Greco-Hellenic cultural complex and its local re- sumptions everywhere. Christianity will pay the price for its failure to integrate or accept the Jewish difference, Jewish irreducibility. Henceforward it will insist on denying all difference. It will hold all foreign manner of being, all cultural irreducibility to be illegitimate "superstition." Henceforward Christianity will forbid a multiplic- ity of belonging. Faith will be the only belonging there is.

Paul is rightly credited with rescuing the Christic model from confiscation by the Judaizers and putting it at the disposition of the Gentiles. But he pleaded no less vigorously in favor of the Jewish irreducibility. The thinking of this Pharisee, this Roman citizen, this Christian preserved its triple belonging. Clearly faith is not a principle of membership in anything. Faith is precisely what per- mits the articulation of Judaism with the Roman ethos, of ethnico- religious particularity with politico-economic ecumenicity, of heterogeneous, separating temporalities issuing from different pasts with a common, plural future. To be sure, for Paul the gospel is "the power of God leading everyone who believes in it to salva- tion, the Jew first, then the Greek" (Rom. 1:16). That is, salvation is from the Jews (cf. John 4:22), and for them first. The law brings only the rending exasperation of sin, with the dizzying fascination of transgression. Obsession with guilt proliferates all the agonizing prescriptions, all the self-justification, all the bad "good conscience" at once. Law separates, sets in opposition. It has been found wanting. Gospel liberation is addressed first to the Jews, who have experienced in their very flesh, in the dregs of their soul, the collapse of revealed tradition, and it is from within this experience that the gospel is formed and born as that tradition's resolution and fulfillment. That the Jewish difference does not represent humanity's future does not mean that that difference is condemned. Israel is not "disqualified" by the simple fact of being that which is transcended or surpassed in Jesus of Nazareth. The Jewish past, with its riches, its oracles, its prophecies, forms part of the conditions of the very emergence of Christic human beings, who integrate all of these in their destiny. Jesus bears a gift to the humanity of the future: his tradition, transmuted in and by his person.

What Jesus does for his tradition, each of the rest of us must do, from wherever we are, for our own tradition. The Jewish Scriptures are not given to us to worship, but to share, by and in a spiritual communication, not only with Jesus but also with all the other Jews who have incorporated them into their own person—who, *ad instar Christi*, "after the manner of the person of Christ," have opened their person to the love of persons come from other horizons, all bearing their burden of particularity metamorphosized by the acceptance of others. The Scriptures exist and have meaning only after they have become the living substance of persons. In the exchange struck between persons, all recognize as their own what belongs to the other; here Judaic irreducibility or singularity takes its just place, the place conferred on it by the currency and efficiency of the Christic model, which implies and summons other experiences, in their difference, in order to be effective. In a like context of communication, what limits could possibly be set to the contribution of Judaism or anyone else?

Indeed, for Paul, the Jews' rejection is not to be imputed to their sole responsibility. It is also the index of a deficiency in pagan Christianity. Arrogant and annexionist, this pagan Christianity is incapable of arousing any jealousy on the part of Jews for its spiritual quality. As Jewish Christians abstain from participation in the development of a common Christian liturgy, dogma, and ethics, pagan Christianity develops tendencies in these areas that wound their Jewish brothers and sisters in their sense and experience of God and life. To Jewish Christians, pagan Christianity seems at once disincarnate and grossly mythological. Despite its extension, despite its imperial Christology, it is singularly narrow and could never really recapitulate the Jewish experience (nor, a fortiori, replace it).

We see the immense process of *déconstruction* and simplification to which Christianity will have to submit before it can again be possible for Jews to be Christians in good conscience, in all loyalty to their own and to their memory. The road is still long. Or is it already too late? Shall we ever commonly see Taoist Christians, Hindu Christians, Buddhist Christians, Animist Christians? When we dream fondly of an African Christianity, we have to be willing to dare to think this far. When we wonder whether Africans, conscious of their identity, their continuities and solidarities, can be Christian, we are asking a question about Christianity's original meaning, at a point further upstream than where dogma begins, as near as possible to its origin.

We ask the reader to consider Part Three with us, then, as an inchoate, groping search for an authenticity and veracity that alone are worthy of faith.

Part Three

THE MARGIN OF CREDIBILITY

In Part Two we took a searching look at the Christic phenomenon in order to be able to see and appreciate it in the milieu of our own experience. That experience is itself inserted into the advent of a world society, a pluralistic society, which has had an extraordinary effect on civilizations and religions. The new order of things imposes coexistence upon civilizations and religions at the price of endless adjustments and reinterpretations. As a cadre of coexistence, this new order of things is called "civil society." As a cadre of potential reinterpretations, it is called "culture." Thus it determines the negative conditions of credibility and calls for explication. There could be no better way of understanding the procedure and purport of the chapters of Part Three than to examine the constraints to which they must submit.

CIVIL SOCIETY

Modern society, in principle and as a matter of principle, is an "open society"—even if it is not always actually so. Numerous religions and civilizations can coexist within it—or should be able to—each without fear of violence on the part of the others. Any pretensions to monopoly of the true and the human are felt as a threat, likely to unleash the old demons of holy frenzy. The old passion does not admit of discussion, does not admit of the possibility of retraction without treason or apostasy, does not admit a differentiation among orders of truth, or the latter's character of incompletion. Such pretensions comport antisocial, antihuman virtualities, prepared as they are to risk collective survival for their own particular authentication and triumph.

Civil society, on the contrary, sets for its task and highest goal the maintenance and safeguarding of the survival of a given historical community, and of the human community, basing its activity on an acknowledgment of the relationship among human beings as such. It stops short of, or withdraws from, the differences that the logic of religious or ideological membership have a tendency to ontologize—to carry to the absolute in order to create radical oppositions and a struggle to the death, physical or symbolic. Civil society intends to be the transcendence of *totalitarian* passion.

Henceforward, religion or ideology (even "scientific" ideology) can be judged not according to its own idea of itself, nor according to the truth of its content, but according to the *form* it takes in its expression and realization. This form will be required to be nonviolent and compatible with the social organization of work, the battle for survival, and the general well-being. Religion will have to calculate in advance the profane consequences of its holiest maxims, its most divine inspirations, its most sincere convictions. It will have to accept the fact that decisions will no longer always be made in function of its own estimate of the essential and the nonessential wherever it becomes urgent and necessary to conquer determinisms, fatalisms, and states of affairs that have become intolerable—even when religion has sanctified them from time immemorial by creedal beliefs and express doctrine. Thus civil society imposes on religion an ethics of historical and social responsibility, a pluralism of convictions and "gods," and the nonheroic commitment of compromise that rests content with provisional, penultimate solutions, but solutions that provide for the survival and tranquillity of the greatest possible number. Civil society is, as it were, the practical and ongoing rejection of all systems under which countless human beings have suffered, and suffer still, sacrificed to the unverifiable "science" of a promised goal in the afterlife, or at the end of history, without surety or pledge. For civil society, the universal is what is common to all, what is waiting for all to do. It does not seem likely that Christianity will escape this structure. It does not seem likely that this structure will fail to trace rigorous conditions for Christianity's credibility, the form of the believable and the universal.

THE TIME OF CULTURE

The twentieth century is seeing Africa as a project in itself and in charge of itself. This time is a "space" in which manifold human formations, each with different temporalities, find themselves juxtaposed. Each has emerged individually at a moment in history to which it refers as its "origin." Each appears as the result of what human beings have made of their conditionings: their biological nature itself, their physical environment, their language, and their chance encounters with other groups from which they have borrowed, or from whom they have protected or defended themselves. Each of these human formations is thus a unique solution. Each is a singular manner of organizing the bond among generations, the lines of communication and relationships among the living, with the dead, with the earth, and with material or symbolic things and products. In other words, each is a unique manner of organizing the opposition between the within and the without. Thus the originality of these groups is but the expression of their basic historicity, the constant and ongoing genesis of the humanity of their members in narrow, mortal liaison with contingent places, movements or migrations, and other events.

When the humanity of various groups is thus formed by investiture in particular content, issuing from their "dialogue" with a singular nature and a singular temporality, they immediately assign absolute priority to what differentiates them from one another. The foreigner will be a mere semblance and caricature of a human being. Convergences, similarities of content are sought only where none can be the victor, where one is forced to admit and accept the humanity of the other, in whole or in part. These instances are the exceptions.

When you are caught in the same socioeconomic space, and the constraints of a common production of the real conditions of material life are imposed upon you, you readjust your traditions, your symbolic representations. You unify your "gods" in a pantheon, you endow yourselves with a natural or spiritual genealogy that minimizes or erases your differences, that founds and legitimates your being-together in the absolute. Thus is born the civilization of heterogeneous fortress towns and peoples, whom need and fate has gathered together, transforming fate into destiny, predestination, divine privilege, and "mission."

The meeting of civilizations—these exceptions—can at first be a violent collision, a "scandal." One civilization will attempt to annex the others. Or perhaps instead it will treat them with a high-and-mighty disdain, reserved for obscene caricatures of humanity.

When victory is impossible, civilizations with their respective religions enter into "colloquies." They begin to take inventory of their similarities or complementarities and look for a "convergent spirit." This is when they begin to reveal themselves to one another, each in its partial character and its partiality. Now the concept of culture is born, that by which human beings grasp themselves as genesis, as self-production, from what they are no longer, toward what they are not yet. Culture is the human being as process of communication, exchange, and transformation of things into objects and signs. It is the human being as strategy of reduction of violence by means of rules, by means of the play of symbolic distances. Culture is the human being as negotiation with death, for death is now reintroduced into the circuit of word, communication, and exchange, in the midst of life and for life's benefit and exaltation. The birth of humanity—for humanity is constantly being born anew—is the story that the history of "cultures" never tires of telling. This is what renews itself and grows to world dimensions, in and by civilizations. In the beginning is the phenomenon of the human being, at whose interior develop the religions of faith. These appear only after long delay—in no wise as the human being's determining instance, but as a facet or dimension of culture, of construction of the real by human beings who are themselves being transformed by these religions. The age of the human being is more global, more vast than the age of revelations—and more varied.

Chapter 9

The Articulation of the Community of Faith

Social skill can be defined as the ensemble of possibilities possessed by subjects in virtue of the fact, and solely in virtue of the fact, of possessing the "practical mastery of the symbolics of interaction" in their community by membership in that community. It is the same with the habitus of faith. Faith engenders in believers dispositions that permit them to act, according to the interior law written in their "heart" by the Spirit of the community, in the face of unforeseen situations constantly renewed. The practices produced in this manner by the habitus of faith maintain a conformity to the implicit anticipation of their consequences, that is, de facto, to fidelity to the past conditions of their principle of production: in the case before us, the principle of the constitution of the Christic model. The Christic model, we recall, is the "fulfillment of the Scriptures," that is, the resumption, in Christ's life and death, of the structures and figures of the religious history of his people for the purpose of composing from it his personal becoming. This is why the structuring figures of Scripture, fulfilled in his Person, are at the same time the structuring figures of the community of faith, organized in the form of Christ, or the Word, and why they make of it, literally, "Christ, continued and expanded."

The continuity and permanence of a Christian history depends on the formal autonomy of this system of dispositions, that is, on the logic and discursive quality of its identity, in its undividedness from itself and its separation from others, in its correlation with itself before its correlation with others. Thus there are, first, structures and figures by means of which human beings say they are what they are, by which they signify the "force" that gathers and preserves them as a people, giving each member to all. Second, there are structures and figures by which they mediate, for one another, real life in its manifold forms.

Human beings activate the first kind of structure and figure to the effect not of deploying the field of their power, and of the presupposition of the human self, but to that of signifying the invisible might that renders this possible. They speak and act under the appearance of not doing so, of suppressing themselves in order to show forth the absent presence of forces that have begun without them and that will continue after them, but which are the real conditions of their consciousness, and which give them to themselves as finite. This manner of designating the elusive origin, the inaccessible end and foundation, proceeds symbolically, in the form of a dramatization, by re-presentation.

The second type of structure regards the human being in its self-determination. It regards the spontaneity of life. It converts into symbolic happenings the concrete processes of the production of life and its material conditions. Henceforth life is given as meaningful, in its immanence, through which an original spontaneity is bestowed even as it slips away.

In this wise, structures of mediation articulate with those of representation, to form the people that lives by the Bible, that lives by the system of possibilities the latter offers once it is personalized by Jesus in the place and locus in which he spoke and died.

STRUCTURES AND FIGURES OF REPRESENTATION

Representation takes two forms: archaeology and cult. In archaeology we recognize and express the delayed presence of our origin. What constitutes human beings in their existence and their capacity as subject stands off at a distance, in the play of temporal mediation and a succession of generations.

Before oneself are one's ancestors, who seem nearer the origin, nearer that which was "in the beginning." This is why archaeology generally takes the form of genealogy. The latter is expressed in a series of relationships that are connected in linear order. Thus the origin is presupposed and betrayed by transitoriness, antisymmetry, and reflexivity. This ordering and these properties are not the same as those by which human beings are agents and operators, by action or thought, as they take a position above them, or enveloping them in and by the enveloping movement of presence and return to self. It is a matter of an Exteriority that implies the human being. The paradox is that human beings must take account of this Exteriority in the cadre of their presence to themselves, in the cadre of the initiative of their autonomous spontaneity. They attain this only by "re-presentation," that convention that consistently marks exterior and constitutive character, and effective, existential self-implication. It is the problem of shedding light on the divine "prevention" with respect to oneself (which makes one be and speak by speaking as if one were not speaking, by being as if one were not) that is resolved by the attitudes and conventional modes of speaking which erase their "artificiality" by anonymity, by their intangibility and "traditional" character. These traits are also the positive mark of the relationship of order in terms of authority from which there is no appeal, authority that one cannot dispute. The divine prevention is grace, to be sure. But it is sovereignty, as well, and has "no need" of its creature.

This language of representation, as it is not that of the spontaneity of the subject, is made of "institutional" words, and obeys preconceived, constant forms and schemas, which one must produce in well-defined circumstances, and which are brought forth by personages—that is, human beings stripped of their individuality and fulfilling a recognized function by submitting to rules imposed publicly or tacitly.

The archeological representation, the representation expressing the constitution of the world and of "true" humanity, first takes the form of story. Myth is story. History, even when it recounts "something that happened," is transformed into myth from the moment it treats of the happenings that have constituted the people in its humanity. From the moment the subject is implied and "recounts" its own genesis, that subject sees himself or herself through preconceived forms. Mythic representation is not neutral. Its recitation is an obligatory act of allegiance, an act of obedience and submission to the force of prevention and bestowal. There is a prescribed attitude, then, where words and texts are concerned that transmit the history of beginnings, the history of the "Fathers."

One does not discuss it. One could not have redone it, told it in a different way. One does not enjoy free disposition over it. Is it not the definition of the sacred to be that which is not discussed, but which "forms the plan of all discussion," which is not the object of one's free disposal, but is protected by a taboo devoid of all utility or "rational" or "reasonable" justification?

Representation, then, is a manner of conduct, and it develops its rules and institutions for the maintenance of the relationship of order and authority that it sets forth to be observed in life. Custom is the ensemble of modes of conduct that develop by way of commentary on the accounts of one's original constitution. Custom proceeds from the Fathers and "locks up" within itself the "spirit" of the first beginnings, the spirit of the origin. For this origin is a delayed one, bursting forth in manifold creative schemas of activity. This is why custom has the strength, the sacrality, and the immutability of these beginnings. Charged with this originating, necessary force, custom projects it into space and structures community in accordance with a relationship of order. To the good order of the generations corresponds a good order among the people, as they faithfully keep the prescriptions and observances that God has given them by the ministry of the Fathers. After all, the figures sketched by the Fathers represent God in his activity of constitution. Custom is "archaeopraxis."

Functions and Servants of Representation

Thus there are functions and structures in the service of representation. The accounts will be preserved and faithfully transmitted, and the manner of understanding them correctly and without distortion will give rise to doctrine, to dogmas, which will say nothing but what the stories themselves tell: God's initiative or prevention, his sovereignty, his separation from creatures, and the attitude of acknowledgment and gratitude that all these call for on the part of the human being. Ministers are persons who deploy the sacred order, proclaim it, and exhort the faithful to live it by observing the laws promulgated by God to the Fathers. The primary function of hierarchy is to represent authority. It carries out this function by maintaining the bond of the generations; but also by keeping watch over the preservation of the Scriptures and their correct interpretation (that is, their "authoritative" interpretation, meaning that of the divine prevention); and, finally, by seeing to the integrity of modes of behavior and customs that make it possible to realize a relationship with God "as God actually is."

The principal attribution of hierarchy is the pronunciation of judgments of conformity with revelation and tradition. God is mystery. His self is hidden. But he has traits, or causes events, which "reveal him." How may one recognize these as such, and distinguish them from others? By the attitudes to be adopted before the God on whom one's existence depends: the attitudes of thanksgiving and adoration. It is for and by the human person that the question of revelation is posed. Revelation is God's ray of light, piercing the dark, and received in the measure of each one's capacity. Incommensurable as are the human persons with what is divine, they become its perfect finite symbol. It is this finite character that imposes the need for judgment of conformity and tradition, a judgment appealing to the spirit that transforms, according to the Spirit of Christ, to an affinity with Christ, and with the church he structures and informs. God's manifestation is earthly. History changes the perception of it, for successive generations are unlike one another. What must be reaffirmed is the good order of the representation, by the correlative attitudes of gratitude and obedience to God, and not to some "intermediary" or some idol. Here is why the concrete content of these attitudes is not determined in advance, once and for all. For the rest, the task of the hierarchy is to watch over, first and principally, the constitutionality of acts and institutions, the constitutionality of what is done and what is made. Hence hierarchy will now require other ministers of representation no less tautological and formal than themselves.

Thus we have preaching—the apostolate—with its agents and the functional structures that correspond to them. Representation is the modality according to which God communicates himself to human beings, in a presence that is personal and real, but mediate.[1] It is personal inasmuch as God refers human beings to the divine ipseity, by referring persons to themselves as persons, to whom God gives to be in his own likeness in quality of free spontaneity. It is real because it is constitutive of reality from a point of departure in creative power. It is mediate because it has its identity in an other-than-itself; it is mediated by others.

Preaching is representation. Those proclaiming the word do not preach themselves. They speak "in the name of God," let the word go, "let it be," let it have free rein, its own efficacity. Faith comes by hearing, for the apostolate places one in the presence of God, who alone converts or arouses faith. Thus understood as the manifestation of the divine activity and power, preaching is constitutive of the community. It is the preaching of the Word, or preaching in the form of word, that engenders new members and initiates them, that nourishes those it gathers, and maintains them in their new status as members of the People of the Word. It is the Word that structures, that awakens each of them to self-consciousness. This is the people that lives by every word coming forth from the mouth of God, the people that cannot subsist and arrive at a comprehension of itself except by interpreting itself as having been instituted by the active presence of God. The distinguishing characteristic of preaching is the homologization of what is transpiring at any given moment with this instituting activity, the proclamation of the Lord's Today: What he did of old, that he continues to do in new figures. The preacher lists the evils from which God delivers his people, the enemies he subdues, and the processes by which he convokes this people for such-and-such a task, for such-and-such a change of direction. The preacher enumerates the modes of behavior that correspond to the acknowledgment of the reign of God and of his sovereignty over the present, over the history we live today, and in the days to come as well. Preaching is actualization with respect to a situation ever unique and unrepeatable. It presupposes commitment and risk on the part of the servants of the Word. But those servants are not propagandists: they must deploy the power of the divine activity that arouses and inspires, that cures, and that saves them. Just as the servants do not preach themselves, neither do they crusade for a cause that has nothing to do with their own existence—an exterior divinity, an idol, or an organization. It is the creative spirit that confesses, groans, prays, and pressures. Thus preaching's message is not a neutral one. It points to examples to imitate or avoid, it interprets events in terms of specific divine activity, and it represents the relationship between God and human beings obtaining at any given moment. It never omits to supply a recommendation for an appropriate attitude, the attitude corresponding to what God does and what he demands, and corresponding to the practical acknowledgment of his transcendence.

There are several manners of being in the service of the representation of the "God who speaks." God becomes present and communicates himself by those who speak in his name—his spokespersons—in virtue not only of the content of what they say, but also of the form in which they say it. The difference in forms corresponds to the difference in the ways of making reference to God, of "letting God be." Each form corresponds to one of the modalities of the apostolate.

The servants of the Word can be *messengers*. Messengers are defined by the message that they have the mission of proclaiming. They have no authority or jurisdiction, no command over their addressees, just as these latter need render no account to the messengers, but only to the originator of the message, the one who has actually addressed it, as they discover for themselves the appropriate response to receipt of the message and its content, in terms of behavior.

Messengers may be mere *heralds*, going before the lord and master to proclaim his coming or promulgate his decrees, to inform the multitudes of his coming actions. The messenger is his mouthpiece. Today's missioner is a messenger, not an envoy. Envoys are the personal representatives of their principals, and "live and dine" with them. The envoy, having shared in the master's project from the start, can be his "alter ego," for the envoy retains access not only to the spirit animating the master's undertakings, but to their very letter, their tone, their accent. Thus envoys have a unique privilege, that of personal intercourse with their leader who is their friend as well, and in whose creativity they share. It is the apostles who, strictly speaking, are the envoys here, and they have no successors. They alone may fix the letter of Scripture. They alone are the foundation of the church.

It does not follow, however, that today's messenger—the servant of the Word—is a mere functionary of representation. The messenger's task is obedience to the faith. What these messengers profess is their judge, for condemnation or deliverance. Furthermore, these messengers do not supply information, but exact attitudes and deeds—the only sign of the auditors' having understood the content of the message and grasped its nature.

The *witnesses* (the martyrs) take a stand for God, and declare themselves to be in solidarity with him, testifying to a co-membership with God of such quality or intensity that the witness cannot subsist where conditions prevent God's name from being invoked or hallowed. The martyr is the one who literally dies of these conditions. When existence in the form of word and love is radically contradicted and opposed, when idolatry rages and tyrannizes, authentic life takes the form of witness. What is at stake is not such-and-such a belief, such-and-such an article of faith, but a mode of existence, in the image and likeness of God, in freedom from all alienation, from all idolatry, and from the confining narrowness and divisions that oppress creative energy. In this procedure it comes to light who is "faithful"—the one on the side that affirms the transcendence of God, the eminent dignity of the person, and the illimitation of love. The witnesses have no need of actively provoking persecution, of being its instigators. They do not go "running after death" or the martyr's crown, seek no test of strength or "trial by blood," either for self or for others. It is simply that they cannot survive where the "abominable and destructive presence" (Matt. 4:4) is installed in place of holiness, where it is impossible to live and be nourished by every word that comes forth from the mouth of God.

The *prophets* speak in the name of God. God seizes, possesses the prophets, using them as his medium. Through censure of public mores, threats of chastisement, reproaches, admonitions, and promises of victory and glory, the prophet declares the will of God as the determining factor in history, politics, and the national or collective destiny. The prophet is not a simple messenger. With the latter there is greater distance, more objectivity. With the prophet the cleft vanishes. The message is received and delivered in the same instant: the personality of the prophet is its vehicle and its form. The message is that of all times, even if prophecy actually arises in crisis, when simple hierarchical and priestly tautology is not efficacious or has fallen into insignificance and meaninglessness. Prophecy takes place amid the tumult of history, of social and military conflicts. The prophet shows the ways of fidelity to God, in and by change, anguish, and misfortune. God is not only present in the eternal return of the seasons of the world and of life, in a people organically integrated and rooted in a soil; he is also where options can prevent dislocation or precipitate it; he is in the forces of up-rooting and exile, stimulating them or holding them back. The prophets are not politicians. Rather, in extreme situations they teach the limits of power, of calculations of relative strength, of alliances, and of all the political techniques and ruses. The political does not save. Salvation comes from elsewhere—from a vital spasm that summons up creative resources of fidelity, hope, and the practice of justice, a vibrant thrust that calls on personal dignity, refuses to yield to distress, and bends only before the sovereign God. In the school of misfortune and suffering, God metamorphoses and ennobles.

The prophets proclaim misfortune in order to conjure it away, in order that it not come. Otherwise the prophets promise its end. In exile, they can already see the return and restoration. After prophecy fails, *Apocalyptic* arrives on the scene. The prophet still calls on those in power, threatening, exhorting, promising, staking everything on their capacity for conversion, criticizing established society, calling it into question so that it may amend itself, pleading with the powers that be to come to their senses, to mend their ways, and thus spare their nation the wrath of God. Is this prophet indeed not often one of their own? There are temple prophets court prophets, whole colleges of prophets—pressure groups. They lack neither influence nor credit, even when they are not heard or followed. Prophecy is an *institution*.

The *apocalyptists* adopt precisely the contrary stance. They are not permitted to plead. Here the addressees are deaf, blind forces—the frigid monsters. The prevailing structures of oppression and evil have not been rectified. Now they must be purely and simply destroyed. Intermediate solutions are no longer in season. The world has been cut in two, between those who alienate and kill, and those who are alienated and killed. The apocalyptist's horizon is not restoration, but the end of the world, the abolition of the shape of the present world with its political regimes and its social and economic organization. It is no longer a matter of reforms, vouch-safed at the pleasure of the benign holders of goods and power, via a slow, prudent integration of the poor and repressed into the order established against them. The monster, the person-devouring Beast, is mortally wounded now. Victory is fated, absolutely certain—as certain as that of Good over Evil or God over Satan.

The kingdom to come will be in radical discontinuity with the old world of tears. So the apocalyptist counts on forces from Elsewhere, from On High—on God's triumphant action, at work this very moment, however anonymously.

If the overthrow of the structures and powers of evil is absolutely sure, how can energies fail to mobilize, to hasten their collapse? Is it therefore this appeal to total subversion that inspires in the apocalyptist all these substitute names and code language? Surely it is. But the apocalyptist takes refuge as well behind the salvific and re-creative might of God, which nothing can resist, and which, once it has sallied forth, does not come back until it has accomplished what it has set out to do. For this reason the apocalyptist is sometimes not content with speaking as a simple instrument of God, as God's spokesperson. Sometimes this spokesperson is actually God's ambassador, his envoy, one in whom God's final power is already active, without distance—hardly a simple messenger, but the promise, the pledge, and stake of a new beginning.

All these persons correspond to functions that develop structures and a language through which they express their intentionality: the recognition of God at first hand, the acknowledgment of God for himself in his constituting power and might, in creation *ex nihilo* and in creation continually renewed. Hearing God in his Word is not "immediate operation." The Word passes by way of the mediation of those who efface themselves as mediators by the play of signs and attitudes, by a discourse of lived representation.

Cult and the Servants of the Presence

How may one "represent" to oneself the incomprehensible presence of God? What figure, what "shape" may we imagine it to have? How may we signify that it summons us, that we "stand before it," as it were?

Representation, with its "rules," its conventions, has the task of expressing the inexpressible, manifesting the invisible by means of the visible, the nonmediate by the immediate. Cult, or public worship, is thereby a representative "action." It is an institutionalized word, institutionalized as prayer, and appears on the scene as something that makes silence speak, and absence present.

Cult is the gathering of the people of God in a time and a space.

Cult is the only "place" where that people can be physically pointed out. Cult is the premier representation of the divine presence. The assembly is the Spirit in the form of community. The assembly is God's being-there, in virtue of the fact that all the human beings here present communicate in the same self, from which they receive themselves, and to which they have given that which separates themselves from others, their as-to-oneself. Here and now, God is all in all. What opposes human beings to one another in the world without, is, as it were, abolished here. The "neither Jew or Greeks, slave or freeman, male or female" (Gal. 3:28) is verified first in cultic time and space.

Emptied of everything, this time and space have been delivered up to absence, and withdrawn from free and common disposal. To enter here is to enter into the silence and mystery of God. Liturgical performance prescribes the acts and attitudes that signify introduction into this circle, and exit therefrom. The space can be a temple, an open place at the foot of a tree, or a rug unrolled at one's feet. In each case, its confection and orientation obey imperative norms.

It is the same with the attitudes to be adopted and the words to be pronounced in the course of the performance of cult. The attitudes considered appropriate make up the element permitting recognition of the presence. They are a manner of "reacting" which molds an emptiness, a concavity, in the shape and form of that presence— its "negative," so to speak. There are different attitudes. They can be grouped in three categories: those corresponding to affects, those accompanying knowledge, and those that are reactions of the will.

Cult commands attitudes that presuppose that the presence of God affects our sensibility, impresses us, so that we experience fear and trembling, joy and reverence, attraction and fascination. Cult "orders," it commands not only these feelings, but also the modes of behavior that demonstrate them, and the words that express them. One shouts for joy, cries, groans, and falls down in adoration *on command.*

God's presence also strikes the intelligence, which professes its faith and tells "the wonderful works of the Lord." It predicates qualities and attributes of him. Finally, the will, too, is moved, and tends toward him. It takes decisions and conceives resolves. It places itself in the hands of God and seeks to identify with him, to communicate with him. These thoughts and these desires have their appropriate language.

Through these attitudes, God provides an avenue of approach to him as a presence that impresses. His reality betrays itself here as something translatable into a coherent discourse, something capable of being represented.

But the translation, in order altogether to avoid being treason and mystification, must avow that it does not correspond directly to another language, but that it is a construction of the ineffable, the unspeakable in a system of the speakable. The words it employs have a sense, but they cannot establish any isomorphic proportionality between what is of the divine order and what is its derivative. The religious affects are not *caused* by "supernatural" stimuli. The translation asserts that the human being, who receives himself and herself from God is his and her existence, is before him *as* a child before its father, *as* a servant before the king. More generally, the translation concerns the representation not of God directly, but of human beings expressing their creatureliness, and professing God as that which is presupposed as giving them to feel him, to understand him, and to will him, but who, as he is in himself, is not the object of their faculties.

The tongue escapes fraudulence by silence. Cult envelops its words in silence. The word pronounces silence and leads to silence despite the vocative, despite the I and the Thou, despite the nearness of the Presence supposed *as* within earshot. The mute murmur of the heart does not escape God—not to mention that a dead, totally incomprehensible language can evoke the strongest sentiments and "feelings."

The reality of the divine presence in cult is imposed by its fecundity. It gives birth to laws, customs, and a whole code that states what is compatible with participation in the liturgy—a set of ordinances regulating it. Rules of behavior are formulated prescribing how one must conduct oneself before God and vis-à-vis the other members of the assembly. The decisions taken concerning a correct attitude toward the holy place of God's presence are to be executed. Missions are organized for realizing outside, in the world, what God has accomplished in symbol in the assembly. It is the same with the "works of mercy" to be done in his name, the service of charity by which the kingdom of universal reconciliation is anticipated symbolically. Thus there develop manifold *diakoníai,* in representation of the presence of God beyond grasp and understanding.

Prayer requires no special consideration. The institutional word ordering the attitudes to be adopted before the presence is prayer. Prayer is something learned, and the most spontaneous prayer is ground out by ancient mills and handed down or reinvented. One can only add that the essence of representation is delivered here in its nakedness—as human beings' representation of themselves as being received from God and not yet returned to him, so that the absence of the kingdom of God yet to come is felt as a presence-in-negative.

This, then, is representation in its two aspects, genealogical and cultic. To be sure, they compenetrate, they exchange modality; for the constitutive events are commemorated, and ancient liturgies are recounted and are at the origin of current customs and laws. Dogma enjoins an opinion while at the same time expressing the divine nature, which the corresponding affect and attitude alone attest. Dogma is "doxological," as we say, at once opinion and an act of obedience and praise. Finally, Scripture is transformed into an object of cult, as the immediate presence of God, arousing reverence and self-effacement on the part of human beings.

STRUCTURES AND FUNCTIONS OF MEDIATION

The human being of faith is still a child of Adam. The absence of the Utterly Other, conjured up by representation in the power of the moment by symbols, gestures, and words, is the basis of the human being's absolute need to be fulfilled through the mediation of the other, to receive God in enigma, as neighbor and fellow, in and by the gift of reciprocal humanity that makes life meaningful. Through the conditionings and mediations assuring its production, preservation, and quality, life is lived and interpreted as the experience of a creating and redeeming love. The community of human beings is "reborn spiritual," and reinfuses its vital processes with the vigor of its origin and principle—now become manifest—in the form of a might that creates autonomies and persons. Proceeding by this general operational principle, henceforth willed for itself, persons produce their definitive being, by their choices, by the integration of constraints and determinisms into their personal destiny, and by the reciprocity of a community where death itself enters into the circuit of exchange and communication. Here, relationships and institutions are structured and oriented in a manner calculated to render verifiable—subject to check and control—the claim to live by principle, and on the Principle.

The relation of representation to mediation flows from this principle. The end is to become the world of the original principle. Representation is a necessary moment, but abstract and difficult to realize. It has been a "revelation of God." By evoking past events symbolically structuring the present and prophetically proclaiming the future, representation has been the bestowal of God's profession as simple unity, above time and time's foundation—the bestowal of God's recognition in the immediacy of a descending relationship.

What we have described of the language of representation has shown that such immediacy does not exist, that it is not offered directly. Just as no one has ever seen God, so also no one knows or experiences descending relationships, but only the uphill labor of the sensible transmuted into symbols, concepts, and schemas. To know is to discover the trajectory of this labor of concept or image, a labor begun again and again. The industrious practice of love of neighbor verifies, by limiting it, one's claim to love the distant, invisible God. Representation creates "elbow room" for a verifying praxis. It has a regulatory function. Representation has nothing of the absolute about it; it is relative to present life, as that life marches to its fulfillment. It is intermittent, provisional. This is why its forms, or even its possibilities for exercise, are in strict dependence on lifestyle. Representation is called upon to disappear when human life as such becomes God's representation, his living symbols. Certain sacraments proclaim in advance this state where sacraments will be no more, for all will be sacrament, and produce what it signifies. This is how it is with marriage, with the Eucharistic meal, and—we might add—with death.

The gospel has defined the meaning of representation in the well-known lapidary, unanswerable logion: "The sabbath was made for man, not man for the sabbath" (Mark 2:27). When all is said and done, it is human beings in their humanity who must do God's representing. Their concrete humanity is not a "simple," atemporal unity. It is process: They *become* their definitive being. Humanity is articulated in differentiated moments, each expressing the totality of life and giving rise to specific relationships and institutions. We are not philosophizing when we say this. We are rereading, in the light of the Christic model, the Scriptures, whose meaning it (he) opens, and whose repetition it (he) makes possible.

Covenant signifies that henceforward human beings will live their concrete existence as interchange with God. Israel subsists only by covenant, which means that its historical being will comprise physical and biological conditionings as God's gift. Its relationship to the world will be mediated by its relationship to the land, which is a gift on the strength of a promise. It will be the same with the tie of blood: Isaac and the posterity of Abraham are born not of the will of the flesh, but as it were of the Word and Mercy of God. The survival and historical becoming of this posterity are still rooted in the divine commitment to multiply it and give it a universal destiny in which all nations will be blessed. The conditions for the continued validity of existence according to the covenant are these three relationships: to a land, to a family, and to a nation. Around these are built the relationships to property and work, those between the sexes, and those of the commandment of obedience. The human being who is sanctified is a sexual, working, and political being. In these three modes of that human being's existence, the human being is a being of relationship, and is fulfilled only by visible reticulation with the other, by the institutionalization of this complexus of relationships with the other.

The life that acknowledges these three mediations as constitutive —as uncircumventable dispositions by which the human being arrives at the fullness of his and her call to personhood—is not profane, even though it must not be identified with the cultic life. It has no need of being sacralized from without. It has no need of religion, and must be lived in a faith according to which the term of the representation is the human being as such. This end is not only to come in the resorption of all contradictions. The living of imperfect existence without hesitation or reticence, without second thoughts, seeking a sober happiness therein, welcoming the astounding brilliance of its joy and beauty, and accepting death and its thousand prefigurations as they strike down human undertakings as "vain"—this, too, is wisdom, and a wisdom undissolved by revelation or event. This wisdom is an integral, paradoxical part of the Bible, and indispensable to it and its ministers. It manifests the essence of mediation, and its priority.

The Land: Property, Work, Justice

Human beings are not the earth's partners. They have been drawn from it, and will return to it. To be sure, they have received the power to administer it—but only as God's "lieutenant," only in God's place. They are not its master. The unbridled appropriation of the soil is one of the great evils denounced by the prophets. The Jubilee, as an ideal, had the purpose of returning the land to its place, of sparing it the frantic exploitation of the greedy and of restoring to it those who had been deprived of its usufruct.

To do justice to the widow and the orphan, to feed the poor—this is behavior giving witness that one acknowledges possession of the land as a gift of God. Justice is appropriate conduct. It is the cosmic virtue: respect for harmony, for good order through equity for all is beneficial to rooting and fertility. Injustice affects the course of the world, the cycles of nature. It provokes drought, famine, pestilence, flood. It also provokes withdrawal from enjoyment of the earth by exile and deportation. These sanctions are executed by God in his immanence. Israel always relates its misfortunes to the absence of justice. When injustice reigns, death prospers. Injustice is exaggeration and immoderation. People no longer invoke or divinize the dark forces of fertility, it is true; they no longer render homage to the Baals in the mystery celebrations and the rites of the fields. But idolatry of property and toil is still thriving. There is the Sabbath, then, to recall that the land is a land of liberty, after the experience of the house of servitude. Work is not servile; it is a vocation, a task entrusted by God, for God blesses the work of one's hands. The imperatives of ecological respect and of justice are but two aspects of the adoration of God as Master, as sole Landlord. One communicates, and one becomes, by means of things and by the intermediary of the persons whose substance things represent. Human beings *are* the land, they *are* their toil. No one may alienate or hate one's own substance. "This is not done in Israel."

Family, Patriarch, Hero

The land is the land of "our Fathers." After long wandering, after the hard experience of being without a country, it is the Fathers who settled here. The land of the Fathers became the paradigm of happiness, of paradise regained, of the New Land where God will be the Father of all men and women, once he has engendered them altogether new in the Spirit. But arrival in this New Land is possible only on the basis of meeting God in truth in the framework of the family. Here one experiences God's creative might, and first and foremost in the fertility granted by him. The life he gives is the first of his blessings, and the foundation of all others.

It is here, in the family, as well, that obligation toward others is immediately present, in solidarity with those to whom we have been given, or who have been given to us, in a co-belonging that lays the groundwork of all ulterior justifications and explanations, in a relationship above ethics, beyond good and evil. We are not respecting our father and mother when they are nothing more than paragons of virtue. It is as our parents that they are respectable. The ensemble of laws regulating our relationships, both *ad extra* and *ad intra* and permitting us to engage in communication and exchange, begin with what is withdrawn from our free individual disposition and enjoyment in the bosom of the family. The first subject of the Golden Rule is the family—not to do to a member of another family what one should not wish to have done to a member of one's own, and to do unto others as one would have others do unto one's own. Under this formality the educative task of the family is accomplished: the induction of an ethic wholly and entirely based on family values with their own proper instances, like fidelity, a sense of honor (not to dishonor one's father, one's mother, one's name), continuity, and survival.

A cult develops, centered on respect for life, attention to its cycles, recognition of its gratuity. The father of the family presides over it. Thus in the case under consideration, Passover is celebrated first in the family. The emergence of a clergy—specialists who monopolize the performance of rites and the duty of education—does not relegate the family and its religion to a stage of the past and render them no longer appropriate to a humanity come of age. The family enjoys a particular autonomy, of a character such as to make it a moment that can never be dispensed with. There are always those who make it their *whole* modality of existence, while admitting that there are other modalities of authentic existence as well.

These considerations will help us to shed light on the figure of the *patriarch*, he who represents the origin. He is a founding father—one of those who inaugurate new lines, a new race of human beings, for having desired and hoped in a better life, albeit in wandering, tribulation, and incertitude. The partriarchs are the point of departure of a continuity, a vector extrapolating to things to come. They are not remarkable for their high deeds of arms, their prodigies, or even their virtue. They are the ideal figures that attest the continuity of one and the same destiny, one and the same adventure, which they inaugurate and partake in by generation.

The partriarchs are not judged on moral criteria. They are beyond good and evil, like the *civilizing heroes* who, by their inventions, ensure humanity's survival and confer on it a new quality of existence, thanks to metallurgy, husbandry, music, or any one of a great number of contributions they may make.

The task and function of ensuring the basic biological and cultural conditions for the transmission, conversation, and affirmation of the humanity of the human being would seem to be one in which the totality of meaning can be embodied. The creator is necessary for humanity's survival, for its recoveries, just as much as, if not more than, the moralist or the pious one. In any case it is improbable that he can be correctly understood from the point of view of these latter—who have the obligation of legislating upon him—without impoverishment or distortion. It remains the task of the patriarch and the civilizing hero to attempt to transcend themselves in their own lineage, by striving to make possible the race of those who look for God, who truly seek *his* face, instead of the substitutes and usurpers that produce manifold fear and misery. These are figures still for today. Today's children must become tomorrow's parents, and leaders must still break with the determinisms of torpor and custom. There are periods with a greater need of heroes than of saints, for heroes live the human condition in its banality and teach us how to stay human.

The Political

The prophet may well declare the limits of power, denounce its abuse, and proclaim its end in tragedy or definitive ruin at the consummation of the ages. "Revelation" shows that the political sphere is not the sphere of ultimate fulfillment. To be sure, by a mysterious paradox, renunciation of legitimate force and the right to self-defense issue upon the royal road of the cross, the road of the supreme creativity of weakness, helplessness, and failure.

The political as such is no less irreducible for all that. Antecedently to revelation, "all authority comes from God," and it is thanks to this authority that human beings are naturally together for their survival, as they recognize a power that can exercise moral demands and physical constraint in the name of the common good. This instance maintains its autonomy even when theocracy endeavors to reduce it to the revealed-sacred—to religion. Such confusion does not contribute to the moralization of politics or the reinforcement of faith. The political is all the more clearly affirmed in its specificity when it is in pagan hands and the people of revelation taste subordination. The authority of Cyrus and the emperor of Rome "comes from God." The magistrate who punishes and gives satisfaction represents the power of Good, and without the tranquillity of order the messengers could not go forth to cry the Good News to the ends of the earth.

It is true that the cross has already vanquished evil and vindicated weakness and nonviolence. To be sure, power must be delivered from evil—its own evil, might without law, without any other end but itself, without the legitimation of continuous consent. In short, power must be delivered from institutionalized excess and murder. This regeneration and salvation of power can only be envisaged under the form of the conversion, ever begun anew, of those who exercise it, and the education of those who submit to it. But conversion and education already presuppose a minimal renunciation of violence and a starting option for reason. It is not the function of the political to presuppose conversion and education. It is the function of the political to posit them effectively, and make them the basis of all subsequent relationships.

If we look closely, the political works almost the opposite of revelation. There is no "election," no divine "prevention." The function of authority by law, in order to exist at all, always supposes a virtual act of consent on the part of the citizen to the right of that authority to prescribe, and to the citizen's own obligation to comply and obey. What prevail here are rules, measures, formal procedures to ensure that the laws by which the citizens are already bound will actually be respected and reduced to action. No priority is attached to good intention, intimate depth, or the inspiration attesting to the constancy of the divine initiative, which can burst in at any moment.

There is more. The mode of association of the citizenry is not that of a community of salvation. The state does not save. The state ensures the life and continuance of the collectivity and protects its goods. Time is the measure that limits its responsibility to "worldly," forseeable consequences, and limits projects to determinate periods. It is a matter of objectives only, not ends. Hence the state penalizes without regard to rectification of intentions or conversion of heart. It is not content that is pursued, but form, a form that gives all persons the conditions of acting without undergoing the detriment of their person or goods. Nothing is sacred here; everything is the contingent product of human beings' willing-to-be-together in history, in that which changes, is transformed, and passes, by means of expedients that are opportune and consented to.

David and Solomon are not saints, but "good kings," who bestowed prosperity and renown on their people. David is even a figure of Christ. In what sense? In this sense alone, but in this sense indeed: that we are forbidden to say that the cross and failure are norms of political behavior and of action undertaken with a view to ensuring the biological and historical survival of a people. An evangelization that rejects the political is the death sentence of the evangelized, as in the Amerindian apocalypse, where "Christianization" has meant historical liquidation.

The Sage

First, who is the sage, the "wise one"? The sage is that able person who, by discipline, experience, and practice, has acquired knowledge and "know-how." Wisdom is the domain of the art not only of transforming "things," but of transforming that raw, chaotic material that is life itself. It is the art of living daily life and of finding happiness there by moderation and prudence. Wisdom is good health, good sense, and the renunciation of empty hopes and illusions. For if human beings are to take seriously the happiness or contentment they find in equilibrium, reserve, the rejection of useless anxieties and ambitions, and the simple pleasures of drinking and eating, it will be because they have no other life to live. The human being is a mortal animal. There is a time for everything: ephemeral joys are part of the human condition, just as are death and suffering, maliciousness and foolishness. These negative realities are not to be eluded by words. They cannot be evaded by dramatization. They are monotonously perduring, and no undertaking has ever freed humanity of them. Here there is nothing new under the sun. The foolish and the wise, the just and the unjust all know the same lot without distinction: pain and death. Suffering does not envince sin, nor excellence its absence. Death is the great leveler of lives and values. The high achievement is to remain alive, to live intensely and fully with what one cannot change, holding at its true worth the marvel of the instant, however fleeting its gladness and bliss. Life is the actuality of currently living and leaves nothing behind.

For the sage, revelation represents "nothing new under the sun." The communities that are its beneficiaries share the common condition of foolishness, absurdity, and death. Revelation adds nothing to what experience and intelligence bestow upon all, once introduced into the system of culture; that is, once it is integrated into the system of habits, of acquired competency, of production, of becoming. Incorporated into culture, it chokes itself. The wisdom of the sage arrives on the scene later than revelation and points toward the courage of maturity. It no longer has the naïveté to confuse Israel with humanity, or to attribute universal, absolute import to particular happenings of its provincial history. The age of majority is thus marked by the strength to save appearances: it accepts the fact that suffering, endurance, and the direct savor of life are part of the primitive truth of existence, valid in and of itself and incapable of being "reduced" to something else. One must seek the contentment available in human measures and affirm life before death swallows it up.

It will not do to be too hasty to rub out the antimony by proclaiming the definitive, all-saturating response of the gospel. How Jesus gathers up all things in himself will be manifest only on the "last day." Meanwhile there is life's polyphony, and it may not be refused. The orders of truth are multiple, and the manners of being human irreducible one to another. Human being-together is the enigmatic form of the unity of human beings, which is asserted by the fact that the different manners of this being-together mutually limit each other, cause mutual problems, and have meaning only by their mutual relationship. Each taken by itself is contradictory, destructive.

This being the case, the office of sage is a permanent one. We may not ask the sage to be the person of rite or prophecy. The sage bears testimony of the insufficiency of representation—dare we say, revelation?—captive as it is of images, particular loci, and the imaginary. A humanity alive is the being-together of these functions and these irreducible experiences. Their oneness is not available to our contemplation, nor to our fruition.

It follows as well that an individual or particular "church" is not in possession of the "faith" in its totality, in all its modalities. The partial character of faith is transcended only in a community admitting and accepting a diversity of gifts and functions, in the communication of different ways of living and being human. Faith excludes private proprietorship: it is not such as to enable or encourage each one to invest all its treasures in a manner calculated to ensure his or her self-sufficiency.

Finally, it follows that the order, or degrees of relief, in which the constitutive elements of the Christic reference are set, depend on situation, conjuncture, and epoch.

Chapter 10

Rules for Conversion

Christian performance is not the simple execution of a structure of objective or formal relationships, the implementation of a mechanical model. In order to pass from the indicative, which deploys the articulation of the constitutive structuring figures of the Christic model, to the imperative of realization in particular forms, one must limit oneself to the conditions of the current conjuncture—to the circumstances of time and place. Here it is the crossplay of multiple relationships and the itineraries of a singular history, with its resources, its specific impasses, its expectations, and its proper tasks, that are determinative.

Among the characteristics of the present age, we have, from the beginning, the ambiguous presence of a Christianity of exteriority and superimposition, characterized by the constant risk of acting as a screen, an obstacle, between oneself and one's person, between oneself and the real, between oneself and the God of reality. Our task is self-delineating, as it were, in view of this basic situation, and is expressed in the following questions: What are the transformations to which a Christianity of exteriority ought to be subjected? What are the operations to which it will be meet to subject it in order to do justice to the legitimate demands of civil society, the culture of the age, and the ethic of responsibility in history?

This chapter is an invitation to a reform of the understanding. We shall seek to indicate the appropriate processes for the conversion of inert, legendary content into propositions capable of being accepted by the awakened mind. Our viewpoint will be that of persons referred to themselves by reference to God, persons who speak of God not intending to say *what* God is, but by reason of and under the form of our relationships with God, by reason of and under the form of our finitude.

When "God" is the subject of a proposition, we immediately understand the proposition as being enunciated in the language of "as if." For this is the language that refers us to the act of our speaking of the "prevention," or interference, that grounds us by a mode of signifying that cancels our own presupposition of ourselves and points to our non-necessity. Furthermore, this mode of signifying by the "as if" undergirds the divine self-presupposition with respect to the spontaneity of the human beings, to whom God gives to be for themselves, to whom God gives self-determination. This divine self-presupposition, present to everything and in everything, is not the human being's and *non facit numerum* (is not in the same line of addition or subtraction, the same series of being). It can be spoken of only in "representation," only in the "as if" mode.

In other words, we are rescued from sheer credence and false conscience only if we recognize and acknowledge the *metaphorical* character of the notion of revelation, and the Word or Will of God, in order to draw from these the "theoretical" consequences for Christian practice. One must keep this language's "representative" structure and function constantly in view. The rules of conversion demand it, as they effectuate the return of content to the original simplicity of the source by turning the subject into a predicate so as to form a new proposition, by reversing a modality and turning it into its antithesis, by reducing or transforming a given "quantity" into another expression.

RULE 1: A PERSONALIZING TRUTH

Christian truth must be personalized in order to become believable.

This proposition seems a banality, a commonplace in current religious language. To all appearances it is woven into the Reformation current, which reacted against the ecclesiastical scleroses called "juridicism,""bureaucracy," and "clericalism." The

Christian horizon, we are told, had been shrunken and shriveled by an "authoritarianism" and "moralism" that was producing only bourgeois virtues of respectability and social and religious conformity, routine practices that happened to be in season, enhanced by a rigid orthodoxy. The birth of the churches of the Reformation is said to have restored a Christianity of participation, a more evangelical, less legalistic Christianity more solicitous of the "social aspects" of the revealed message than of individual salvation, and according the primacy to "personal contact" with Christ and God thanks to direct access to the Scriptures, the treasures of tradition, an understandable liturgy, and genuine mediation. The result, we are informed, is a committed, "involved" church, and a Christianity of far more shining witness in the bosom of the City of Humankind.

Obviously, we shall not be concerned to take the contrary position. We shall expand this concept of the reform churches, since it is not just a matter of the credibility of churches, but of Christianity itself. Our point of departure does not primarily place us in confrontation with an internal crisis of the churches, but subjects us to another type of question: What is the current meaning of Christianity as perceived from other horizons of history than those of the Christian or post-Christian West? How may we integrate into our historical destiny a Christianity of exteriority and imposition? To undertake a revolution in the ecclesiastical institutions and a quest for indigenizing adaptations while we evade the question of foundations and turn our backs on the question of the relevancy, pure and simple, of Christianity, the relevancy of its language, would be to doom ourselves to sterile agitation, and to place ourselves in continuous danger of bad faith, distraction, and idle amusement. The flight from God, and God's dissimulation to oneself, can take the form of conservatism: one buries oneself alive in the quicklime of institutions. Or it can take the form of reformism: one simply runs amuck, or else engages in a Quixotic quest that makes short work, to be sure, of many a windmill along the highway.

Let us reformulate, then, what we mean by a "personalizing truth." It is via what we accomplish, what we know and desire that we emerge as a self-reflecting human subject and assume responsibility for our being-in-the-world with others. The true is the very act of our constitution as person, according to differentiated modes but always "in situation" and in the present, within the limits of the time and space in which we live. No affirmation of truth is dissociable from this constitutive movement. No affirmation of truth is separable from the understanding that we have of it, from the manner in which we signify it, or the circumstances in which we enunciate it. Truth is ever the advent of a liberty new and alive. To be a person is the truth shining through. "The truth will set you free" (John 8:32).

In this perspective Christian doctrine can and should be understood in its entirety as the description of the modalities of the human being's emergence as a person in the determinations of the action and the word within this world, in availability to the creative might which refers one only to itself, and which in justifying itself justifies all—that is, manifests itself as gratuity for no reason other than itself and its manifestation.

In such an understanding of Christian doctrine, we shall be placing ourselves at the very heart and center of the Trinitarian faith. The Triune God is referred only to himself. God is thus outside the field of projection and anticipation of self of the being-in-the-world of human beings and cannot be utilized by the latter to satisfy their own needs, fill their lacunae, solve their problems, or have an effect on themselves as by means of a phantasm. The doctrine of the Trinity refers to God in his very ipseity, in such wise that human beings who recognize God as such—that is, God in his incommunicable mystery, or Self—are redirected to their own ipseity as human beings, to their being-in-the-world as the constitutive form of their humanity and personhood.

The only "certitude" we may have that we are not adoring an idol, a projection of our desire, is to return to ourselves, to be given over to ourselves in order to be and to do what we can be and do "by ourselves," alone, without vicarious substitution, to be given over to ourselves as the means of nothing, *ad instar ipsius Dei*, on the model of God himself. For God does not surrender himself to our contemplation, either in the introspective motionlessness of prayer and spiritual reading or in the reception of the sacraments as such. There is no privileged means of getting to God. There is but the real act of becoming a person who justifies "all means" and gives sense to them. The glory of God, that is, the splendor of his brilliance, is human beings alive, coming to be, producing themselves, together with others, these free spontaneities that are the means of nothing and recognized as such by word, respect, and the reciprocity of gratuity. "Knowledge of God" is not detachable from becoming a person, from the becoming of this particular person. This is why God is "incomprehensible" and can never be objectified. And this is why his "designs" are unknowable, why one cannot read them in any book.

Thus apprehended, the Trinity is the transcendence of monotheistic and polytheistic idolatry. Monotheism and polytheism are still anthropomorphisms, all the more tenacious for their ignorance and oblivion of the fact that they are a representative language. In order correctly to grasp the doctrine of the Trinity, one must restore its polemical content, give it back the mark of its historicity. Then, and only then, will the originality and efficacy of its conception of the divine appear. The experience conditioning this conception was that of an encounter of two different cultures and their calling each other into question in singular fashion. The experience was that of the confrontation of Judaism and Hellenism and their transcendence, which resulted in the exclusive victory and endorsement of neither. The Trinity, with its fascinating aura of abstraction and connotation of multiplicity, is the transcendence of the anthropomorphic, solitary, "jealous" god of the Jews, the principle of exclusion. It is the refusal to give God a name and is a deliverance from the equivocations of such an operation. God is not a mere historical personage, whose career begins with the oldest "memories" of the Jewish people, and whose character, "habits," and illustrious deeds can be learned in the Holy Scriptures. No, revelation is not the disclosure of the mystery of God. He is also the "hidden" God, the unknown God adored by the pagans and acknowledged by them in enigma. He is both, all at once. But the Trinity is also the rejection of polytheism, which is the idolatry of phantasms of desire and departure from oneself in favor of the dark and fascinating powers of sex, blood, might, possession, rhythmic cycles, and fate.

Monotheism had engendered a bending back upon self, the exclusion of others, the refusal of difference, and the spirit of conquest, of the reduction of others to oneself. Polytheism had finished in disintegration by syncretism, immoralism, and opportunism that cared not a whit for the truth. And it was too docile to triumphant force. But the notion of "trinity" was dialectical and negative. It gave no new name to God, made no attempt to comprehend his identity more adequately, or lift the veil of his nature, his intrinsic constitution. It said what God is not. It said that he is neither one nor many, but beyond the one and the many, the same and the other—beyond all representation. It said that there is no isomorphism between him and either oneness or numerical multiplicity. Neither totalitarianism nor anarchy can subject what he is to their authority. Unicity can be an idol just as plurality can.

Thus understood, the doctrine of the Trinity could prescribe a mode of thinking, or better, a mode of conducting oneself and existing, a mode of living in society As a designation of the mystery of God, it enjoins on the human being the thing called adoration— that total availability that is open to accept what is radically other from itself, the surprise of a god who is coming always, under the ever new form of the birth of a person. It delivers the human being from the sacred, that is, from facts, names, places, personages, all objects immediately identifiable with the presence of God, with his mark or brand, with his tracks, his traces, all things pretending to afford immediate access to him other than by the "discursiveness" by which the human being is posited in effective re-presentation of him. The doctrine of the Trinity goes so far as to emancipate the human being from every a priori, even the religious, whether theistic or antitheistic, thus leaving the person vulnerable—naked to the novelty of the real as it wells up unceasingly. Its function is not to crush human pride, scandalize reason, and force the sacrifice of the intelligence by demanding adherence to a contradictory formula; for its function is not to propose the contemplation of a pure Without, outside the human being, with no function in the genesis of the concrete humanity of the human being, in the latter's becoming-person. All theology, not alone triadology, would easily find its place under the imperative of personal and personalizing truth.

RULE 2: HISTORICIZATION

Faith must be a process of historicization.

Let us recall the result of the investigation we conducted in Part Two. Christianity, we found, is historical not because its founder can be assigned a certain place in an objective chronology, but because it was, part and parcel, a response in history to a situation born of history, that is, of the shock of the collision of cultures and civilizations, a response to questions born of the advent of history.

We were forced to conclude that the "essence of Christianity" is a "having become," and not a nature that is always there but hidden. Christianity is novelty, something added to "nature," the product of culture and freedom in the area of meaning. This having-become is produced in "dialogue" with reality, in response to questions and challenges. It is born of the risk of liberty, which confronts choices and dares to take a decision, to submit to determination, in such wise that, however excellent it may always be to describe its necessary conditions, one can never deduce its sufficient conditions, those of its reality and current actuality. Its necessity is a posteriori. Its necessity is coherence and efficacity imposed after the fact, after the indecision of the struggle, after the agony of Good Friday and the mute despair of Holy Saturday. The death of Jesus will already have been required, along with the testimony of the apostles. Nothing had been rehearsed. Having-become is understandable only against the background of the obstacles it has overcome, the mechanisms of protection, attack or defense, it has developed not only to survive but to be competitive with or in harmony with others in a given environment.

Having-become is a determination, then, an affirmation and a negation at the same time, a self-limiting affirmation whose function is to integrate what limits it. Considered as creative novelty, having-become is simple affirmation and overflows its limits and conditionings, for it is repeatable; that is, it is capable of having its limits varied, it can contract them or expand them. But when it renounces all limits, it falls into indetermination and meaninglessness. Having-become has no other relevancy or pertinence than to maintain the memory of its birth, its growing up, and the route it has traversed. It must remember what has given it its contours, its shape. In order to understand and repeat, one must reinvent the motion that cuts out the shape, the form, from the thickness and indetermination of life or action. Remaking this motion, this deed, upon affirmations that had been jolted loose from their form, so that their contours were obliterated and they had become absolute and thereby nonsignifying is called "historicizing." Historicization is a process of self-limitation on the part of a timeless and absolute language and praxis. Transformation to operation consists in inserting or introducing into time something that is situated only "in the beginning," at the "origin." It consists in translating into the life of town and marketplace what occurs only within the sanctuary of the temple and liturgical assemblies. It consists in producing-without what one professes is transpiring within, in the sanctuary of the soul and heart.

Thus faith changes myth. It grasps it by the collar and makes it tell. It makes it tell the genesis of a people born of nothing—ill-fitting, servile tribes, created by history. Rites are no longer merely repeated. They are not content with being celebrated. They remember, they recall. Indeed they "prophesy," that is, they furnish motives for hope, diagrams of action with a view to the future. The chosen people is a cosmic person issuing from chaos, dispersal, and servitude. It has exited from nothingness. Its history is the drama of life and death in alternation, through military and political conflicts, through defeat and exile. Historicization is an inversion, a reversal, a kind of Copernican revolution. Previously, the cosmos provided human beings with the models from which to understand themselves and organize their existence. Now historicization sketches their diagrams for the interpretation of social life. Word, pact, the relationships of commandment and obedience, war and friendship—all enable them to form a picture of the world's creation and of God, with his sovereignty and his activity.

This process can stick in a naive anthropomorphism, but this in no way militates against its decisive orientation of human beings toward the symbolic universe of word and desire. It repatriates them in the sphere of the responsibility and action of representations that tend to constitute autonomous entities and parallel worlds. This task is never finished, accomplished "once and for all." Word, wisdom, law (or custom)—indeed Israel itself—will become hypostases, supernatural realities, dominating human beings and even tyrannizing them. Jesus' obsession was to bring all these things down from the stars, as it were. To fulfill the Scriptures is precisely to historicize them. To endow myth with currency is not to rewrite it, but to resurrect it as an event in political and cultural life.

Historicization is the destruction of a cosmological and metaphysical dualism, via the projection of supernaturalistic repre-

sentations into the world. These representations *are*. Historicization begins with this situation of fact, this sort of transcendental
illusion. It calls on human beings' responsibility, their ethical commitment, and enjoins them to recover their footing on terrain
where they may have lost their footing, as they renounced their own
benefit in favor of entities, hypostases, and fate. Metaphors, fi-
gurative or spiritual meanings, must be circuited in series with
the literal sense. The letter is the stylobate of the spirit, and its vehicle.

The rule we are here proposing is an invitation to reduce everything to what occurs among human beings, who speak, desire, suffer, and die, who oppose or cooperate with one another and
accomplish their destiny and definitive being in so doing. This is
what historicization does. Where today there are only metaphors,
"mystical realities," historicization recalls that these are an ancient
euphemistic language for good and evil that is altogether real and
terrestrial and heralds a return to realism as a revolutionary task.
The resumption of an ancient category or mode of life in a new
context, on an enlarged scale, with the help of acquired knowledge
and modern means, is a utopian step in the dynamic, positive sense
of the term. It is the culmination of this historicizing process.

This resumption is not rationalization, it is not demythologization. The possibility of the resumption of different evolutionary
"phases," the necessity of putting them on circuit today is a rejection of the evolutionist postulate that sees in the "higher religions,"
of which Christianity is one, the term of a spiritualization, of a
refinement of religious notions and feelings to such an extent that
they are now perceivable only by the fine point of the soul or the
intellect. These ideas and feelings are metaphysics, we are told, but
with a parallel "mysticism" permitting them to be experienced and
lived. Deliberately we descend from these cloudy heights; we
mount up from these dark depths. The old Dionysian progress
through degrees of light is unknown here. Now we know but the
interminable cycle of the entities and hypostases, the endless goings
and comings of metaphors for sensible, social reality, metaphors
for the waking state of those who know that they are often asleep
and dreaming. Demythologization presupposes mythologization
as a process, not merely as fossils from another age.

What we have said about fulfillment, about the Christic model not being repeated but being reinvented, is the foundation of this imperative of historicization. In Jesus structures, or "types," are transformed into events in his life, and these in their turn structure the thought and life of the community of his disciples. In Jesus the eternal myths are realized in the vicissitudes of his historical existence. Historicization is really the engraving of a timeless exteriority upon the age and time of a person—in the temporality of personalization.

RULE 3: ESTHETICS

Christianity must become a redemptive esthetics.

Persons are living souls, animated bodies, and it is as such that they are redeemed. Christianity is not a metaphysics made sensible by the prowess of an arduous mystique. It is not the preserve of a spiritual elite. Its heart is not accessible only to the sages and saints of this world as they respond to the criteria of perfection set up by human beings and subject to the fluctuations of mentalities, ages, and civilizations. The Christian mystery is that of the life and death of the human being, the mystery of the resurrection of the flesh. If these expressions are not to be understood as simple metaphors, we cannot escape the task of examining the manner in which Christianity views life in its elementary conditionings as sensing and suffering, feeling and passion, or undergoing.

The corporeal radication of religious discourse must be at once its point of departure and point of arrival. The human being of whom we speak is the one who "is born, ingests food, copulates, and dies"—no less than this in any case, and if more, then not by omitting or neglecting these acts of life, but by investing them with value, by sanctifying them. What is elementary is the platform, the set of bases to which one must ever again descend. There is nothing in the intellect, not even the theological intellect, that has not first been in sensory living. If Christianity is redemption of fallen human existence, it must have to do first and foremost with these elementary acts, subject as they are to abuse, contempt, and negligence. Sin, whatever be its "essence," has its discoverable, indicable shapes and figures in the degradation of birth and dying, eating and drinking, sleeping and seeking shelter, engendering progeny, and suffering or rejoicing.

The transfiguration of these is the sign of the presence of the kingdom of God, and no equivocal one. We call it "redemption." Redemption forms part of the penultimate realities, the ones we can see, those that make it possible to "verify" the ultimate, invisible ones, and to anticipate them in hope. Redemption is to salvation what love of neighbor is to love of God. God, no one has ever seen—and those who pretend to love him while not loving their own brothers or sisters are living an illusion, lying to self. In like manner we have never seen a saved human being. We do not *know* what salvation is. We can only believe in it and hope for it.

Redemption concerns the here below, time and history. Salvation tells of the invisible, of eternity, of the beyond. Salvation promises endless happiness after death, when there shall be no more tears, or needs, or sin. Redemption knows only healing, the happiness of repenting and the groping path, succor borne to the "neighbor" in peril, unprofitable servants, the rare joy of brothers and sisters dwelling together in unity, the still more rare joy of having overcome one's fear and suffering in the name of justice, the sparks of the divine that light our night. Salvation holds discourse upon a universe where God acts, hears his servants, and delivers them, where he does not disappoint, where he judges, condemns, sanctifies, and reigns. Salvation assures us that the biblical word is the source of all authority and the rule of all truth, that the human being seeks to become God, and that disobedience to God is the source of all evils, while obedience is the foundation of peace. This is the discourse of salvation.

The world of redemption gives us to see nothing of all this. We do not *know* where and when these "Christian things" take place, and the conviction with which we affirm them does not dissipate the kingdom of ambiguity in which we live, where the victories of good and beauty are laborious and never definitive, where divine institutions have a perfectly "worldly" form and are distinguished by no discernible "perfection." The world of redemption is the one where every proposition calls for its visible process, every idea has its material referent. It is indeed the place of finitude, of death, the place "under the sun."

The drama begins when one wishes to deny density, deny reality, and thereby fail to recognize the good order obtaining between redemption and salvation. The trouble begins when one opposes one to the other, seeking to substitute the one for the other and vice versa. The common error is to suppress redemption, the next-to-last realities, and assert the last to be the more important ones, the only ones that "count," that is, the only ones that exist. The Christian life now becomes a "spiritual life," God's "invisible kingdom" deep in our hearts. Now the Christian life is the anticipation, in prayer, "holy obedience," saintly desires, and the sacraments, of the life of paradise. All our attention and energies must be mobilized in the service of the interior life and the invisible but constant activity of the Word, which of course we ought ceaselessly to be proclaiming. The bodily life—with its constraints, and the activities of its maintenance, its production, and its transmission—is to be lived distractedly, furtively, with indifference or cynicism. For the saint, the life of the body is but a rumor, to be squelched by mortification and asceticism, as the interior, heavenly music waxes ever louder and more distinct. But we have at our disposition a vocabulary made to order for the task, an invariable system of concepts and laws permitting us to judge life, to understand it from without, in all its swarming prodigality. These expressions and these values attributed to things are constant by virtue of what determines them. Their referents are spiritual and divine, and belong to the order of grace, which is an eternal order.

The Christian responses provided from within a like conception are necessarily clapped on from the outside. They do not correspond to the questions as actually posed. The reason for this is simple. The penultimate things lead to the ultimate ones, and the latter have the power of polarizing and dynamizing the former. For the human being, however, there is no means of thinking and knowing the mediations or paths by which these last, invisible realities could redound upon the world of the next-to-last realities. The temporal human being cannot conceive of this descending relation. Temporal irreversibility is the very mark of finitude. The passage from eternity to time is unknowable. No one can place oneself in God's view of things. We can speak only of the manner in which he "converts" us to him, the manner in which we are drawn out of ourselves.

When one places salvation in competition with redemption—

when one undertakes to persuade people that biological and social life as such is nothing, that it receives its value and its zest from without—there is nothing for it but to have recourse to a "methodism" of salvation. This "methodism" will consist in an indictment of life: the regenerate, awakened human being is the suspicious human being, who, in health, in the simple acceptance of existence, in the activity of reason in quest of solutions of human dimensions, sees misfortune, hopelessness, and pride all unbeknownst. The serenity of persons who accept their mortality is but anguish, dissimulating to itself its tragic depth. In all one's enterprises, such a person is delving abysses underfoot, marching toward destruction and catastrophe. But there is grace, there is the saintly life: life transformed by a sense of guilt, a sense of one's own corruption, life persuaded of its unreal, illusory character, but consecrated and saved by practices, works, inspired by the gospel, inspired by Christian things and customs.

"Methodism" is a song exploiting weakness and fear. It succeeds only where human beings, alienated by misery or prosperity and the obsession with self that flows from these, have already renounced themselves. This "methodism" is systematic autosuggestion, calculated to make one see white where there is black and deny the disparity between the system of religious practices and concepts and the swelling, teeming complexity of life. "Methodism" is a Procrustean bed, for it is a Christianity of exclusive salvation. It will have to be converted into a redemption of terrestrial, biological existence.

The sacraments could once more effect this redemption, which they signify, for they resist de-Christianization: they resist the erosion of the "methodism" of salvation. They have espoused the essential moments and rhythms of life. They indicate the manner—ever to be rediscovered, reinvented, as it were—of ascribing value to these moments and rhythms without wafting above them, by celebrating them, by sojourning intensely in them, by making them into knots of relationship, of exchange and communion of human beings with one another. They create a cosmos of meaning; they actualize a life in the form of word and love. This is the sense in which the sacraments arise from an esthetic praxis. They humanize the elementary acts of life, rendering human beings "beautiful and good," and draping their animality in the splendor of a most noble language. The matter of the sacrament, then, is human life as such. The sacrament's purpose is not to impose a membership or an indelible mark or character. The community in the form of word is without closure. One is born to it every day.

The sacraments will deploy a like efficacy only if they are a point of arrival and a new point of departure, only if they are but one aspect, or one part, of a more general esthetic strategy. They presuppose that the basic conditions of the "elementary" life are ensured before and after their liturgies. The sacramental liturgies must not be allowed to be palliatives, substitutes for the lack of nourishment, education, and care. They must not mystify those who are in misery, lulling them to sleep or consoling them by holding out hollow hopes. Further, the sacraments and their celebrations ought to be prolonged by an ethic of the beauty of the body—a body pledged to the metamorphosis of resurrection. There is a politics of the body that does not make of it a slum hovel as in the hagiography of the bygone age. There is a religious culture of the body that does not let it lie fallow, that does not abandon it to its anarchical petulance, but makes it the harp of the Holy Spirit. Whatever disfigures, whatever constitutes a provocation to condemn human beings, to turn one's face from them, or treat them as objects, is to be guarded against and combated.

Christianity has been remarkable for its compassion, for its unsurpassed dedication to the human being disfigured by misery and disease. It has taught people how to make good use of both. The leper, the person covered with sores, has even been cherished as another Jesus, the reincarnation of the Man of Sorrows. But the Christian is far from having learned how to dominate gladness without killing it. Christians have not been educated to the joy of living, but have contented themselves with "training," with killing the "beast" in themselves. This has surely been necessary, but it is by no means sufficient. The *manner* has never been the object of attention. The means have not been regarded. They have been justified by their "supernatural" end. Morality is not esthetics, however. Prohibitions do not always soften mores after the manner of music. They do not have a cathartic effect. Because it has ignored or rejected the polyphony of life, Christian morality has not developed an art of living for the ordinary person. It has only opened the way to one-dimensional mutilations and vulgarity. Sexuality spontaneously comes to mind as an example—cheapened, repudiated, and thereby delivered over to merciless cynicism and exploitation. It has become the geometrical center of guilt, fascination, and alibi. This is only one of the areas in which bad taste has caused harm.

Christians have been at great pains to draw dogma, morality, and politics from Sacred Scripture. And they have always succeeded by dint of great ingenuity. Actually such operations are assured of success from the start. Their results are of the order of the probable, and one finds what one seeks. The Bible does not hold our concerns. It is altogether foreign to the questions that exercise us. No matter, we take up our concerns and questions and place them there. And along with them we fraudulently slip in the answers. Then we "draw" the latter "from Scripture." "The Bible has a nose of wax, which you may twist every which way," it was said in medieval times. But was this the true function of the Bible? What of making us dream, what of being the means of our self-projection beyond ourselves?

All knowledge thus snatched from Scripture is artificial. The "biblical concepts" of this or that are those of nobody; they are robot photos made by a great number of individuals scattered over the centuries, of every age of life and both sexes. The unity of the Bible is mainly that of an encyclopedia, which gathers between the same two covers a great number of disparate compositions. A unity of this whole would have to be the expression of a supra-individual consciousness, a transhistoric subject, unfolding and developing through the centuries. Such a subject never existed. To call it "Israel" is to build, out of the Book's bric-a-brac, a being "on paper." Any coherence or semblance of objective unity is obtained at the price of violence to the real, and of falsification: for what is sought and found here has not hitherto existed, because it is the solution to be discovered in response to the events in function of the circumstances of a new, fresh age, of irreversible moments. If the dogma of the Trinity can be read in the Old Testament, beginning with the book of Genesis, however mistily and in outline, then it falls into insignificance. In this case, everything is in everything and vice versa.

Likewise the Bible will disappoint us totally if we "examine" it to "discover" a morality for our time. Lying, massacring, committing adultery and incest in the name of the Most High will scarcely do. The ethical prescriptions of the Bible bear the mark of bygone ages. They are testimonies to history. They, rather, teach today's human beings the distance separating them from biblical times, the difference in scale of a bygone universe from ours today, the chasm between the problems of the first millennium B.C. and our two millennia since. Morality drawn from Sacred Scripture is worth no more than politics drawn from the same source.

What the Bible offers us are figures, types, myths, stories, images, and words. The Bible talks, it sings. You can paint it, you can put on plays from it, you can draw examples and illustrations from it. Some of its passages, some of its personages, some of its words flash in our night, set us vibrating, and transport us outside ourselves, beyond ourselves. The Bible is a treasury of metaphors, thanks to which we can represent our existence to ourselves, transpose it to ourselves and for ourselves. The Bible is alive today only by its esthetics and for esthetics. What it expounds are the forms that have structured, at one moment or another, consciousness or communities of Jews, images that have uplifted, moved, or educated them—that is, that have escorted them out of their as-for-themselves, that have expressed them in their co-membership with the world and the divine in the unrepeatable welling up and gushing forth of this world and this divine. The Bible survives in the fragments representing what the Jews perceived and felt of existence in its epochal novelty. Distress, solitude, the humiliation of exile, defeat—as well as joy and triumph—here become the lived experience of a God and of reality.

Many who will not fall down before the God of Jews and Christians will yet be ravished by the stories the Bible tells, or by the psalms, for example. Gospel scenes and words will still console and strengthen those who do not believe the "divinity" of Jesus and reject the other "hedges" with which the Christians surround him. In fact, numerous Christians today maintain Christianity only in its esthetic form. Many religious statements and beliefs, in order to be uttered without offense to intelligence or good taste, have to be sung, danced, or played in order to be accepted by the mute, primordial depths of the feelings. They must arrive there despoiled of their dogmatic arrogance and their transcendent violence, for they are coming home. The divine, such that the human being can appropriate it, such that it concerns the human being, can only make its transitus through the sense, and don sensible form: "God sensible to the heart," to the eyes, to the ears, to the body, and to the imagination. Esthetic conversion is the last bend in a road of humility. It places us in the silent, discreet presence of God. Faith is not distinguished by the wealth of its thought. Scripture or systems of dogma or morality can still be used as means of power. They are performatives and have a tendency to favor the establishment of a power relationship. But esthetics is satisfied with making us hear the polyphony of life, the music of its transfiguration. It disposes us to live in beauty, laud, *eucharistía*, and all aspects of our mortal condition.

One of the great events of our experience, and perhaps of our age, is the advent of esthetic human beings. Their fashion of attaching to the past, to traditions, is neither dogmatic nor rationalistic. They have no intention of worshiping what their fathers venerated, nor of burning it at the stake either. They are not concerned about a choice between the thesis of the unsurpassable wisdom of the ancients and the Ancestor, and the antithesis of the antiquated imbecility of these same ancients or Ancestor. Their minds are elsewhere. For them, traditions are treasures of forms and models, and the most durable of them are styles that cannot be reproduced without fakery, but which ever inspire and enchant, which lend more zest to the present, our present, and more assurance to our own quest for the beauty that abides. For these styles procure us the necessary space and distance to play our own game, ephemeral but unique. They refer us to the irreducibility of sensation, of the sense of situation. This sense is the presence of the human being to the simultaneous totality, momentary and epochal, of things and beings—a totality that, in human beings, is the explosion of the origin, revealing human beings to themselves as a total part of the world. The esthetic human being endeavors to be equal to the new currency of totality, where the past appears only in fusion with the vivacity of the present, in the instant being lived by living human beings, sons and daughters of their times.

The esthetic human being is not necessarily a "distinguished esthete." Esthetic Christianity is a "popular" Christianity. It lives by stories, music, and icons, more than on dogmas and moral teaching, more than on tautological commentaries on the authority of the word and the gratuity of salvation. Esthetic Christianity is the hypothesis that arises in the midst of the theses and antitheses, freely passing through all barriers and boundaries, and playing havoc with the game rules of confessional membership and the criteria of religious adherence. In modern culture, Christianity perdures as an esthetic "preserve," always open to everyone. Anyone at all can draw from it at any moment. Shintoists will buy by the millions recordings of Gregorian chant, of which Catholics have grown weary and which Protestants have disdained for centuries. A communist will recount, with great cinematographic verve, the Gospel according to Saint Matthew, to the great surprise of many Christians concerned to dissimulate or demythologize the origins of their faith.

So goes the world, remembering Jesus of Nazareth in the transversality of cultural communication. The Spirit breathes where it will, making of Christianity a constitutive element of the consciousness and sensibility of the human being in process of becoming, penetrating where the sacred shock troops of Scripture, dogma, and imperial truths have failed to make a breach. After the vociferations of the preachers, the clang of arms of the warriors of the Eternal, the strident blast of the priestly trumpets have all died away, God himself comes: on the murmur of the breeze, the song of spring water, the endless lament of a spiritual.

RULE 4: UNIVERSALIZATION

Universality is made, not given.

The long discussions in Part One, the presentation of the Christic model in Part Two, and the considerations thus far in Part Three ought to have dispensed us from the obligation of tarrying on the question of Christianity's universality. Yet they do not, for evident pedagogical and historical reasons. The abuse of this notion is the too frequent pretext for seeking refuge in creedal belief. Its allegation impedes thought and clotures all discussion. It is the form more and more often taken by the argument from authority.

Neither in fact nor by right could Christianity be said to be universal in the obvious or current sense of the term. Factually, the whole world is not Christian. Christianity is minoritarian today as it was yesterday. Long confined to the Mediterranean basin, it left there and spread only by dint of a European expansion, in the form of migrations and the colonization of indigenous peoples. Other forms of expansion have since replaced this, but it is given to no one to know the day or the hour in which the whole of humanity will stand under the Christian allegiance. If this were ever to be, we would still be dealing with the circle of a historical humanity, and not of all possible humanity.

Why not universal by right? In default of a universal extension, must we not still affirm a universality of *intension* of Christianity? No. Here, as well, we see that in its very constitution Christianity is tied to something less than universal. It is bound up with singular events, with the life and death of a particular person. Historicity affects with its particularity not only the immediate content of Christianity, but its very form as well. Therefore it cannot be reduced to the general, the original without complicated discursive detours. Because it occurs in history, it cannot pretend to be the foundation of what precedes it, except by pretending that it has always been. It must postulate its preexistence. It must postulate its own timeless transcendence. By the same token, "revelation" as an event is no more essential, no more necessary and salutary a mediation than historical Christianity. Revelation manifests that which has always been: the eternal act of the redeeming love of God. This is what saves, and not its historical unveiling in one place and one person.

Is it not the essence of mythology to speak of the eternal and the divine in anthropomorphic terms and the categories of space and time? Then how may the privilege of this manifestation be saved? The Logos, we shall be told, anticipated a final and definitive manifestation through a dissemination in the teachings of philosophy. The rites of the nations prefigured the Christian mysteries. The orality of the sages is a presentiment of the gospel maxims in all their grandeur. Revelation is maturity, a full unfolding, truth's bright day that knows no sunset or twilight.

Such a language of comparison, however, presupposes a homogeneous level, in which realities of the same nature, or at least having an implied relationship of part to whole, encounter one another, where differences are measurable. A like postulate leads us away from the level of the universal, and makes that which founds or constitutes into that which is founded or is constituted.

How may one hope to prove that the other religions are reducible to Christianity without begging the question, that is, without doing so by means of Christianity, from its viewpoint? How may one do so without taking one's point of departure precisely in that which is to be demonstrated? If we proceed to the demonstration by means of something else, by language and reason, it is at once evident that Christianity is not immediately identical with reason, and furthermore that this identity, like the nonidentity of the other religions with that which measures all things and itself as well, will have to be proved. Surely this will be a difficult undertaking. In the first case—where Christianity itself is our middle term—we admit an initial nonidentity: we admit that Christianity is the projection of the supreme instance, with a self-representation in the other-than-itself. Thus the identification will be nothing but the eternal return to itself of that which is by itself. In the second case—where we use language and reason—we conceive a reality that is other than the supreme revelation and opposed to it. It will then follow that Christianity is but the *revelation* of truth, that it is therefore of the order of event, that it belongs to time and will pass with time.

The dogmatic assertion of Christianity's universality yields up a meaning, its meaning, only by the place and function it enjoys in the eschatological discourse of faith. What do we mean by this? In faith judgments, the predicate "universal" signifies "eschatological." Eschatology, as language, indicates the integral order of reality, that order according to which God, having "prevented" us by his anticipating love in creating us, draws us to him, converts us to him, as to our end. To qualify the church as universal or integral, as catholic, is to describe it as an act, the act of proclaiming conversion to the kingdom of God. In and by his very convocation, in and by his call, God proclaims himself *as* the one given to be known in himself and for himself—that is, as the end that attracts and gathers up the whole of humanity. The church is universal in the measure and to the extent that it acknowledges God in his mystery, "lets him be" in his mystery. The church is universal to the extent that it is conversion, the place of risk, the place where one awaits the God who is on his way, who is the means of nothing. However small it be, it is catholic by the integrity of its witness, its hope, and the creative vigor of its love.

Be converted, for the kingdom of God is at hand. Universality presents itself as a task. The kingdom of God is proposed—it is

here, but it "becomes" for us only by transformations performed
in us, by our emancipation from the servitude of the passions and
tyranny of the world, by the changes brought to bear on our relationships to possession, power, and sex, such that we have entered
into the process of universalization and the kingdom of the end-
time. Thus the concept of universality comports at once that of the
divine activity and the imperative that enjoins on the human being a
corresponding practice in the world. The authenticity of any reference to God in his mystery is verified by the return to earth, where
the universal to be achieved will only be able to take the form of the
tasks proposed to, or imposed on, human beings as their common
obligation, as necessary to their "survival," their emancipation,
the creation of an order that breaks with the old servitudes and
ancient discriminations based on age, sex, race, religion, learning,
power, wealth, and all the rest. These great tasks are realized only
from a point of departure in collectivities as they are at the moment. Here, in historical, traditional communities, they receive
their concrete determinations. At this point the Christian religion
intervenes as an acting historical factor, as an agent of effectiveness
at the heart of communities where it has struck cultural root. In the
transversality of communication among nations and civilizations,
the Christian religion brings its specific contribution to the creation
of a new earth in the desire for new heavens, which latter are the
work of the "divine majesty" and are his exclusive prerogative.

Thus understood, the doctrine of the universality of Christianity
affords no pretext whatever to deduce the duty of conquest, or
exclusive privileges to be arrogated by the revealed religion. It
furnishes no title of hegemony, no right to break in where it is not
welcome, no pretense to expansionism. Intolerance and the claim
to a monopoly of the truth are an abuse of the universality of Christianity correctly understood. The rejection of difference and particularity in the name of universality is a tragic non sequitur. The
Abrahamic religions will recover from revelation disease and Book
sickness only by a radical conversion to ethical nonviolence, only
by conversion to disinterest and the "hypothesis."

Ethical Conversion

We have not ceased to call for ethical conversion in many ways.
The assent of faith under pain of immorality should have taken the

form of self-determination and responsibility, and the latter should have had to suffer the profane consequences of its inspired words and deeds.

Authentic Christianity presupposes emancipation from the passions. But more often than not, this emancipation is merely presupposed. It ought to be posed, for itself, in the formulation of doctrines and practices, in the form of a will to the universal and of rational freedom. Lacking this, religion feeds on passions, and feeds them in its turn. It plays on the reflexes of fear, the spirit of gregariousness, and resentment. It undertakes to fashion the happiness and salvation of individuals and peoples without or even against themselves. Faith communities and chosen peoples are continually claiming to be exempt from the obligations of humanity at large. Based on privilege and the arbitrary, they maintain a perpetual violence. Ethical conversion implies the renunciation of this *violence on principle*, and requires that one give one's theoretical maxims and practices the form of nonviolence-in-principle, a characteristic of the universal on its negative side.

A profound revision of Christianity's turn of thought would ensue. Compared with other religions, the Abrahamic ones seem to have been ground out by predatory, warrior mills, and to have been marked from the start for violence and the will to conquest. God here is the lord of hosts, a god of armies. Mission is the holy war, continuing in another form but altogether capable of reverting to the crusade of jihad. The dominant note of its prevailing theory of life is combat. Its world-view is that of competition, valor, spilled blood (one's own or another's), and the accumulation of spiritual spoil and booty.

Truth is that which is opposed to error. What is not within the truth is against it and is an enemy to be confounded. The holy books breathe menace and imprecation. They fairly ring with noise and fury of battles of every kind. Have they contributed to bring human beings war rather than peace? Our concern in asking this question is not to pronounce judgment on the past. The task before us is the liberation of the powers of reconciliation. Only ethical demand and ethical form will deliver religions from their fundamental particularism. Then they themselves will bestow historical reality on morality, on the will to the universal. Then Christian hope can take on meaning. Hope is the unimaginable hyperbole of a present characterized by reason and meaning, in which claim and fact, truth and might, word and existence coincide in complete adequacy.

Faith: Free and Gratuitous

The Christian undertaking is insidiously corrupted by the lack of disinterest or sense of gratuity. All is predetermined by an ulterior motive. Everything is transformed into the means of something else, made the occasion for expressing or attaining another reality than that which determines the process of signification or action. The most banal human acts, the most ordinary gestures of courtesy, and profane works with their roots and ends elsewhere are interpreted as means of "getting the gospel through" (as if the gospel were contraband goods), of "making Christ present" (as if one had to disguise him to do it), of sowing the good seed on the sly, for a surprise (and we chortle knowingly to ourselves as we watch it silently sprout up). Tolerance and a friendly welcome are understood as an "anonymous," unconscious rallying to the truth of the faith. How may apostolates live by a like duplicity, which they create and exploit! It is not surprising that contact with apostles who have taken this path provokes uneasiness in every man and woman in love with liberty and transparent honesty. Christianity loses credibility.

Christianity forgets itself when it accepts the transformation of the short relationship of charity into the long and anonymous relationship of justice. Christians are experts in beneficence. They have often paid with their persons and their lives for their love of the unfortunate and the outcast. They are ceaselessly exhorted to think of others, especially of the "very poorest." Along with prayer, alms is the center of piety; it is the mighty "means" of pleasing God. Thus Christianity at first felt disconcerted when anonymous organizations began to take the multitudes in hand through procedures and functions that demanded no heroism, created no relationship of personal obligation, and had no other aim than to "be effective," to "help the recipients." In like manner, Christianity was at first insensitive to institutionalized injustice, to the established disorder that generates violence and misery. To be done with the Sisyphean toil of good works seemed perilous. There would be no more devotion, no more merit. Christians would be deprived of occasions of "doing good," of preaching by example and deeds. As to structural reforms and revolutions, they always have something Luciferian and utopian about them. They fall in the category of prideful revolt against the order of things fixed by a divinely created nature. They constitute a practical denial of original sin, of the radical evil that human beings now so saucily seek to uproot by their own strength.

A charity of beneficence also has its shortcomings. In spite of all its ineffectiveness, it has engendered a good conscience, and the devotion with which the professionals of charity have carried out their tasks has not necessarily shielded them from spiritual complacency and hardheartedness. Charity has shown itself capable of corrupting benefactor and beneficiary alike. It has established an unseemly relationship of dependence between them, calculated to favor the will to power in the former and the abject renunciation of self in the latter. Thus the authenticity of charity and the liberty of faith suffer from an unhealthy relationship. The gospel commands that no one be called "father," "teacher," or "benefactor" (Matt. 23:8-9; Luke 22:25) and orders that, in the accomplishment of the greatest tasks, we consider ourselves "useless servants," for we have "done no more than our duty"(Luke 17:10).

How may one be in no other debt to anyone than that of love except via the activity of anonymous institutions, services to the community available to its members as such, and justice? It is not seemly to have the human being's survival at the mercy of the good will of others. It has been to the discredit of the great religions that they have subordinated the acquisition of the bare necessities—the right to have one's humanity acknowledged, the right to life—to conversion and acceptance. The human being of another faith, or without faith, has passed for less than human, and passes for such today. The great religions have lost all sense of gratuity and freedom. To have the faith became a necessity, the condition for biological survival. It must no longer be thus. Faith will be free and gratuitous or it will not be.

The Hypothesis

One must delve beneath the religious thesis and antithesis and discern the hypothesis: the conditions of possibility or actuality forgotten by both. The hypothesis does not necessarily condemn the theological debates as metaphors of the interplay of profane elements. Via the circuitous route of social, political, economic, and biological conditionings, it forces them out of the closed field of the chapels and thrusts them into the world, where they will have to undergo the test of their verification. Christian practice is often the result of a like displacement when it is creative and fertile, as happens in popular piety, as happened with the founders of religious orders. Conversely, the bankruptcy of the greatest so-called religious contributions, and even of certain "religious geniuses," could be read as a failure to go beyond the theses and the antitheses, beyond the collision of contrary unilateralisms. The Reformation has stuck on the same plane as the Catholicism it set out to oppose. The hypothesis embraced the birth of nationalism and of the modern state, the advent of an unbridled subjectivity, the subjectivity of a society of profit-at-any-cost—a society of capitalism—and the beginnings of scientific rationality and, finally, colonial expansionism.

These phenomena have failed to capture the attention of theologians. All energies have been invested in internal wars, in conflicts of interpretation of the Scriptures, with the surreptitious collaboration of the unrecognized forces of "profane" history. The latter have finally been unmasked—after having taken over the churches. They have managed to render church quarrels vacuous by depriving them of their object. Ignoring or minimizing the hypothesis, the churches failed to mobilize in order to stem the tide of European violence unleashed on the world and blaspheming the name of God, and so the tide surged on unchecked. The churches are powerless to thwart the rise of nationalism. Religious dissidence and resistance to reform have even favored and legitimated that nationalism in its outrages and excesses. The churches have been slow to value the benefits of civil society at their true worth, and some of their teachings have exacerbated their deliria of subjectivity, their egocentric, anthropocentric obsession with individuality, to the extent of the exalted affirmation of God's omnipotence in contrast with the nothingness and absolute corruption of the human being, thus endowing the latter with an infinite negativity.

We could continue this sort of meditation on the history of the church. It would behoove us to ask ourselves why, for several centuries, the churches have seemed condemned to wage a rearguard action against the things that eventually would necessarily become the framework of their thought and the condition of their survival, as they constitute the condition of the survival of everyone: the sciences, technology, the freedoms. Why are the churches so dedicated to singing paeans to yesterday while they engage in their tardy, superficial, and opportunistic *aggiornamenti*? The quest for the hypothesis that forces one to transcend the closed circle of conventional religious language suggests the limits and the maladies of that language. What do we mean by this?

Christianity is heir to a language—a vocabulary, a system of concepts, a type of "explanation"—with which it cannot and should not tamper.[1] In Christianity the essence or truth of the world and of history has already been revealed once and for all. What now is, as well as what is still to come, can in no wise be modified. Thus Christianity's function is not to contribute to the discovery of the real by helping to articulate its current processes according to coherent sets and systems, but to proclaim its truth, whose monopoly is in the hands of this same Christianity. Truth is not the fruit of investigation or patient observation. It is wholly and entirely in the system of Christianity's invariable concepts. In the face of a changing reality, Christianity will keep on saying the same thing. That which occurs—novelty—is already anticipated in the Christian discourse. One subsumes this apparent novelty by "going deeper" with the discourse, by paying more attention to the interrelationships among the categories, and thereby discovering their infinite virtualities. Changes are but the occasion for this going deeper into thinking and concepts already totally given in the language of revelation, the articles of faith, and dogmatic conceptualization. The real is an obstacle calling for the integral deployment of the logic of faith, which is already the logic of things and of historical becoming. Thus there is no exchange between reality in the ordinary sense and the spirit, which seizes and expresses itself only upon contact with revelation's objects and categories.

The passage from this logic to the real, whose truth the logic expresses, suffers from a lack of mediation. It can only be proclaimed authoritatively, dogmatically. Proceeding as it does from itself unto itself, and confronting itself alone, the Christian language is coherent and irrefutable. Nothing can give it the lie, since it is on its very principle the truth of all things, as if in virtue of a stipulation or a tautological definition. Victory is all the more certain in view of the Christian theory of its own error and failure, which exist only on the part of the subject who claims to see them in Christian discourse. Its insufficiencies are outside it; they are those of the carnal human being whose heart is darkened by sin, the blind person who either denies the existence of light or enters upon a disquisition concerning color. The doubters would do better to doubt themselves instead—doubt their "health," refuse to believe their "eyes," and say that what appears to them to be black is really white, when "faith" so ordains. Thus dogmatism will see death only in victory and solitary monologue, the prisoner of the limits of its own vocabulary.

This erects a screen around the real, and Christian discourse progressively cuts itself off from it, a little here and a little there as the world and humanity grow larger and discover themselves in their rich complexity when unprecedented situations arise. Christian language, being or seeking to be a theory of practice and effective action as well, shows itself to be more and more powerless to transform the real in precise proportion to its locked-up logic and the multiplication of its certitudes, in proportion to its growing capacity to produce doctrines relative to all situations and all professions. The passage from Christian conceptuality to a reality to be *understood* without mediation is what we call "dogmatism." The correspondence or harmony between the two is preexistent. The passage of this same conceptuality to a reality to be *transformed* without mediation will depend not only on assertion, but on an act of the will. A dogmatism that fails to recognize the real leaves no room for anything but voluntarism. However, this voluntarism cannot defy the real, cannot challenge it, for it is a language that comes into confrontation with itself alone. Will ends by willing itself. It becomes pure will to liberation. Real action can only betray and blemish it. It protests each particular enterprise as falling short of its own pure expression. Only symbolic, ritual action is equal to expressing the pure, self-willing will. Historical, nonreligious action is the object of condemnation or denigration.

The world follows its course, nevertheless. An abyss of inadequacy yawns between the world and the language of faith as the latter mediates itself by the pure will of itself—that is, by willing its own noneffectiveness—and strives to restore its losses by reratifying its dogmatic affirmations and regulations. It is because the truths are no longer firmly held, we are told, and because doctrines are adulterated, that all goes ill. Also, we are told, it is because solid Christian virtues are abandoned now, and religious practices are falling into desuetude. The whole crisis is a result of the relaxation of the dogmas and ethics and will dwindle into thin air on the day that we return to pure orthodoxy and the strict observance of the commandments of God and the church.

The function of hypothesis is to burst through the enchanted but vicious circle, to deliver the real from the limits of a Christian vocabulary and explanatory schemata, doomed as they are to inefficacy, opportunism, and inglorious regrouping following rearguard operations. Refusing to recognize the limits of the very thing that would seem to be its reason for being, the reason for its privileged power, Christianity will die of its victory, irrefutable and incontrovertible. To recognize one's limits is to sacrifice oneself. But "whoever loses his life . . . will find it" (Matt. 16:25).

Chapter 11

Sketches for a Plan of Action

Limiting the discussion here to the conditions of our own social space—Africa—as it is inserted into the vast world, we propose in this chapter to sketch a Christian existence that will do justice to the demands of an ethic of responsibility in history. A reform of the understanding, by and in institutional, communitarian practice, will bring us back to the situation with which we began—this time, however, to transform it. The program of action demanded in a given place or at a given moment should keep as close as possible to the initial experience.

Let us begin, then, with the actual deeds and processes that African churches have established in their historical positiveness, as the work of others and as the accomplishment of their missionary project. We shall seek to discover how these founding acts could be turned inside-out, in such wise that these same churches would be constituted in interiority, as their own work, and the expression of their self-evangelization. A meditation on Christian expansion in Africa would reveal that its driving force consisted in a thrust from the bases of Christendom, from a whole people, with its various social strata. Central or specialized organs channeled this thrust into strategies of territorial occupation, the employment of local resources and personnel, and the doctrine founding and legitimating this undertaking. We would see how, in its practice as based on human relationships—by creating centers for the diffusion of knowledge and technology, institutions for human beings' education and protection, and a cadre of social "understudies" among the people—the "mission" renewed the environment and its people, opening the latter to the universal. Now the task is to ask how these positive acts, once freed from what misdirected, perverted, or canceled them (the "colonial mortgage," confessional and nationalistic rivalries, racism, and the discredit cast on manners of being human differently), could be resumed in a fundamentally changed context, consisting in Africans no longer being objects, but subjects, so that they might now "work on themselves."

The result would provide the framework and material for exchanges and discussion among those engaged in actual ecclesial practice. The latter alone can be the source of real strategies and programs of action that will lead them to be reconciled with themselves and to take themselves in hand.[1] Here we should like to insist once more on the necessity of better adjusting these plans of action to the freedom and ethical responsibility of faith in history, that is, to the specific challenges arising from deep within the African situation. We shall put these latter in the form of three injunctions, each with an explanation and commentary.

1. *In a framework of generalized domination, the liberation of the faith will have the* form *of power and self-determination, rediscovered and rectified.*

The end pursued by the resumption of the founding deeds of African churches is not to reproduce (not even by indigenizing it) a Christianity whose acculturation is that of other times and places and erected into a way of life. The reality seems to call for the transformation of the human condition as such, the transformation of the system of relationships currently prevailing among human beings, among Africans, and between Africans and the others. The horizon here is one of the risky hope of a metamorphosis that will be the anticipation of "salvation"—its symbolizing or, better, its effectuation in our world and for our time.

Colonial Christianity juxtaposes two sets of salvation themes, each of which has its effect even when they are opposed. In the first form, salvation is entry into the supernatural "world" in this life itself. It is there, in the supernatural dimension, that what is essential and decisive for the human being has developed, and it is transpiring still. One has access to this world by means of adherence to "truths necessary for salvation," and certain conditions consisting in obligatory rites instituted by God in his free sovereignty and benevolence. It is the soul that enters into this universe, endowed as it is with a spiritual penchant or "knack" for communication with God, his angels, and his saints, by grace. Once the soul is in full communion with them—once the veil is lifted, the veil of the body—it will be in beatitude, vision, and heaven. Heaven is the place of salvation, or, by metonymy, salvation itself, just as hell is its opposite, the place of perdition and perdition itself.

The time of salvation, too, is autonomous. It begins with the "fall" of humankind, continues with the promise of redemption by God, and culminates in the time of Jesus. Jesus' life by itself constitutes an archetypal, foundational time: for in virtue of the fact of his "twofold nature" of human being and God, what Jesus accomplishes immediately takes on a transcendent, transhistorical dimension. The facts and deeds of his earthly existence are "mysteries"—the direct projection of his divine being-there. This is why they swell the liturgy and are the object of adoration and contemplation on the part of the faithful. The life of holiness is the life more and more absorbed by the mysteries of the life of Jesus, and by the company of the angels and saints—without neglecting the duties of one's state of life and the practice of charity toward one's neighbor. But these tasks, these earthly relationships, must be wrapped in prayers, "consecrated," in order to become transparent, in order not to have to be a screen between God and the human glance directed toward him. The world is a place of passage, exercises, and testing; the supernatural is its parallel, covering it and overlapping it, capable of acting upon it, of traversing it, as the soul acts on the body and the higher on the lower, a fact attested by the power of prayer and by miracles.

In the second approach, the second set of themes, "salvation" is proclaimed in the subject's *certitude* that God is the sole author of salvation, to the exclusion of any contribution on the part of the human being. Salvation comes where there is faith, where there is human beings' firm adherence to what the Word of God reveals, namely, that God alone accomplishes what human beings cannot realize by their own strength. This deed, proper to God, is already manifest in faith. Because faith is the acknowledgment of God's sovereignty, because it renders to God what is due to him alone, his unshared glory and grandeur, faith is to be attributed to the action of God himself. God is the author of faith.

Such a faith can be said to be obedience, the profession of submission to the authority of the Word of God in Scripture, which alone gives the knowledge necessary for salvation: our powerlessness, our nothingness, as opposed to the omnipotence and all-reality of God. Salvation is acknowledgment of the Bible as the Word of God, the incarnation and tabernacle of that Word whose content is salvation gratuitously bestowed in Jesus by the sovereign freedom of the God who is above every creature, and who never delegates his sovereignty, but acts directly and without any mediation upon the soul, which he judges, condemns, consoles, and justifies. Ultimately the sign or expression of salvation is the perception and *sense of contrast or antithesis* between the absolute power of God and the total nonpower of the human being. Salvation is manifested only by this absolute *confidence in God* and total *diffidence in the human being.* Nothing else betokens salvation—not behavior, not good works. It is independent of all intramundial transformations. It does not create new persons, but only "new hearts," objects of the activity of the invisible reign of God for their having confessed that God is all and human beings are nothing. The pledge and promise of salvation is actual and obedient obedience to the church, which proclaims free and gratuitous salvation by means of faith alone, and the absolute, nondelegable sovereignty and power of God, always exercised directly. The sovereign authority of the Bible and the Word of God continues to prescribe and teach, directly, currently, and personally, the commandments and knowledge that are necessary for salvation.

At this juncture *another possibility* appears on the scene, reducing the status of both salvation-descriptions just presented to that of simple thematizations of the Christian experience. They cannot be its absolute expressions. The judgment that thus qualifies them negatively states the following: *(a)* These descriptions of salvation are bound up with a bygone age and to social conditions that have furnished the form of their expression. *(b)* They persist beyond the duration of the circumstances that gave them rise. They represent the presence of the past in the present, as to the possible, finite categories and attitudes of the human being with respect to the divine—the figures of religious consciousness.

This very persistence is possible only in view of what is currently at work on these expressions that have come out of past times and other places: namely, the current situations and conditions that these expressions now have to assume *obliquely,* as these situations and conditions oblige them to be reinterpreted in order to preserve any relevance. A *new* thematization will find it necessary and unavoidable *directly* to design the present conjuncture, with its aspirations and specific tasks. Its originality will consist in being the only thematization in which present experience will be expressed most completely in its irreducible novelty, for it will have to do justice to novelty as novelty.

The other merit of a new thematization will be to unveil the other interpretations' "forgetfulness" of their insufficiency when they wish to see themselves absolutized. These thematizations appear, as they hide the conditions of their production, as simple projections, the first into the mythico-cosmological element, the second into the mythico-psychological element. They fail to recognize themselves as language and representation and tend to substitute themselves for the structures and functions of mediation by which God is attained as reality without parallel worlds. At this point they no longer come face-to-face with anything but themselves, in a false "universe" that cannot be contradicted.

Another language is needed at this juncture. The context is one of domination. The reality denoted by the word "domination" is reducible to a lack on the part of groups and collectivities, and at times individuals as well, of a minimum of the power to build and grow as societies and persons—the power to ensure their own mental coherence and to have taken hold of the production and reproduction of the material and symbolic conditions of existence. If domination is this capability of disposing of the human substance of others, then the question of power becomes inseparable from that of the freedom of faith. A "faith" refusing to face this question would be the reflection of a situation of dependence, an alienated credence that would play its powerlessness by investing it in imaginary, "spiritual" power and freedom. The faith of human beings, once they become the agent of their destiny again, can only be in the *form* of rediscovered, rectified power and self-determination. The structuring that will render its content perceptible, enunciable, and hence real for us, will be that of a power of actual, historical self-determination.

Power and self-determination, then, inasmuch as they restore life to the dead and liberty to slaves, will be able to be the sacrament of salvation, at once the effect and the condition of salvation, its "demonstration" and its production. Power and self-determination in the service of the creation of life—"letting others be" in their consistency and for themselves—will constitute the radical rectification in question. Miracle is power become service, and thereby multiplying life, bursting the vicious circle of violence and the will to power that institutionalizes murder and feeds on the "flesh" of others and their abjection.

In this context, the task before us is to develop significations from within the very interior of the movement by which societies and persons structure themselves and come to be. A like approach does away with models and systems parachuted in from the outside, imposed, or inculcated, as destructuring. The models and systems must be invented, discovered in the immanent process of self-determination. It is easy to see how the political model can disqualify certain "Christian" practices and theories as productive of domination, when they propose "salvation" as the interiorization of ready-made truths, as the "incarnation" of the faith in Africa—the deduction of a way of life, from a point of departure in already constituted doctrines, as ethical and dogmatic inculcation. Everything acquires meaning and sense only when sprung from the enlightenment afforded by the lived movement of self-determination of a society and persons who join forces in order to see themselves into being, in order to conquer fatalism and the banality of evil and unhappiness, and to deliver themselves from the servitude that ever feeds on the rejection or fear of the Christic law enjoining us to lose our lives in order to save them and rise again.

2. *In reforming themselves, the African churches will reach, from within, the alienated, sick society of which they are total parts.*

The empirical, particular church that is in Africa is a real part of the African historico-social ensemble. It is subject to the same economic and political conditions, the same mechanisms of the depreciation of the human being as all the rest of that ensemble. In attacking these alienations just as they are present within itself, the church would contribute directly to the remaking of the global society of which it is an integral part. This is the specific purport of the second proposition: the African churches, in reforming themselves, will touch from within the alienated and ill society of which they are total parts.

In the context of self-structuring, models and authorities imposed from without lack validity, legitimacy, and mobilizing power. By presenting themselves, straightway and from without, as an instance of reproof, of the recall of eternal principles and moral education, the churches insert themselves into society according to a manner that is only a legacy of colonial times. This fashion of striking a relationship with society in the West is the product of an endogenous evolution, which makes the church at once the co-equal and the auxiliary of the state and the established power—a situation in which Christianity is the cultural tradition of all and the faith of some, the customary religion of a great number and the active ideal of a minority. The voice of the church has the tonality of the interior voice of a civilization, the voice of its conscience. Its pronouncements are not its monopoly, but the heritage of all: the basic references produced in dialogue, even contradictory dialogue, with Christianity.

Evidently the church does not occupy in African cultural consciousness the place assigned to it dogmatically. Hence neither can it play the corresponding roles. It cannot operate by means of protestation, denunciation, and the "social doctrine of the church." Its incapability of functioning in such wise should not be a matter of blame, nor should it be laid at the door of the cowardice of its dignitaries in refusing martyrdom. As the church does not represent an instance springing from the moral experience of Africa, neither can it appeal to its consciousness of the same. Trust and legitimacy are to be earned. What the church has accomplished to the time of this writing, it has accomplished with the resources, personnel, and protection of the Christian West. The contribution of African Christians to African civilization is yet to come. Their current power is but borrowed, subordinated, auxiliary.

In order to arrive at a creative autonomy that will enable the church, as by a kind of bonus, to become the promoter of the spiritual liberty of others, it is only necessary for the church to be itself converted to liberty, in its teaching, its activity, and its relationships. The church should not conform to the world within it so that its exercise of authority, its relationship to the "people," its use of church resources, its "tribalism," and the mechanisms of its decision-making would all be indistinguishable from those of that "world."

It should be possible to initiate an ecclesial practice that would reverse, within itself and for itself, the general tendencies and manners of acting. The church would thus begin to heal the portion of society it constitutes from the ills that afflict the whole body, and thereby contribute from within to the well-being of all.

3. *Communication among the churches is necessary. This will suppose, in each, the courage to be itself and the ability to receive and administer "fraternal correction."*

It goes without saying that the various churches of Africa have the obligation to open themselves to communication with all who claim Christ. Thus it is the manner and conditions of this communication that should occupy their attention and ours.

Because they are frankly given as particular and plural, each church posits the need for the others, by which and thanks to which each is passé, by which each transcends itself. The deficiency of all the churches is that they are so far from being the origin and principle. None can claim to possess the fullness of truth. Thus it is in reciprocal recognition and acknowledgment, in exchange and confrontation, that they will discover the principle of unity and an active universality, in the sense of a process of universalization and unification whose fulfillment will be the end of history. Meanwhile the human being journeys in partiality, and each church should be speaking the divine transforming action that is under way in the historical and social space in which it finds itself immediately inserted. Nowhere and at no moment does totalizing practice, or the absolute, synoptic viewpoint, simply emerge. Unity and universality are in the process of communication of the particular, different churches.

Does not such a conception tend to cut off the African churches from the riches of Christian tradition, the riches of the Christian past? Does not Christian authenticity oblige them to "go to school in the West," inasmuch as they need to integrate within themselves the indispensable wealth of spiritual experience accumulated from the beginning of Christianity up to the relatively late birth of the African Christianities? What are we to think?

We might answer as follows. The African churches spring from a unique encounter, an intersection of different axes, those of the African world and those of other universes. At this intersection, one lives one's own past as a present, in what that past retains that can act on the common consciousness. Of course, the past of others becomes present as well, at this rendezvous of history. But the past of others, and everything proper and particular to it, interests the individual only via the mediation of its present—in the relationship that this present strikes with the individual's own, in virtue of what the two wish and are able to make together of the present, conditioned by their respective pasts and determined by the position each occupies in the world's field of tension, of forces.

In the reciprocity established in this manner, Christian traditions and treasures come to one as living realities. Any other mode of appropriation, which would seek to "economize on" the mediation of those whose past this history is—those who register in this history the living continuity of their cultural consciousness—will seem to the person to be illusory. It will be foreign to the communication process, in which one has access to someone's past only if one receives it from that someone as present at this present moment. One cannot simply "break in," for that would thereby denature the other's past and preclude its comprehension.

Hence the necessity of communication among the churches, a communication that supposes and calls for differences and diversity and lives only on the mutual gift of these. Such a communication will imply autonomy, and must be sought for itself, without the constraint of material and intellectual dependence or dogmatic blackmail.

It is notorious that the African churches have little interest in one another, that they hope for nothing from one another. Their survival depends on their bilateral and vertical relationships with the rich churches of Europe and the United States. Foreign material aid seems more necessary than the grace of exchange and fraternal correction among sister churches equally poor.

Beggar churches of the periphery cannot administer fraternal correction. They speak only to conform themselves to the implicit or explicit expectations of those who come to their assistance. They approach the latter only to solicit them or thank them. Even their criticisms, when not disfigured with spite and resentment, are suspect of being a ruse of the weak and miserable to stir up the bad conscience and generosity of somewhat insensitive, distracted rich people. And sometimes their call for help sounds like the cry of distress of the emancipated, caught in a spell of dizziness before the terrifying chasm of freedom, with its loneliness and its responsibilities, and begging their old masters and mistresses not to abandon them.

The African churches will not succeed in sidestepping the question of the role of force in their relations with the churches of the West, and the question of domination. These problems cannot be brushed aside with, "The church has always been above economic and political interests, above the interests of nationalism and imperialism." Why not? For the very reason that we have called the African churches to account. The churches of the West are a segment of the capitalist world. They suffer from the alienations and ills of the society of which they are integral parts, and to which they spontaneously conform. They exhibit the same will to power, the same spiritual self-satisfaction that springs from wealth, the same idolatry of victorious strength, material success, and "apostolic profit," the same rejection of other ways of being human, and all the rest. Only the irreducible existence of other "worlds" can deliver these churches from these passions.

Clearly, recourse to the same Bible and agreement on the same symbols and the same articles of faith do not furnish a sufficient basis for understanding and action that will be faithful to the Christic demand. For it is on the level of practice, centered around non-religious concerns with water, food, land, and shelter, that divergences arise that maintain the old discords and foment new secessions. Christian faith is not a reference outside the sphere of these conflicts that set human beings in conflict with respect to possessions and power. It is on the plane of a "leveling of potential" among groups and individuals that the Christic model has proposed to exercise its ministry of reconciliation.

This is where the Christic model has been carved out as the act of razing the walls of separation. Thus there are no Christian "truths" that can be transmitted independently of the redemptive act that abolishes the old opposition between Jew and pagan, master and slave, ignorant and learned, and so on. The tradition of a simple deposit, an inspired book, a corpus of beliefs immediately fits into the field of tensions and divisions in which each individual and group will make use of it as an offensive or defensive weapon, an escape or an alibi. Agreement on principles and formulas is empty and without force in a like context, a context such as prevails in the world today. The accord must be reduced to action. We must take note of the shipwreck of discourse and of the practice of orthodoxies, and continue the journey.

Epilogue

The Manner

The only way to blaze a trail to responsibility in one's adherences is by doing it oneself. The eternal truths find their temporal, mortal modality in this or that concrete word, pronounced as it vanishes into thin air, in this or that concrete unprecedented initiative, taken and undone all in the same moment. Word and initiative flash forth in the presence of a moment, and disappear. In this momentary birthplace of the truth, the exercise of the truthfulness we have just accomplished will take up its abode.

To restore all things to this native soil of credibility has been the method I have followed, in its simplest act and essential form. Do not ask me, then, where I speak from, who I am, and what audience I wish to help or harm. I am a human being like you, I shall die, and I was not born a functionary of the Truth nor a professional in the service of "Christianity." I write in order to doff my masks before they blot out my face.

Not being this, or not believing that, is unimportant. The only important thing is the *manner* of not being or not believing. The sharing that it initiates is located beneath allegiances, doctrinal allegations, and programs. It founds and justifies them. As Kierkegaard put it:

Altogether equal in importance to the truth, indeed, even more important than the truth, is the manner in which it is accepted—and it would not be of much use to lead thousands to accept the truth, if, precisely by the manner in which they accepted it, they were to find themselves excluded from it.

229

Notes

INTRODUCTION

1. Thomas Aquinas, *Summa Theologiae, I*, q. 45, a. 7.

CHAPTER 1

1. In reference to this matter, the Latin American precedent is a help to understanding the African situation. I have read P. Duviols, *Les campagnes d'extirpation au Pérou* (Centre d'Études Andines), with great profit.

CHAPTER 2

1. I have borrowed this expression from E. Ortigues, *Le temps de la parole* (Neuchâtel, 1954). I owe much to this book generally.

CHAPTER 7

1. I owe my information to a course given by Father J. Goetz on this subject in the theologate at Lyons-Fourvière. I have made free use of my notes.

CHAPTER 9

1. I have borrowed my definition, and the description that follows, from the great work by Hans Dombois, *Das Recht der Gnade.*

CHAPTER 10

1. At issue here are the limits of dogmatic language, which has nevertheless become the raison d'être of the churches and the basis of their power. I owe much to L. Bod's analyses, and have occasionally para-

phrased passages from his remarkable article, "Langage et pouvoir politique," *Études,* February 1975, pp. 177–215. The influence of this article is already discernible above, in my Introduction.

CHAPTER 11

1. Cf. "Pour une catholicité africaine," *Civilisation noire et Église catholique: Colloque d'Abidjan, 12–17 Septembre 1977* (Paris: Présence Africaine/NEA, 1978), pp. 331–70.

Index

Aaron, 99
Abraham (patriarchal figure), 132, 133
Accidents of God, 12
Acosta, 44
Adam, 52, 55
Africa, in twentieth century, 165
African churches,
    African Independent Churches, 63, 69, 74
    communication with all Christian churches, 224-227
    liberation of faith through power and self-determination, 218-222
    reform from within, 222-224
African spirituality, 77-83
Alienation, 112
    of belief, 73-74, 85
    caused by Christianity, 24-29
Animism, 20
Anthropology,
    Christian, 36
    of God, 145-146
Apocalyptic, 96-97, 175-176
Apostasy, 96
Apostolate, the (preaching), 170, 171-176
Atheism, 3-4
Authority,
    functioning of, 186
    source of, 185
Baptism, 58, 95-96, 103
Bar Kochba, 90

Belief,
    alienated, 73-74, 85
    irrefutability of, 9-11
Bible,
    esthetics of, 203-205
    historicity of, 119, 122-123
Caiaphas (high priest), 91
Capitalism, 213
    church and, 226
Casuality concept, 36
Catechisms, 34
Charity, see Love
Christianity,
    African, 56, 63, 69, 74, 161, 218-227
    alienating character of, 28-29
    atheism and, 3-4
    authentic, 75-76
    bourgeois, 58-63
        African resistance to, 63-83
        dissociations characteristic of, 61-63
    civil society and, 164-165
    compassion of, 202
    conflict with Essenes, 99-100
    conflict with Pharisees, 100-102
    conflict with Sadducees, 98-99
    cultural destructiveness of, 24-26
    essence of, 195
    ethical conversion, 209-211
    exporting of, 4-5
    faith as key to, 159
    historicity of, 194-198

Nationalism,
  Christianity and, 213
  evangelism and, 61
  see also Political, the
Nazarenes, 157, 158
Noah, 151
Orthodoxy, language of, 40-42
Paganism, 40
  Christian view of, 19-26
  "pagan" Christianity, 160-161
Particularism, regressive, 72-73
Paschal mystery, 65, 69, 72, 134
Patriarch, 132, 133, 184
Paul, 129, 159, 160
Person, *see* Human being
Pharisees, 92-93, 100-102, 156, 157
Phinehas, 94
Political, the (the nation), 185-186;
  see also Nationalism
Polygamy, 38
Polytheism, 193-194
Post-Christian, 3
Poverty, created by Christiantiy,
  27
Praxis, imaginary, 73-74
Prayer, 179
Preaching, *see* Apostolate, the
Prometheus, 137
Property, concept of, 40, 182
Prophets, 174-175
Pythagoreans, 97
Qumran, 140
Redemption, 198-206
Reformation, the, 190-191, 213
Refutation, language of, 32-33, 48
Religion,
  civil society and, 164
  spontaneous, 78
  see also African spirituality;
  Christianity
Representation (of divine Pres-
  ence),

Christic model, 150-155
cultic, 176-179
functions and structures of,
  168-170
genealogical (archaeological),
  168-170
human beings in service of,
  169-179
insufficiency of, 188
mediation and, 180-181
significance of, 127
Revelation, 34, 55, 171
absolution of, 1-15
vs. fetishism, 11-14
metaphysical character of, 190
the political and, 185-186
re-creation and renewal, 71
the sage and, 187, 188
Sacraments, redemption and,
  201-202
Sadducees, 91-92, 93, 98-99
Sage, the, 186-188
Salvation, 42, 67, 68, 159
Christian, 82, 116-117, 218-220
Essenian, 99
in gnosticisms, 140
as object of cult, 179
Pharisaic, 102
proof from, 9
redemption and, 199-201
sacrament of, 221-222
Sadduceean, 93
state and, 186
Segneri, 45
self, alienated expression of, 112-
  113
Sexuality, 37-38, 131, 138, 203-
  204
Sicarii, 94
Sin, 31, 37, 40, 81, 143, 198-199
an assault on God, 66
Social skill, defined, 167

Other Orbis Books. . .

CHRISTIANITY IN CULTURE
by Charles H. Kraft

"This book will be welcomed by any biblical or theological student with serious interest in cross-cultural perspectives. The author has brought together here almost all possible information on Christianity in culture. Part one is devoted to the clarification of perspective, especially the needs in view and the reality under scrutiny. Part two divides the cultural matrix into the culturally individual and human community, explained through various cultural forms, patterns and processes. Parts three through six deal with the divine action, the way divine revelation affects cultural transformation and its transcultural significance."

Worldmission

ISBN 0-88344-075-X *463pp. Paper $14.95*

BLACK AND REFORMED
Apartheid, Liberation, and the Calvinist Tradition
by Allan Boesak

"In this collection, Allan Boesak continues to raise for those of us outside South Africa the issue of liberation of all people in that country. He creatively relates the black struggle for freedom in South Africa to the liberating message of Jesus Christ without sacrificing the universal note of the gospel." *James H. Cone,*

Union Theological Seminary, New York

ISBN 0-88344-148-9 *192pp. Paper $8.95*

FAREWELL TO INNOCENCE
A Socio-Ethical Study on Black Theology and Black Power
by Allan Boesak

"Boesak provides a framework of review of current black consciousness, black power, black theology, and liberation theology and then offers a helpful, evolving black ethic. All the major black American and African theologians are included in summaries of these issues and are treated in adequate fashion. Boesak indicates his knowledge of the issues and in a brief concluding essay probes a black ethic that arises from oppressed peoples (e.g. black) and urges a reversal of much 20th century materialism 'to recapture what was sacred in the African community long before white people came—solidarity, respect for life, humanity, community.' "

Choice

ISBN 0-88344-130-6   *197pp. Paper $6.95*

THE FINGER OF GOD
Sermons on Faith and Socio-Political Responsibility
by Allan Boesak
Foreword by Paul Lehmann

"Boesak is a South African student chaplain, and the excellent sermons collected here were written for his audience of young, liberated black Christians. Addressing hard political questions in a biblically centered fashion (scriptural passages introduce each sermon), Boesak more than meets his own criterion for good political preaching. Notes with background information on specific people and events will help American readers."

Library Journal

ISBN 0-88344-135-7   *112pp. Paper $5.95*

AFRICAN CHRISTIAN SPIRITUALITY
edited by Aylward Shorter

"Shorter presents a fine essay on African spirituality, identifies its themes, and locates it in context. Then he proceeds to give us an anthology—selections from contemporary Africans. He includes prose and poetry, introduces us to statesmen like Senghor and Nyerere, Catholics like Kayoya and Mwasaru, Protestants like Sawyerr and Okollu."

Spirituality Today

ISBN 0-88344-011-3   *160pp. Paper $6.95*

AFRICAN CHRISTIAN THEOLOGY
Adaptation or Incarnation?
by Aylward Shorter

"An exploration of approaches to the understanding of African traditional religion in preparation for creative dialogue between Christians and traditional believers. . . . This is probably the best brief discussion of the approaches to the study of African religion now available and should be in every collection of books on the subject."*Religious Studies Review*

ISBN 0-88344-002-4   *175pp. Cloth $7.95*
ISBN 0-88344-003-2   *Paper $4.95*

MISSIONS ON TRIAL
by Walbert Bühlmann

"Wit and humor punctuate this masterpiece. The writer is at ease even while dealing with sensitive issues. He makes Christian missionaries of all denominations speak their heart out soberly and self-critically and, for that reason, convincingly."   *Indian Theological Studies*

ISBN 0-88344-316-3   *160pp. Paper $5.95*

WEST AFRICAN CHRISTIANITY
The Religious Impact
by Lamin Sanneh

West African Christianity is a broad historical study of the development of Christianity in West Africa. Past historians tended to glorify the white missioners to Africa; many contemporary historians almost vilify them. The author, a Black African Christian and an Assistant Professor at the Center of World Religions, Harvard University, details both the strength and weakness of the European outreach which has produced the fastest-growing church in the world. Selected by the Editors of the *International Bulletin of Missionary Research* as one of the Fifteen Outstanding Books of 1983 for Mission Studies.

ISBN 0-88344-703-7   *304pp. Paper $11.95*

POLYGAMY RECONSIDERED
African Plural Marriage and the Christian Churches
by Eugene Hillman

"Hillman's knowledge of theological and sociological writings is evident but not oppressive; the book is well written, with touches of humor. It is the best treatment available of this specific question, and is also significant for its broader implications. Index and extensive bibliography."
Choice

ISBN 0-88344-391-0   *236pp. Cloth $15.00*
ISBN 0-88344-392-9   *Paper $7.95*

AFRICAN WIDOWS
by Michael C. Kirwen

"This study, based on a sociological survey of four Tanzanian societies, examines the problem of the African custom of leviratic marriage: the cohabitation of a widow with her deceased husband's brother, a custom prohibited by Christian churches even though for many widows there is no other decent way to live. Kirwen's findings present a strong case for the position that this type of marriage is not incompatible with Christian theology, but is merely at variance with Western marriage customs."

Theology Digest

ISBN 0-88344-009-1   *246pp. Paper $8.95*

NEW COMMUNITIES, NEW MINISTRIES
The Church Resurgent in Africa, Asia, and Latin America
by Michel Bavarel

A journalistic account of small Christian communities in a variety of cultural and geographical settings throughout the Third World. The vitality of the young churches is dramatically portrayed as a picture of the Church as the Church must increasingly become. This is a book of living witness. It teems with the witness of the new countries, the "young Churches" that live the Gospel today in the Third World, in another culture, and in a situation of poverty as their daily lot.

ISBN 0-88344-337-6   *128pp. Paper $5.95*

A CASE FOR AN AUXILIARY PRIESTHOOD
by Raymond Hickey

"A cautious, highly convincing work of first-hand pastoral theology, relating the teaching of Vatican II about the centrality of the Eucharist on the life of the local church to the hard facts of the African countryside as the author himself experienced them. In no other book have the arguments for a major modification of the pattern of priestly ministry in Africa and the introduction of a married priesthood, drawn chiefly from the best of the existing catechists, been so carefully marshalled."

The Tablet, London

ISBN 0-88344-021-0   *154pp. Paper $7.95*

AFRICAN THEOLOGY EN ROUTE
edited by Kofi Appiah-Kubi & Sergio Torres
"These papers, presented at the Pan-African Conference of Third World
Theologians, show Africans thinking for themselves about the sources,
presuppositions, and priorities of their faith, using literature, art, traditional religion, and current events, as well as the Bible, as resources."

Religious Studies Review

ISBN 0-88344-010-5   *224pp. Paper $10.95*

THE SONS OF THE GODS AND THE DAUGHTERS OF MEN
An Afro-Asiatic Interpretation of Genesis 1–11
by Modupẹ Oduyọye
"Modupẹ Oduyọye knows the rules of biblical criticism set down by the
scholars of Europe and North America, and he draws upon them to good
effect. Yet when he chooses to read the Hebrew Bible through the eyes of
African creation myth and with the tongue of the Hamitic language
group, the effect is extraordinary. Without attempting to solve the complex riddle of all that Jerusalem of old had to do with Ethiopia and East
Africa, Oduyọye persuasively shows that the exquisite sensitivity of African religion to the realm of the spirit is a living witness to a biblical consciousness much richer and more pluralistic than we had realized. We
ignore to our impoverishment and even our peril, Oduyọye believes, this
biblical sense of human participation in the divine vitality and of spiritual
kinship among the creatures."   *W. Sibley Towner*

ISBN 0-88344-467-4   *126pp. Paper $12.95*